THE DIG

Academic work, l   y become
digitised. This bc   e impacts,
possibilities, polit   university,
using digital tech   dentifying
the implications   mic publishing protocols   he ways in
which academics   and relationships with stu   s of using
digital media and   g, research
administration an   ctives. The
contributors span the spectrum of early to established career academics and are
based in education, research administration, sociology, digital humanities, media
and communication.

Deborah Lupton is Centenary Research Professor in the News and Media Research
Centre, Faculty of Arts and Design at the University of Canberra, Australia.

Inger Mewburn is the Director of Research Training at the Australian National
University, Canberra, Australia.

Pat Thomson PSM is Professor of Education, School of Education at the University of Nottingham, UK.

THE DIGITAL ACADEMIC

Critical Perspectives on Digital Technologies in Higher Education

Edited by Deborah Lupton,
Inger Mewburn and Pat Thomson

Routledge
Taylor & Francis Group

LONDON AND NEW YORK

First published 2018
by Routledge
2 Park Square, Milton Park, Abingdon, Oxon OX14 4RN

and by Routledge
711 Third Avenue, New York, NY 10017

Routledge is an imprint of the Taylor & Francis Group, an informa business

British Library Cataloguing-in-Publication Data
A catalogue record for this book is available from the British Library

Library of Congress Cataloging-in-Publication Data
A catalog record for this book has been requested

ISBN: 978-1-138-20257-3 (hbk)
ISBN: 978-1-138-20258-0 (pbk)
ISBN: 978-1-315-47361-1 (ebk)

Typeset in Bembo
by Sunrise Setting Ltd, Brixham, UK

CONTENTS

FIGURES

CONTRIBUTORS

Kim Barbour is a qualitative new media scholar and lecturer in the Department of Media at the University of Adelaide, Australia. Kim's research looks at online persona, the strategic production of identity through digital media, and particularly focuses on the use of social media. Her research often focuses on artists or other creative practitioners. Kim is the co-founding editor of the *Persona Studies* journal, an online, open access journal. She has published articles in *Celebrity Studies*, *M/C Journal*, *First Monday* and *Platform: Journal of Media and Communication*, and her paper 'Performing professionalism | Validating artistness' won the Grant Noble Award for best post-graduate paper at ANZCA 2014.

Jessie Daniels (PhD, UT-Austin) is Professor of Sociology at Hunter College and The Graduate Center, CUNY, USA. She is the author of five books, including *Being a Scholar in the Digital Era* (Policy Press, 2016) and *Cyber Racism* (Rowman and Littlefield, 2009), along with dozens of articles. Since 2007, Daniels has published a scholarly blog called *Racism Review*. Forbes named her 'one of 20 inspiring women to follow on Twitter' and she can be found there under the name @JessieNYC.

Katherine Esteves currently works as an eLearning designer at the Australian National University, Canberra, within the College of Law's College Education and Innovation Support Team. She has worked extensively as a web designer, graphic designer and multimedia specialist as well as teaching within the higher education sector and specialising in distance education and educational technology.

Martin Forsey is Associate Professor in Anthropology and Sociology in the School of Social Sciences at The University of Western Australia. Martin is an educational sociologist/anthropologist with particular interests in the social and cultural effects of schooling and the internationalisation of tertiary education. An award-winning teacher, Martin has an abiding interest in the scholarship of teaching. He also has an extensive list of research publications including books on neoliberal reform of government schooling and school choice and a range of papers reflecting his interest in qualitative research methods, social change, schools and society, education and mobility, among other things. His profile also reflects a strong commitment to interdisciplinary research.

Katharina Freund currently works as a senior eLearning designer at the Australian National University, Canberra, designing and supporting education technology initiatives. She researches digital communication, education technology and media as an independent scholar.

Sara Goldrick-Rab is Professor of Higher Education Policy and Sociology at Temple University, USA, and founder of the Wisconsin HOPE Lab, the nation's only translational research laboratory seeking ways to make college more affordable. She is the recipient of the William T. Grant Foundation's Faculty Scholars Award and the American Educational Research Association's Early Career Award. In 2016 *POLITICO* magazine named her one of the top 50 people shaping American politics. Her latest book, *Paying the Price: College Costs, Financial Aid, and the Betrayal of the American Dream*, is an Amazon best-seller, and has been featured on *The Daily Show with Trevor Noah,* the *New York Review of Books* and CSPAN's Book TV, among other venues.

Tseen Khoo is a lecturer in Research Education and Development at La Trobe University, Melbourne, Australia, and the founding convenor of the Asian Australian Studies Research Network. She has been a Monash University Research Fellow (2004–2009), University of Queensland Postdoctoral Fellow (2001–2004) and a research developer at RMIT University. Tseen has published on higher education funding policies and academic cultures, early career researcher experiences, Asian Australian cultural politics and diasporic Asian studies. Tseen is a former editor and current editorial board member for the *Journal of Intercultural Studies*, and was a founding editorial advisor for *Peril* (an Asian Australian arts and culture magazine). She is also on the editorial board of *Australian Universities' Review*.

Stephanie Kizimchuk is an early career researcher and teacher within the Australian higher education sector. Currently she is a PhD candidate in cultural history and memory studies at the Australian National University, Canberra, and an education-focused academic based in the Teaching and Learning Directorate at the University of Canberra. Stephanie is also an Associate Fellow of the Higher Education Academy, regularly teaches at both the Australian National University and the University of Canberra, and is an experienced education technologist, designer, online facilitator and moderator.

Narelle Lemon is an Associate Professor in Education at Swinburne University of Technology, Melbourne, Australia. Narelle's research is focused on engagement and participation in the area of building learner capacity to engage with cultural organisations and community arts programmes, arts education and social media for professional development including Twitter, Instagram, Pinterest and blogging. She is especially focused on social photography and the generation of visual narratives to share lived experiences. Narelle blogs at *Chat with Rellypops*, Tweets as *@Rellypops* and has recently begun a new project to promote stories of how creativity and mindfulness are applied to people's lives from various disciplines in the community. This *Explore and Create Stories* series is curated on Instagram through *@exploreandcreateco*.

Deborah Lupton is Centenary Research Professor in the News and Media Research Centre, Faculty of Arts and Design at the University of Canberra, Australia. She is the author/co-author of 16 books, the latest of which are *Digital Sociology* (Routledge, 2015), *The Quantified Self: A Sociology of Self-Tracking* (Polity, 2016) and *Digital Health: Critical Perspectives* (Routledge, 2017), and she has also edited three further books. Deborah is the co-leader of the Digital Data and Society Consortium. Her blog is *This Sociological Life* and she tweets as @DALupton.

Megan McPherson is a practising artist, educational researcher and has taught in a university art studio for almost 20 years. She is interested in emerging research design and methodologies, feminist and queer theory and professional practice in arts and education. Megan is a PhD scholar in the Faculty of Education, Monash University, Melbourne, Australia, where she is conducting a transdisciplinary research study of the role of the critic in studio pedagogies. Her research work in the university includes a number of studies that investigate peer learning and peer assessment in the creative industries, e-learning approaches in the university studio, higher degree research creative practices and ethics and professional development for teaching in new-generation learning spaces. Her tweets and Instagram can be found at @MeganJMcPherson.

P. David Marshall is a Research Professor and holds a personal chair in new media, communication and cultural studies at Deakin University. He has published widely in two areas: the public personality/celebrity and new media culture. His most recent books include *Contemporary Publics* (Palgrave, 2016), *Celebrity Persona Pandemic* (Minnesota, 2016), *A Companion to Celebrity* (Wiley, 2016), *Celebrity and Power* (Minnesota, 1997; second edition, 2014), *Advertising and Promotional Culture: Case Histories* (Palgrave, 2017) and *Persona Studies: Celebrity, Identity and the Transformation of the Public Self* (Wiley, 2017). He is one of the co-founders of the *Persona Studies* journal and his current research continues to develop Persona Studies as a new and important field of research. He is also embarking on a major project, *The Cultural History of Fame*, designed to be a six-volume series that explores fame and celebrity across human history.

Inger Mewburn is the Director of Research Training at the Australian National University, Canberra, Australia, where she is responsible for designing, measuring and evaluating centrally run research training initiatives and doing research on research candidature to improve experience. Inger blogs at www.thesiswhisperer.com.

Christopher Moore is a lecturer in Digital Communication and Media Studies at the University of Wollongong, Australia. His research in Game Studies examines the affective dimensions of multiplayer, first person and virtual reality experiences. Most recently co-editing the journal of *Persona Studies*, Dr Moore's research in the Digital Humanities explores the role of digital objects in the presentation and personal surveillance of the public self online.

Sara Page is a social researcher based at The University of Western Australia. Her background work has been in psychology and sociology, with a particular curiosity for how the macro (society, culture and its structures) is reflected in the micro (individual experience and biography) and vice-versa. Her current interests are in the use of digital technology in higher education including mobile and flipped learning; with a specific focus on interrogating the student experience of these innovations.

Bonnie Stewart is an educator and social media researcher fascinated by who we are when we're online. Co-ordinator of Adult Teaching programs at the University of Prince Edward Island, Canada, Bonnie leads digital strategy and professional learning initiatives. Her research focuses primarily on digital literacies, networked scholarship and the intersections of knowledge and technologies. A networked educator who began working in online education in the 1990s, Bonnie was involved with Massive Open Online Course (MOOC) research in its early Canadian incarnations. Bonnie has published in *Salon.com*, *The Guardian UK* and *Inside Higher Ed* in addition to peer-reviewed venues, and does her best thinking aloud on Twitter as @bonstewart.

Pat Thomson PSM is Professor of Education, School of Education at the University of Nottingham, UK. She is the author/editor of eighteen books, the most recent being *Inspiring School Change: Reforming Education Through the Creative Arts* (2017, with Chris Hall, Routledge), *Place Based Methods for Researching Schools* (2016, with Chris Hall, Bloomsbury), *Educational Leadership and Pierre Bourdieu* (2017, Routledge) and *Detox Your Writing: Strategies for Doctoral Researchers* (with Barbara Kamler, Routledge, 2016). She blogs about academic writing and research on patthomson. net and tweets as @ThomsonPat.

Ben Williamson is a lecturer in the Faculty of Social Sciences at the University of Stirling, UK. His research focuses on educational policy and technology, with a particular emphasis on the involvement of networks of commercial, philanthropic and scientific experts in data-driven educational governance. He is the author of a forthcoming book on big data and the digital future of education, and has previously published his research in a range of education, sociology and policy studies journals. Ben maintains a research blog at https://codeactsineducation.wordpress.com/ and on Twitter he is @BenPatrickWill.

Jonathon Zapasnik is a PhD candidate in the School of Literature, Languages and Linguistics at the Australian National University, Canberra. He has taught undergraduate courses in Gender and Cultural Studies and is a learning adviser at the ANU Academic Skills and Learning Centre. Jonathon is an Associate Fellow of the Higher Education Academy.

ACKNOWLEDGEMENTS

This book has its origins in a workshop entitled The Digital Academic convened by Deborah Lupton at the University of Canberra in December 2014. This was followed by a public panel discussion with some of the workshop presenters the next day, held at the Australian National University and convened by Inger Mewburn. Presenters at the workshop were subsequently invited to develop their presentations as chapters for this volume, several of whom agreed to do so. Their chapters are complemented by others we knew who were working on relevant research who we asked to contribute as well. We thank the University of Canberra for funding the workshop and the travel of the participants, the Australian National University for funding catering for the panel discussion and accommodation for some of the workshop presenters and University House for providing reduced accommodation rates. Finally, we thank the participants at the workshop and panel discussion for their presentations and thoughtful discussions and all contributors to this volume.

1

THE DIGITAL ACADEMIC

Identities, contexts and politics

Deborah Lupton, Inger Mewburn and Pat Thomson

Introduction

On 5 August 2016, a short piece for *The Guardian* online site (Anonymous, 2016) provoked discussion among academics on its site and various social media platforms. The piece was published in the 'Academics Anonymous' section, in which authors are not expected to reveal their identities, presumably to encourage potentially controversial opinions to be aired. Titled 'I'm a serious academic, not a professional Instagrammer', the author, who identified as a 'young PhD student, not some cranky old professor', working in science, criticised faculty members and higher degree students who were active on social media. In the article, the author described a 'selfie epidemic' in which 'We document every moment of our lives', and bemoaned that 'this culture has infiltrated the world of academia'. She or he went on to describe other academics 'live tweeting and hashtagging their way through events', suggesting that they were thus too occupied to pay proper attention to the speakers. The author characterised this behaviour as a way of self-promotion, and indeed went so far as to accuse colleagues of 'showing off' as 'proof of their dedication to the profession'. She or he not only criticised academic social media users for publicising their academic activities but also for expounding 'strong opinions' in these forums.

A week later, the piece had been shared over 3,000 times on social media and attracted over 300 comments. Another article was published in response, this time with the author's name revealed: Dean Burnett (2016). His piece was entitled 'I'm a non-serious academic. I make no apologies for this'. Taking a jocular tone, Burnett made fun of the anonymous author's claims, particularly that scientists should not be communicating with anyone outside their field or the world of the university and that academics who use social media are frivolously wasting their time. As he questioned, with tongue firmly in cheek: 'Who would have thought that academia would behave similarly to the human society of which it is a part? It boggles the mind.'

While it would probably be going too far to characterise such debates as culture wars, they signify the growing use of social media and other digital media in academia. The discussions in response to Anonymous' critique reveal some degree of controversy among academics about which media should be employed and in what ways. More broadly, these exchanges and viewpoints raise some interesting questions about contemporary academic work and its relationship to digital technologies. Since the advent of the personal computer in the mid-1980s, and the internet and the World Wide Web in the 1990s, the university sector has witnessed major changes in the ways in which teaching, research and communication with colleagues are conducted. Universities were among the first adopters of email as a mode of communication; initially as part of local networks of staff members within universities, extending to other universities and organisations as the internet developed. Since the introduction of mobile computing, Wi Fi and cloud computing, the university sector is now thoroughly saturated with opportunities for academics to communicate instantaneously with each other and with students and people outside the university across geographical regions.

Academics can choose from a plethora of digital tools to conduct teaching and research. Regular assessments are made in which the future of academic work is predicted to change even more radically in response to digitisation. At their most extreme, some pundits have predicted a future in which most university teaching will take place online, with little face-to-face instruction or interaction anymore. Dystopic predictions stretch to the complete 'unbundling' (Robertson and Komlenjenovic, 2016) of the university – it becomes a non-institution which contracts academic staff working from home to 'deliver' online courses developed by specialist commercially based teams.

This vision is not without some basis in reality. Simultaneous with the advent of digital technologies and their introduction into the academic workplace, academia has increasingly become part of a globalised market, and inculcated with market values emphasising corporate-oriented attributes. In the contemporary global economy, information and knowledge are valuable commodities and increasingly a source of profit (Lyon, 2013; Beer, 2013; Lash, 2007). Academics are part of this global knowledge economy, their teaching and research contributing to the reproduction, dissemination and generation of information. Academics are now highly valued, by governments in particular, for their potential contribution to wealth generation and innovation. Scholarship and learning for their own sakes have arguably become progressively devalued, making way for a vision of the university not as a community of scholars, but as a corporate enterprise – an engine to power economic demands for growth (Giroux, 2009; Burrows, 2012; Slaughter and Rhoades, 2004).

The move towards universities demonstrating the ability of their researchers to have 'impact' and to be 'engaged' with stakeholders and the public, especially in countries like the UK and Australia, is integral to this growing preoccupation on the part of governments to capitalise on academic research and to demonstrate value for the funds invested in universities. Academics have been encouraged to take up such digital technologies as online learning, student feedback and referencing systems as part of their contribution to knowledge generation and the training of future knowledge workers. Most academic journals have become digitised, enabling citations to scholarly work to be automatically monitored and measured using software tools such as Google Scholar, Web of Science and Scopus. Many journals have introduced digital monitoring of such aspects as views, downloads and social media discussions of the work they publish, sometimes displaying the 'altmetric' (alternative metrics) scores individual articles have achieved in receiving attention on social media. Academics are also now often encouraged by publishers and their universities to use such tools as open access publishing, blogs and social media to promote their research and facilitate public access to and engagement with knowledge creation and dissemination.

Despite the progressive emergence of these technologies and their adoption in academia over the past thirty years or so, comparatively little research has been conducted on how faculty use digital technologies as part of their work. How are technologies taken up or resisted in academic work? What are the broader social, cultural and political implications and contexts of these practices? This volume was designed to address these issues and more. In this introductory chapter to the book, we set out the topics we consider most important to consider when discussing digitised academic work, in order to create a context for the chapters included in our volume.

Open access publishing and open education

The expansion in the ways in which tertiary education can be offered online has led some academics to envisage the utopian possibilities for 'open education', offering this level of education to anyone with an internet connection and digital device. The introduction of massive open online courses (MOOCs) is one element of this move, but so too are such initiatives as open access publishing of scholarly materials such as research papers, books and syllabi. Digital technologies have facilitated the sharing of academic publications beyond the pay-walled domains of traditional publishing outlets such as journals and books. Many universities now manage their own e-repositories for their staff members to use to deposit material such as theses, conference papers, reports and preprints (pre-reviewed versions) or postprints (authors' accepted versions) of their manuscripts that have been accepted for publication in journals and edited books. Platforms specifically for academics to connect with each other and share their research publications have developed, the most well known of which are currently Academia.edu and ResearchGate.

While the possibilities for 'opening up' tertiary education and academic scholarship accorded with many ideals related to the untrammelling of constraints to access, these initiatives are also often replete with threats and challenges to the practice of academic work (Weller, 2013; Rhoads et al., 2013). For example, governments may view open education initiatives as opportunities to reduce financial support for the maintenance of university buildings and the provision of university staff members (Hall, 2013). Thus far, open courseware initiatives have tended to privilege some academic disciplines and well-known academics from high-ranking universities, thus rendering others invisible and reproducing a narrow conceptualisation of what counts as valuable knowledge (Rhoads et al., 2013). Open education may become reduced to simple models of delivering online content to as many people as possible, with little recognition of the funding required to ensure the quality of the learning experience is monitored and upheld. The number of academic teaching positions may be reduced even further as software for assessment and digitally recorded or curated materials stand in for a continuing human presence in the learning experience. As Hall (2013) has observed, the open education movement employs an 'explicit (and often deliberate) fusion of conservative and progressive tendencies and discourses', where such terms as 'hacking the academy' and 'DiY Universities' are accompanied by corporatised visions of efficiency, attracting customers and cost-cutting. Research also suggests, contrary to many of the most optimistic narratives, that students accessing open education initiatives like MOOCs tend to be drawn from the ranks of the privileged groups who already have good tertiary education access, and that completion rates are low (Christensen et al., 2013; Pursel et al., 2016).

The realities of attempting to engage in open education and such methods as 'flipped classrooms' are discussed in two of the chapters in this book. Forsey and Page's discussion outlines the benefits and drawbacks of the flipped classroom from the perspective of both students and lecturers. In many ways, the model of the flipped classroom is attractive in a context in which student attendance at lectures is dwindling in many subjects and the face-to-face lecture as an effective form of teaching has been called into question. They draw attention to the shift in norms, routines and expectations from both sides that is required for this mode of teaching to operate successfully, including a departure from the traditional face-to-face university lecture, in which the lecturer stands at the front of a lecture room or hall and delivers content to a largely passive audience of students by talking for about an hour. Both students and lecturers have to devote significant time and effort to making it work, including adjusting to new ways of doing things. The flipped classroom model does away with this lecture-style of content delivery by sometimes providing recordings of lectures that students can listen to in their own time or removing lectures altogether in favour of small-group activities such as discussions or group tasks involving the active participation of students. Referring tangentially to Bourdieu's concept of the habitus, Forsey and Page emphasise that mundane practices and routines must be changed or adjusted: and like any change in habit or mindset, this takes significant effort. They also point out that a lack of appropriate training and resources for lecturers can impede on the success of models of teaching and learning that use these kinds of approaches.

MOOCs are the topic of the chapter by Freund and colleagues. They too draw on their experiences of developing and teaching a MOOC, identifying what they call the 'hidden iceberg of academic labour'. Here again, the unrecognised and unsupported costs of adopting this method of teaching are highlighted. As Freund and colleagues point out, the discourses of 'disruption' and 'revolution' focus almost entirely on the possibilities offered by MOOCs for 'opening up' tertiary education. What these techno-utopian discourses fail to recognise is the nitty-gritty of the intense work demanded of academic and university administrative and other support staff in getting these courses up-and-running and providing appropriate support to meet their educational objectives. This involves not only the intellectual labour required of the course convenors to develop its content and assessment strategies, but also the 'articulation work' that underpins teaching activities in universities, including emotional and administrative labour. A large proportion of this labour remains unrecognised and, indeed, not remunerated, so that developing and running a MOOC can often become yet another form of unpaid labour required of the faculty and administrative staff involved. Furthermore, because this type of labour is largely invisible and devoted to supporting students' learning experiences, like other forms of academic support work, it is often under-valued and viewed as 'women's work'. The tendency to draw on the existing 'precariat' labour force of casually employed academic staff and PhD students raises serious ethical questions for university management.

Another feature of open learning and open access initiatives that has provoked disquiet among academics is these initiatives' departure from previous scholarly ideals. As with numerous platforms and technologies originally developed for altruistic purposes as part of knowledge sharing, the building of communities and social networking (Facebook being the most obvious example), some of the software and tools for scholarly research and communication have become progressively commercialised. In alignment with the commodification and corporatisation of higher education more generally over the past twenty years or so, many of these tools and platforms have been taken over by corporate enterprises, including major education and research publishing corporations, such as Pearson and Elsevier.

Critics suggest that platforms that advertise themselves as promoting open access to scholarly research and then seek to monetise academics' willingness to become members are undermining the ethos of open access. They have pointed out that academics are performing unpaid labour for Academia.edu by uploading their details and their scholarly work – as indeed they do for traditional academic journals, whose for-profit model platforms like Academia.edu have directly challenged (for an example of these critiques, see contributions to The Academia.edu Files, published as an open wiki on the Culture Machine Liquid Books platform: www.openhumanitiespress.org/books/series/liquid-books/). The move by Elsevier to acquire the reference-sharing platform Mendeley and the preprint access platform Social Science Research Network provoked many advocates of open access publishing to express their concern that these sites would progressively lose their original intentions as a result. Boycotts by individual academics, and the cancellation in December 2016 by sixty German universities of subscriptions to all Elsevier academic and scientific journals (Doctorow, 2016) highlights the knowledge ownership questions at the heart of the open access debate.

Academics like Gary Hall have called for scholarly approaches to open access publishing that are far more radical, moving away from individualism, quantification and a focus on publishers' profit or faculty members' self-promotion and 'personal branding' to a more collaborative and generous approach. Hall has challenged the features he describes as 'the Uberfication of the university' (Hall, 2016) by presenting alternatives: those of 'pirate philosophy' and 'media gifts'. These approaches seek to offer creative ways to facilitate free access to scholarly work, rejecting corporate and neoliberal imperatives and encouraging contributions and collaborations in the spirit of the academic gift economy (see Hall's (2017) website *Media gifts* for many blog posts on these approaches and initiatives like the Culture Machine Liquid Books series and the Open Humanities Press with which he is involved).

In summary, open access platforms hold the potential to change not only the shape of academic work, but its potential audiences and impact. An academic in a cloister is a very different creature from one on a stage. The place we see this shift most clearly is in open access practices. Academics are called on to make decisions in a congested, and often contested, publishing and teaching landscape, usually with very little support for this decision-making process or attention to the broader political and ethical implications of this drive for openness. There is much room for further discussions and interventions that can highlight the tensions and contradictions as well as the potential of scholarly open access initiatives and practices.

Digital data and academic work

'Big data', or the huge datasets generated by people's interactions with digital technologies, are often presented as creating great possibilities for enhancing social research and contributing to the development of professional practice. This championing of big data is becoming evident in all areas of education, from early learning and school-based to tertiary level (Selwyn, 2014; Grant, 2013). Teachers and academics are also increasingly expected to use digital technologies as part of their teaching practices (Williamson, 2015; Selwyn, 2013). As we noted earlier, faculty members are themselves frequently monitored and measured using digital data-generating tools. Not only their research outputs and impacts but also their teaching practices are assessed and tracked, using such tools as online student surveys and platforms such as Rate My Professors.

In his chapter, Williamson refers to the new phenomenon of 'education data science', bringing together education research with big data analytics. He argues that this research approach originated in higher education institutions and has now spread to other forms of school-based education. The discourse of 'smart schools' is accompanied by that of the 'smart university', a model of tertiary education in which academics are proficient in employing digital media for teaching and research and are equipped in accessing data analytics to measure and monitor student learning and their own teaching performance. In his analysis, Williamson adopts Bourdieu's concept of 'fields of power' to explain the ways in which particular types of capital (cultural and social as well as economic) are established and reproduced as part of power relations. For Williamson, educational data science is a field of power and its exponents access these forms of capital as part of its ascendancy in educational domains. He examines the ways in which this emergent field has established itself with certain specific credentials, many of which rest on the broader privileging of big data and learning analytics software as superior modes of knowledge.

Digital data – and particularly large datasets – have acquired a reputation for offering innovative and more insightful knowledges into human behaviour, partly by virtue of being considered more 'neutral' and 'scientific' than other forms of data (Kitchin, 2014; Lupton, 2015; van Dijck, 2014). Further important questions to ask of the use of big data, including in tertiary education, include who has control over and access to these data and how are they used not only for educational purposes but also as profitable materials that are commercialised. As Williamson shows, actors such as the large educational company Pearson use educational digital data to promote their products and introduce new styles of learning and analytics for measuring learning. In the process, they are shaping how learning and teaching are conceptualised and practised. Educational data science as a field of power draws on this reputation and seeks to further establish and extend it, with little critical awareness of the shortcomings and possible threats of using digital data. In his chapter and other writings (Williamson, 2015; Williamson, 2016), Williamson notes that the authority of big data is exerted in an increasing number of areas in education, including the tertiary level.

As scholars working in critical data studies have pointed out, digital data are the products of human decision-making and the affordances of hardware and software. Digital data are no more neutral than any other form of data. Indeed, they are increasingly used politically, in ways that pose challenges to human autonomy and privacy (McCarthy, 2016; Gitelman and Jackson, 2013; Andrejevic, 2013). Digital data are used to establish norms against which people (teachers and academics as well as students) are measured and judged. Digital data are being used to conduct surveillance of people for a wide range of purposes, from commercial to social to managerial, and to make predictive inferences about their behaviours and preferences. Academics are not immune to digital surveillance – for example information on internet service provider (ISP) visits is routinely collected, many libraries use filtering software and profiling technologies are used to monitor 'risky' behaviour, such as the online activity of security and terrorism scholars (Tanczer et al., 2016). Such algorithmic authority can be used to limit or promote people's life opportunities (Lupton, 2015; Crawford and Schultz, 2014).

This move towards digital monitoring and quantification has significant implications for shaping academic work practices and identities. As part of this use of data analytics, academics are encouraged – and indeed, in many cases compelled – to collect data about their research and teaching practices, reflect on the apparent insights these data offer them and work to make changes so that their data can be improved. The academic quantified self (Lupton, 2015) has become a key feature of contemporary higher education. Academic workers are subjected to a proliferation of measurements and metrics: from Google Scholar listings of citations for each of their publications to student evaluations of their teaching to national research evaluation exercises, all of which serve to continually formulate 'metric assemblages' of different kinds (Burrows, 2012).

Social media and blogging

It is perhaps the use of social media that is the most contentious in the world of contemporary academic work. Several studies have identified the usefulness for academics of using social and other digital media for professional purposes. These practices can help faculty to publicise their research, engage in networks with other academics and also with non-academics and keep up to date with others' research (Mewburn and Thomson, 2013; Veletsianos and Kimmons, 2012b; Veletsianos and Kimmons, 2013; Veletsianos and Kimmons, 2012a; Lupton, 2014; Weller, 2011; Carrigan, 2016; Gregg, 2009; Kjellberg, 2010; Kieslinger, 2015). For some academics, the use of social media and tools such as blogs have been important in their social activism efforts (Daniels and Thistlethwaite, 2016). Many of these activities can promote the visibility of an academic's scholarship to diverse publics, both within and outside the academy, and thus assist them in their efforts to be public intellectuals. Self-promotion online can work to provide better employment opportunities and options. Effective use of digital technologies can provide academics with higher levels of visibility that encourage others to read and cite their work (Terras, 2012). Whether or not an academic is looking for a faculty position or promotion, the satisfaction of having one's research read by more people can be its own reward. These benefits need to be put alongside some of the drawbacks which include tensions with academic management responding to the market imperatives in which universities are situated and the perennially thorny issue of academic freedom.

The importance of digital media use for furthering an academic career is further emphasised in several of the chapters in this book. In their chapters, Bonnie Stewart, Narelle Lemon and Megan McPherson write about the academic Twittersphere and its possibilities. In the interviews Inger conducted with Jessie Daniels and Sara Goldrick-Rab, both women highlight how valuable blogging and social media use – particularly Twitter – had been for their engagement as public scholars and political activists. In her interview, Jessie Daniels identifies her approach to communication and scholarship online and describes how she often develops journal articles beginning from tweets or blog posts. Alternatively, she communicates about her published articles and books on Twitter or her blog. Other academics who blog and use social media have also made reference to the opportunities they see in this kind of practice for 'thinking aloud' in public and demonstrating the often mysterious ways in which academic scholarship and writing are conducted (Daniels and Thistlethwaite, 2016; Carrigan, 2016).

Not only does this practice mean that authors of these accounts have a chance to express their ideas in early form, bypassing the often glacially slow publication processes of traditional academic publishing, but they can demonstrate to less-experienced researchers how the mechanisms of academic writing and research take place. In her chapter, and speaking from the perspective of an early career academic, Charlotte Frost argues for a reconceptualisation of an 'emerging career trajectory that is less publish or perish, than platform and flourish'. She also sees the work performed on the blog she established, PhD2Published, as a form of practice-led research. In developing narratives on the blog of how to publish a book from a doctoral thesis, Frost was able to make the process of research publicly visible as a process.

The ways in which academics communicate with each other and with students and the public are also transformed via the discursive affordances of social media and open access publishing. In her contribution to this volume, Tseen Khoo discusses the importance of the ways in which marginalised scholars (specifically those working in Asian Australian Studies) have used platforms, digital publications and social media to connect with each other, publicise their work and engage in activism. Jessie Daniels describes how she uses Twitter both to conduct informal conversations, but also, as a digital sociologist, to observe how others engage on this medium: 'listening in on conversations' and 'observing people's behaviour – some of it bad behaviour – on Twitter', as she puts it. This engagement allows her to have her say and to see how others formulate their opinions and views. As a scholar of online racism, this insight into online discussions has been valuable for Daniels' research. This is a kind of participant observation research, therefore, where researchers are participating in online discussions at the same time as they are observing them.

Despite these benefits and possibilities, academics have generally been slow to take up social media use for professional purposes and their institutions have taken varying stances in supporting or encouraging them to do so (Roblyer et al., 2010; Daniels and Feagin, 2011; Daniels and Thistlethwaite, 2016; Carrigan, 2016; Kieslinger, 2015). Each of us (editors) could provide many examples of the resistance we have encountered among our colleagues and students in our home countries of Australia and the UK in our efforts to promote social media as a mode of academic work. In her interview, Jessie Daniels observes that even her students (members of the so-called 'digital native' generation) at her New York university lack interest in wanting to learn about how to use blogs and social media to become engaged scholars.

This continued resistance or simply lack of interest among faculty and students flies in the face of institutional initiatives to encourage them to be more active on social media and to use platforms such as blogs to promote their research. Indeed, not all universities are eager and willing to encourage blogging or social media use. Research suggests that employers across occupations harbour some ambivalence about the promotion of these practices. Work organisations can often see social media use by their employees as positive in terms of increasing morale and feelings of cultural belonging, developing professional networks, sharing and accessing knowledge and information and enhancing communication with clients, consumers and other stakeholders. There is evidence of concern, however, about the legal and policy implications of their employees using social media and the potential for them to waste time using these media or to post content that could be potentially damaging to the professional reputation of the individual and the organisation (El Ouirdi et al., 2015; O'Connor and Schmidt, 2015; O'Connor et al., 2016).

Some workplaces involve specific sensitivities to social and other digital media use by their employees because of professional ethical concerns. Medical associations and medical journals, for example, have warned of the potential ethical issues related to doctors and other healthcare workers using digital media in ways that could potentially flout professional conduct standards, threaten patient confidentiality and challenge the trust relations that are central to the doctor–patient relationship (Chretien and Kind, 2013; Gholami-Kordkheili et al., 2013; Mansfield et al., 2011). Similar concerns about school teachers' use of social media have been expressed. Teachers have lost their jobs because of posting content about themselves or others deemed to be inappropriate by their employers (O'Connor and Schmidt, 2015). In some jurisdictions teachers are banned from becoming friends with their students on social media or giving them access to their profiles (Papandrea, 2012; Asterhan and Rosenberg, 2015). The higher education context involves similar ethical and legal conundrums, related to norms of professional behaviour, the protection of people's privacy and considerations concerning the appropriate manner in which faculty and students should interact with each other on social media. Some universities have instituted policies for staff's use of social media, but many provide little or no guidance to their employees (Jerry and Lidsky, 2012; Carrigan, 2016).

As social media and blogging become more 'normalised', the boundary between a publication and a conversation becomes progressively blurred, with implications for academics that go beyond concerns about finding time or building the right skills to participate in these (constantly) emerging digital spaces. Academics are being encouraged to become performers as well as teachers and researchers – a new kind of academic selfhood, which we will return to later.

The affective dimensions of digitised academia

For some academics, the use of social media and other forms of online self-promotion can inspire ethical disquiet. Academics are subject to what Gill (2010) has described as 'the hidden injuries of neoliberal academia' caused by increasing pressure on faculty to be ever-more productive while being closely monitored and measured and called to account, all in a context of growing precarious work opportunities (see also Burrows, 2012; Gill, 2014). Such critiques draw attention to the affective aspects of academic labour, including responses to the modes of 'dataveillance' that track the work practices of academics and their impact (for example, their citation rates on Google Scholar or student ratings of their teaching performance).

Like most other professionals in the knowledge economy, the introduction of digital technologies into academic work has led to work being ever present. With laptops, smartphones and tablet computers connected to the internet with pervasive Wi Fi almost everywhere, opportunities to switch off work can be difficult to find (Gregg, 2011). While this may lead to a more flexible work experience, it can mean work is omnipresent. For some critics, exhortations to academics to use digital technologies more actively is yet another instance of the accelerated academy and the move towards 'fast academia', in concert with the progressive commercialisation and marketisation in general of the sphere of academic work (Vostal, 2015; O'Neill et al., 2014). The affordances of these technologies, coupled with expectations about academics' performance and the open-ended nature of academic work (there is always another article to be written), can lead to a constant feeling of guilt and anxiety and the notion that one is never working hard enough (Gill, 2010, 2014).

As Freund and colleagues demonstrate in their chapter, dealing with the pressures of developing and running a MOOC course, as well as the often highly emotional encounters they had with distressed students as part of moderating the course, proved on some occasions to create distress and anxiety. These affective repercussions were part of the unrecognised emotional labour of running a MOOC, the focus of their chapter. As they show, while those involved in the MOOC also experienced the pleasures and emotional satisfactions of being involved in a pioneering way of offering education, these were coupled with significant stressors. Freund and colleagues draw attention to the sometimes difficult-to-manage tensions between 'fun' and 'work' in such situations, highlighting the point that as highly educated, reflexive workers, academics can often feel very ambivalent about the use of such digital tools. Academics are aware of their exploitation but often desire the benefits that the tools offer them or those they are teaching. These tensions can be exacerbated when working on short-term (or even non-existent) contracts where the academic does not necessarily have the agency or tools to challenge the conditions under which they are expected to work.

One of the most popular academic Twitter accounts is 'Shit Academics Say' (with over 226,000 followers at the time of writing – there are also Facebook and Tumblr accounts). In highlighting the omnipresence of academic work (and particularly, the imperative to write prodigiously), the Canadian academic behind this account, Nathan Hall, constantly riffs on the 'I should be writing' theme. Recent examples (all tweeted in November 2016) include:

> How not to work on the weekend: 1. define work and weekend as restrictive social constructs. 2. feel sad

> What doesn't kill you makes you profoundly resent your inability to say no

> How to be productive when working from home: 1. Don't nap 2. Don't nap 3. Don't nap 4. Just one quick nap then it's back to writing I promise

The irony of these mordant accounts is not lost to Hall or to his followers. Both he and they are 'wasting time' interacting on Twitter: yet the popularity of the account demonstrates the value of this kind of humour for faculty who are facing the same kinds of challenges and pressures to be productive in the accelerated academy. Indeed, as Hall puts it himself in one of his tweets: 'It's not Twitter procrastination. It's knowledge mobilization 2.0.' One could also add that it is emotional support that is the key value of the material disseminated on this account and interactions shared on it between followers. In an interview (Wagman, 2015), Hall explained that his key motivation, in fact, was to have an outlet for his own frustrations and anxieties:

> there had been a lot of anxiety for me getting ready for tenure. At the time I was feeling fairly burnt out and disillusioned and I actually wanted to see if people felt the same way I did. What I realized is that people online, on Twitter and other social media, were engaged in sharing things more widely, talking more candidly about issues. I felt like I was missing out.

Hall went on to describe the importance of academics having a space where they could discuss their failures and relieve the sense of isolation that many often feel. Hall's sarcasm hides an often biting critique of the high work levels and precarious employment many faculty members are experiencing. Mewburn and Thomson (2013) note that the 'virtual staffroom' function of social media goes beyond the individual, it also allows political critique and mobilisation, as well as expressions of collegial solidarity.

Another cause for concern is the vulnerability that greater visibility can bring with it. Online sites, and particularly some social media platforms, have become notorious for offering opportunities for users to engage in 'flaming' or 'trolling' behaviours, involving making abusive and even threatening comments about and to other users. Academics who use online media for professional purposes can find themselves the target of such abuse. This is particularly the case if they are members of marginalised or less powerful social groups, including women, people who identify as non-heterosexual or cisgendered, and non-whites, or for those whose online comments and writing involve discussion of politically contentious issues. Some academics have been publicly shamed for making controversial statements online, and have even lost their jobs as a result (Carrigan, 2016).

In this volume, Jessie Daniels provides her own experiences of being attacked on Twitter by racist and white supremacist groups because of her discussion of her work on racism and hate speech. She has been verbally attacked not only because of her opinions but also on the basis of her sexuality and physical appearance. In her interview, Sara Goldrick-Rab also recounts her frustration that googling her name results in search returns providing incorrect information about a tweet in which she made a political comment about an American politician. Despite her prolific tweeting on all manner of subjects, this sole tweet eventually created a high level of controversy and led to Goldrick-Rab being sanctioned by the faculty senate of her university. She eventually left that university, as she felt that her academic freedom had been undermined. Despite these experiences, both Daniels and Goldrick-Rab remain committed to their online scholarly practices. Indeed, both emphasise that they see their social media use as essential to their work as academics working hard for social activist causes. Mewburn and Thomson's chapter on doctoral bloggers also shows that several of them were aware of the potential risks of engaging in blogging: but here again, the benefits they received from this practice outweighed any drawbacks.

Many faculty members have either experienced hostile behaviours or witnessed them in their online encounters, and have come to be wary of engaging professionally in social and other digital media for this reason, as Deborah found in her survey of academics who use digital media for their work (Lupton, 2014). When her respondents were asked to comment in an open-ended question about any concerns or worries they may have about their engagement online, many mentioned their fear that their ideas may appear 'half-baked' or that they may say something that would prove contentious and expose them to disciplinary action or the possibility of losing their job or promotion opportunities. The issue of finding the time to use digital media in a work context in which there are many demands on people was also raised by many respondents, as were the difficulties of working out the right tone when communicating on social media. This finding was corroborated in the chapter by Mewburn and Thomson in this volume and was also an issue raised by Marshall and colleagues in reporting the findings of their study into academics' use of digital media. Furthermore, faculty members are often concerned about how to appropriately maintain the boundaries between private and professional content (see also Kieslinger, 2015).

Given that academics are working in a precarious job market, such fears are well founded. Daniels (this volume) advises that junior academics consider the political context of their own institution, including how supportive of social media use those in positions of power are, when deciding how to engage online. She further advises that faculty members of any level of seniority challenge social media guidelines developed by their universities if they appear to be overly restrictive or punitive. Both Khoo and Daniels suggest that universities need to support publicly engaged scholars in situations when they are opening themselves up to vituperation online, particularly those from marginalised social groups.

The performance of academic selfhood

Another important dimension of understanding digital academia relates to issues of professional identities and selfhood. Any form of digital engagement involves the performance of selfhood, including professional selfhood (van Dijck, 2013). When academics use social and other digital media for professional purposes, they are called upon to make decisions about how best to represent themselves, including what platform to use and how to use it. These decisions may involve such features as how academics write their biographical details on their university webpages, on their blogs, social media sites and platforms like Academia.edu and ResearchGate and what images they choose as portraits, as well as the content they go on to contribute and the engagements they have with other users.

These considerations are particularly brought to the fore in the chapter by Marshall and colleagues on academic persona online. They are also addressed in Mewburn and Thomson's contribution on the use of blogging in the formation of academic selfhood by doctoral researchers and Stewart's chapter on Twitter 'orality'. In their chapter, Marshall and colleagues draw on their previous work on the ways in which certain types of personae are configured via online practices. Drawing on Goffman's work on the performance of selfhood, they use the term 'persona' to describe a strategically developed public identity. The use of platforms like social media and practices such as blogging and open access publishing, they contend, are important contributors to academic personae. Marshall and colleagues contend that a range of digital identity-shaping and defining metrics and content work together to configure academic personae: from automatically generated data from such tools as Google Scholar and journal article views, download and citation statistics (which are now standard for all academics) to their more voluntarily created representations of their scholarly work, such as social media posts, podcasts, YouTube videos and contributions to platforms like Academia.edu.

Engaging online for professional purposes also requires developing new styles of communication that can differ quite markedly from the norms of scholarly discourse. In her chapter, Bonnie Stewart describes Twitter as engendering a 'scholarly public' in which oral and literary traditions are challenged and, in her words, 'collapsed', intersecting to create a new space and format of academic communication. The informality and brevity of the Twitter format is directly counter to the formal language conventions of academia. Academics who choose to take up the use of Twitter or other social media, or writing blogs, often need to learn these conventions, including not only how to write, but what the content of the writing should be, how to share this writing and who else to follow and engage with. The skills, knowledge and time required to establish and maintain online profiles for sites like Academia.edu are further emphasised by Marshall and colleagues in their chapter.

As Mewburn and Thomson's study of doctoral researchers who blog found, this practice can be important to various practices of academic selfhood. Drawing on Foucauldian concepts of ethical self-formation and applying these to engagement online, Mewburn and Thomson demonstrate that, for these students, blogging can be a way of discovering how to be an academic researcher. The doctoral students in their study found blogging worked to help them reflect on their research, practise writing and the expression of their ideas as they were formulated and learn to communicate as a researcher working in an academic context. They position academic blogging as a hybrid form of writing, involving both note-taking and correspondence, inviting responses from others. Indeed, in contradiction to arguments that practices like blogging and using social media may contribute to the pressures of the accelerated academy, many of the participants noted that, for them, blogging was a form of 'slow thinking', allowing them to progressively develop their ideas in a shorter and more informal format than typical academic publications demand of them. Here again, the pleasure, sense of achievement, agency, connection with others and self-fulfilment that this type of academic writing can engender were highlighted in their participants' accounts of why they blog. Marshall and colleagues also reported a high level of satisfaction from the participants who were experimenting with using social media, YouTube and more academically specific platforms. Their participants reported such benefits as attracting postgraduate students, better engagement with current undergraduate students, drawing more attention to their research publications and speaking invitations ensuing from their labour of contributing online content.

Nonetheless, for many academics the very concept of 'self-branding', a term which is sometimes used to describe an important purpose of using online media to configure an academic profile, is viewed as highly questionable and unnecessary. The 'branding' notion fits uncomfortably with broader anxieties about cultures of narcissism (particularly as expressed on social media), audit culture and the neo-liberal imperative to engage in self-improvement and self-promotion. Increased public visibility is not always viewed as positive and, as we noted earlier, can have serious repercussions if things go wrong. For some academics, incitements to use digital tools like social media to promote themselves and their research is anathema to their concepts of appropriate professional deportment. Despite increasing pressures on the part of funding bodies, government policies and their own institutions to encourage academics to engage with publics and demonstrate 'impact' outside the university, some faculty are challenged by an unwritten norm that academics should not be seen to be self-promoting or allowing themselves to 'dumb-down' their serious scholarly work in attempts to reach a public forum.

It is here that the words of the anonymous social media critic with which we opened this Introduction are echoed: to be an academic Instagram, Facebook or Twitter user is to be a 'non-serious' academic who is prioritising self-promotion or the utterance of banalities over appropriate academic discourse and communication. This belief is noted in several chapters in this volume (including those by Lemon and McPherson, Mewburn and Thomson, and Stewart). As Daniels comments in this volume, academics are still not rewarded for the knowledge production and dissemination that takes place in digital media. Despite the fact that altmetrics can demonstrate the often significant reach that digitally engaged scholars can achieve, other measures of academic worth and standing are still privileged (Kieslinger, 2015).

Conclusion

If there is one key finding of the research we have here discussed, including the contributions to this volume, it is that there is no escaping the digital – no outside to which we can retreat. As in any other sphere of life in many countries, there are no distinctions now between being 'online' and 'offline'. The nature of the academic workplace for nearly all faculty members globally is digitised to a greater or lesser degree and in ways in which they may have little opportunity to challenge or change. Academic work and academic selfhood in the increasingly digitised realm of higher education are fraught with complexities and ambivalences. The authors of the chapters included here have gone some way to providing nuanced accounts of the complexities and ambivalences in what is a fast-changing work environment. Their contributions include theoretical argument, empirical research and critical self-reflection, as well as two interviews outlining personal experiences of working as an academic in the digitised workplace.

Taken together, a complex, even contradictory picture of digital academic practice is emerging. While each of the contributors would be the first to suggest that their view is partial and incomplete, taken together, the chapters in the book are a persuasive 'take' on the actual lived experiences of the digital academy. As such, the book stands, we suggest, as a marker of and in a particular time in university history – a time when decisions about the ownership and control of knowledge production and the working conditions of academics may change values and practices for better or worse. This book is intended as a contribution to that discussion that can help transcend some of the unhelpful narratives that have circulated about academics who engage with digital practices. We want to move beyond the stale binary of 'good' social media engagement that supports a neoliberal agenda of expansion and growth and its shadow, where social media is facile, banal and a waste of time for the 'serious' academic. We hope that you read the book, adding your own experiences to those that are elaborated here – and, of course, communicating them to us on social media!

References

Andrejevic M. (2013) *Infoglut: How Too Much Information is Changing the Way We Think and Know.* New York: Routledge.

Anonymous. (2016) I'm a serious academic, not a professional Instagrammer. *The Guardian.* Available at: www.theguardian.com/higher-education-network/2016/aug/05/im-a-serious-academic-not-a-professional-instagrammer (accessed 29 November 2016).

Asterhan CS and Rosenberg H. (2015) The promise, reality and dilemmas of secondary school teacher–student interactions in Facebook: The teacher perspective. *Computers & Education* 85: 134–148.

Beer D. (2013) *Popular Culture and New Media: The Politics of Circulation.* Houndmills: Palgrave Macmillan.

Burnett D. (2016) I'm a non-serious academic. I make no apologies for this. *The Guardian.* Available at: www.theguardian.com/science/brain-flapping/2016/aug/05/im-a-non-serious-academic-i-make-no-apologies-for-this (accessed 29 November 2016).

Burrows R. (2012) Living with the h-index? Metric assemblages in the contemporary academy. *The Sociological Review* 60: 355–372.

Carrigan M. (2016) *Social Media for Academics.* London: Sage.

Chretien KC and Kind T. (2013) Social media and clinical care: Ethical, professional, and social implications. *Circulation* 127: 1413–1421.

Christensen G, Steinmetz A, Alcorn B, Bennett A, Woods D and Emanuel E. (2013) The MOOC phenomenon: Who takes massive open online courses and why? *Social Science Research Network.* Available at: https://papers.ssrn.com/sol3/papers.cfm?abstract_id=2350964 (accessed 9 December 2016).

Crawford K and Schultz J. (2014) Big data and due process: Toward a framework to redress predictive privacy harms. *Boston College Law Review* 55: 93–128.

Daniels J and Feagin J. (2011) The (coming) social media revolution in the academy. *Fast Capitalism*, 8. Available at: www.uta.edu/huma/agger/fastcapitalism/8_2/Daniels8_2.html (accessed 12 March 2013).

Daniels J and Thistlethwaite P. (2016) *Being a Scholar in the Digital Era: Transforming Scholarly Practice for the Public Good.* Bristol: Policy Press.

Doctorow C. (2016) Germany-wide consortium of research libraries announce boycott of Elsevier journals over open access. *Boing-Boing.* Available at: http://boingboing. net/2016/12/15/germany-wide-consortium-of-res.html (accessed 6 February 2017).

El Ouirdi A, El Ouirdi M, Segers J and Henderick E. (2015) Employees' use of social media technologies: A methodological and thematic review. *Behaviour & Information Technology* 34: 454–464.

Gholami-Kordkheili F, Wild V and Strech D. (2013) The impact of social media on medical professionalism: A systematic qualitative review of challenges and opportunities. *Journal of Medical Internet Research*, 15. Available at: www.jmir.org/2013/8/e184/ (accessed 23 June 2016).

Gill R. (2010) Breaking the silence: The hidden injuries of neoliberal academia. In: Flood R and Gill R (eds) *Secrecy and Silence in the Research Process: Feminist Reflections.* London: Routledge, 228–244.

Gill R. (2014) Academics, cultural workers and critical labour studies. *Journal of Cultural Economy* 7: 12–30.

Giroux HA. (2009) Democracy's nemesis: The rise of the corporate university. *Cultural Studies ↔ Critical Methodologies* 9: 669–695.

Gitelman L and Jackson V. (2013) Introduction. In: Gitelman L (ed) *Raw Data is an Oxymoron.* Cambridge, MA: MIT Press, 1–14.

Grant L. (2013) Understanding education through big data. *dmlcentral.* Available at: https:// dmlcentral.net/understanding-education-through-big-data/ (accessed 25 October 2013).

Gregg M. (2009) Banal bohemia: Blogging from the ivory tower hot-desk. *Convergence* 15: 470–483.

Gregg M. (2011) *Work's Intimacy.* Cambridge: Polity.

Hall G. (2013) Introduction: 'We're all game changers now'. Available at: http://liquidbooks. pbworks.com/w/page/65026176/Introduction%3A%20'We're%20All%20Game%20 Changers%20Now' (accessed 7 December 2016).

Hall G. (2016) *The Uberfication of the University.* Minneapolis, MS: University of Minnesota Press.

Hall G. (2017) *Media gifts.* Available at: www.garyhall.info/ (accessed 6 February 2017).

Jerry RH and Lidsky LB. (2012) Public forum 2.1: Public higher education institutions and social media. *Florida Coastal Law Review*, 55. Available at: http://scholarship.law.ufl.edu/ cgi/viewcontent.cgi?article=1364&context=facultypub (accessed 7 December 2016).

Kieslinger B. (2015) Academic peer pressure in social media: Experiences from the heavy, the targeted and the restricted user. *First Monday*, 20. Available at: http://firstmonday.org/ojs/ index.php/fm/article/view/5854/4580 (accessed 9 December 2016).

Kitchin R. (2014) *The Data Revolution: Big Data, Open Data, Data Infrastructures and Their Consequences.* London: Sage.

Kjellberg S. (2010) I am a blogging researcher: Motivations for blogging in a scholarly context. *First Monday*, 15. Available at: http://firstmonday.org/article/view/2962/2580 (accessed 30 January 2014).

Lash S. (2007) Power after hegemony: Cultural studies in mutation? *Theory, Culture & Society* 24: 55–78.

Lupton D. (2014) *'Feeling Better Connected': Academics' Use of Social Media.* Canberra: News & Media Research Centre, University of Canberra.

Lupton D. (2015) *Digital Sociology*. London: Routledge.

Lyon D. (2013) *The Information Society: Issues and Illusions*. New York: John Wiley & Sons.

Mansfield SJ, Morrison SG, Stephens HO, Bonning MA, Wang S-H, Withers AHJ, Olver RC and Perry AW. (2011) Social media and the medical profession. *Medical Journal of Australia* 194: 642–644.

McCarthy MT. (2016) The big data divide and its consequences. *Sociology Compass* 10: 1131–1140.

Mewburn I and Thomson P. (2013) Why do academics blog? An analysis of audiences, purposes and challenges. *Studies in Higher Education* 38: 1105–1119.

O'Connor KW and Schmidt GB. (2015) 'Facebook fired': Legal standards for social media-based terminations of K-12 public school teachers. *Journal of Workplace Rights* 5: 1–11.

O'Connor KW, Schmidt GB and Drouin M. (2016) Helping workers understand and follow social media policies. *Business Horizons* 59: 205–211.

O'Neill M, Martell L, Mendick H and Müller R. (2014) Slow movement/slow university: Critical engagements. Introduction to the thematic section. *Forum Qualitative Sozialforschung/ Forum: Qualitative Social Research*, 15. Available at: www.qualitative-research.net/index. php/fqs/article/view/2229 (accessed 9 December 2016).

Papandrea M-R. (2012) Social media, public school teachers, and the First Amendment. *North Carolina Law Review* 90: 1597–1642.

Pursel B, Zhang L, Jablokow K, Choi GW and Velegol D. (2016) Understanding MOOC students: Motivations and behaviours indicative of MOOC completion. *Journal of Computer Assisted Learning* 32: 202–217.

Rhoads RA, Berdan J and Toven-Lindsey B. (2013) The open courseware movement in higher education: Unmasking power and raising questions about the movement's democratic potential. *Educational Theory* 63: 87–110.

Robertson S and Komlenjenovic J. (2016) Unbundling the university and making higher education markets. In: Verger A, Lubienski C and Steiner-Kamsi G (eds) *The Global Education Industry*. London: Routledge, 211–227.

Roblyer MD, McDaniel M, Webb M, Herman J and Witty JV. (2010) Findings on Facebook in higher education: A comparison of college faculty and student uses and perceptions of social networking sites. *The Internet and Higher Education* 13: 134–140.

Selwyn N. (2013) *Education in a Digital World: Global Perspectives on Technology and Education*. New York: Routledge.

Selwyn N. (2014) Data entry: Towards the critical study of digital data and education. *Learning, Media and Technology* 40: 64–82.

Slaughter S and Rhoades G. (2004) *Academic Capitalism and the New Economy: Markets, State, and Higher Education*. Baltimore: The Johns Hopkins University Press.

Tanczer LM, McConville R and Maynard P. (2016) Censorship and surveillance in the digital age: The technological challenges for academics. *Journal of Global Security Studies* 1: 346–355.

Terras M. (2012) The verdict: Is blogging or tweeting about research papers worth it? *LSE Impact of the Social Sciences*. Available at: http://melissaterras.blogspot.com.au/2012/04/ is-blogging-and-tweeting-about-research.html (accessed 3 May 2013).

van Dijck J. (2013) 'You have one identity': Performing the self on Facebook and LinkedIn. *Media, Culture & Society* 35: 199–215.

van Dijck J. (2014) Datafication, dataism and dataveillance: Big data between scientific paradigm and ideology. *Surveillance & Society* 12: 197–208.

Veletsianos G and Kimmons R. (2012a) Assumptions and challenges of open scholarship. *International Review of Research in Open and Distance Learning* 13: 166–189.

Veletsianos G and Kimmons R. (2012b) Networked participatory scholarship: Emergent techno-cultural pressures toward open and digital scholarship in online networks. *Computers & Education* 58: 766–774.

Veletsianos G and Kimmons R. (2013) Scholars and faculty members' lived experiences in online social networks. *The Internet and Higher Education* 16: 43–50.

Vostal F. (2015) Academic life in the fast lane: The experience of time and speed in British academia. *Time & Society* 24: 71–95.

Wagman S. (2015) The McGill prof behind 'Shit Academics Say'. *University Affairs*. Available at: www.universityaffairs.ca/news/news-article/the-mcgill-prof-behind-shit-academics-say/ (accessed 5 December 2016).

Weller M. (2011) *The Digital Scholar: How Technology is Transforming Scholarly Practice*. London: Bloomsbury Academic.

Weller M. (2013) The battle for open: A perspective. *Journal of Interactive Media in Education*. Available at: http://jime.open.ac.uk/articles/10.5334/2013-15/ (accessed 23 December 2013).

Williamson B. (2015) Governing software: Networks, databases and algorithmic power in the digital governance of public education. *Learning, Media and Technology* 40: 83–105.

Williamson B. (2016) Digital education governance: Data visualization, predictive analytics, and 'real-time' policy instruments. *Journal of Education Policy* 31: 123–141.

2

TOWARDS AN ACADEMIC SELF?

Blogging during the doctorate

Inger Mewburn and Pat Thomson

During their PhD candidature, doctoral researchers must become expert in research practice. They must produce a well-argued thesis, which demonstrates a contribution to scholarly knowledge. However, doctoral researchers produce more than a hefty tome and intellectual 'stuff': they also manufacture themselves as 'scholars'. Much of the work of constructing an academic self occurs in and through writing. When researchers make writing choices, they conform, adapt, reframe or resist dominant academic textual genres. Crafting a text involves strategic syntactical and lexical choices, such as who to cite and who and how to critically evaluate – the sum of these choices constructs a particular kind of scholar. When others read this work, they interpret and respond to it: they 'see' the researcher, their text and their scholarship as one. Through scholarly practices such as review, feedback, interrogation, critique and rejection, the writer also forms a view of how her work, her scholarship and herself as a scholar are viewed. These understandings influence the writing. This other/self cycle, mediated through text, is now framed by international and national regimes which use citation indices, subject league tables and various forms of metricised audits. Writing the text and writing the self now extends to writing the institution – and it is this combination of self, text and institution that is folded into the contemporary PhD experience.

Researchers have examined the tangle of text-work/identity-work (Kamler and Thomson, 2006/2014; Thomson and Kamler, 2013, 2016) undertaken during the doctorate. Ivanic's (1998) pioneering study showed that writing the scholarly self is framed by institutional and disciplinary discourses, but that there was still room for doctoral researchers to exercise choice in the kinds of text and identity they produce. Some researchers interested in writing pedagogies have built on this analysis to show, inter alia, that: writing groups provide an environment in which an emerging academic self can be nurtured (Aitchison and Guerin, 2014); if they publish during candidature, doctoral researchers gain experience in inserting both their text and self into scholarly conversations (Aitchison, Kamler and Lee, 2010); and supervision is a site in which text and identity can be productively formed together through feedback, if the supervisor uses a writing-centred pedagogy (Paré, 2011; Paré, Starke-Meyerring and McAlpine, 2011). Some doctoral researchers have also taken the identity/text imbrication as a site to study their own process through the PhD (e.g. Harrison, 2009).

To date, less attention has been paid to the ways in which text and self is formed through publishing online. One exception is Ward's (2013) doctoral thesis, which argued that blogging provided a liminal space through which doctoral researchers could explore their emerging understandings, the scholarly community and what it means to be an 'academic', all tasks integral to being and becoming a scholar (see also Ward and West, 2008; Coverdale, 2012). Thomson and Kamler (2016) also recommend blogging as a means of addressing some of the uncertainties arising from 'imposter syndrome'. This chapter provides new empirical evidence of the ways in which blogging, as a form of writing and academic publishing, produces both scholarship and the scholar. We report on an online survey of 279 volunteer respondents. All were doctoral researchers who blogged. We begin with a brief note about our approach to understanding the academic self.

Forming a self

Foucault argued that a condition of freedom was self-regulation (Foucault, 1988, 1978). In order to avoid external discipline (punishment, incarceration, the asylum), individuals must take it upon themselves to 'produce themselves' – as law-abiding citizens, workers and family/community members – by managing their own behaviour, speech, interactions, relationships, sense of right and wrong, ambitions, desires and so on. The production of an apparently autonomous self, who chooses to practice, evaluate and adhere to an internalised set of rules about the way to live, feel, be and become, is a modern form of governing society, the conduct of conduct writ large (Rose, 1999). Particular kinds of social institutions require particular selves; contemporary retail industries, for example, require workers to produce themselves as constantly cheerful, proud of their company and work, and eager to assist customers (Du Gay, 1996), air crew are required to produce themselves as aids to passengers and the creation of a 'holiday mood' (Hochschild, 1983) and teachers are required to 'want' to work long hours in highly performative, audit-driven schools (Ball, 2003). 'Governmentality', as this process is called, works by people internalising and incorporating expectations voluntarily as part of technologies of the self, rather than primarily through coercion. Thus, the goals of employers are seamlessly integrated into personal objectives.

The technologies that autonomous individuals apply to produce and reproduce their 'professional self' include: *responsibilisation* – taking care of the self in order to do whatever paid work or unpaid work is required; *normalisation* – controlling one's own impulses and emotions and that of those for whom one is responsible so that implicit and explicit social and institutional codes of conduct are met; and *entrepreneurialism* – taking initiatives which not only inculcate desire for self-producing lifestyles and behaviours but also simultaneously advance the spread of technologies which calculate, measure, evaluate and discipline (Ransom, 1997; Peters and Besley, 2007). Foucault's approach is often applied to higher education, where performative pedagogical–managerial processes can be understood as the simultaneous production of particular ways of knowing and being (e.g. Drummond, 2003; Grant, 1997; Green, 2005). These Foucauldian understandings have been brought to research on the types of ethical self-formation that take place on social media. Hassoun (2012), for example, discusses the ways in which social media users multi-task. Social media users either tune out or fine-tune their attention practices – build 'attention temperance' – by developing new forms of responsible self-managing behaviours such as timekeeping and minimising distraction.

In tune with Foucault's later works on ethics of the self, we take the practice of self-regulation to be an expression of freedom, rather than a straight-forward imposition of repressive practices. Here, we focus on blogging as a technology of the self, a generative form of habituated 'self-writing' (Foucault, 1997). Foucault describes two kinds of historic self-writing practices. The first is the *Hupomnemata* – or personal journals. Foucault argued that personal reflections brought together and made sense of a bricolage of diverse ideas, heterogeneous events and scattered readings:

> Writing as a personal exercise done by and for oneself is an art of disparate truth – or, more exactly, a purposeful way of combining the traditional authority of the already-said with the singularity of the truth that is affirmed therein and the particularity of the circumstances that determine its use.
>
> *(Foucault, 1997: 210)*

In other words, writing in a journal is not only a way to bring together ideas from a variety of sources, but also to make them our own and in so doing to make our self a particular kind of rational, thinking person – an academic perhaps, for whom reflection is a key practice.

Foucault also discussed a second writing of the self, 'correspondence', that is, writing with another in mind. Correspondence is an exercise in which the writer gazes at the addressee, and invites the addressee to feel that gaze but also to gaze back at their open 'soul':

> The reciprocity that correspondence establishes is not simply that of counsel and aid; it is the reciprocity of the gaze and the examination. The letter that, as an exercise, works toward the subjectivation of true discourse, its assimilation and its transformation as a "personal asset" also constitutes, at the same time, an objectification of the soul.
>
> *(Foucault, 1997: 218)*

Sharing knowledge through writing can be seen as training for scholarly perusal which is integral to all communication within the academy and most obviously exercised through peer review. Writers imagine critical readers and critical readers responding to their writing: they imagine the scholar and their scholarly self invested in the text.

Scholars have worked with the concept of self-writing in relation to social media. Weisgerber and Butler (2016), for example, argue that blogging, understood as the curation of content, is an act of self-exploration, self-care and self-cultivation. They argue that the online 'notebook' practice works to shape the offline, corporeal self. This is a position we also take, refusing a binary between analogue and digital self-writing practices. Boklage (2014) also mobilises the notion of the *Hupomnemata* to argue that blogging is not narcissistic, but rather is an expression of a civic self. As she puts it:

> bloggers are often those who use the medium to channel their own impressions and pass personal judgments about the social events. They do not claim objectivity or universal value. The very fact of posting personal commentary on the blog indicates that the authors try to approach reality critically and observe it while also finding their own place in it.
>
> *(Boklage, 2014: 40)*

We hold this argument up to scrutiny in the light of the results of our survey, reported later.

Both Weisgerber and Butler and Boklage use the first of Foucault's self-writing 'types' – the *Hupomnemata* – to describe blogging practice. However, we see blogging as a hybrid form of both notebook and correspondence. Our understanding of blogging as a both-together self-writing practice resonates with Sauter's (2014) analysis of Facebook use. She argues that posting on Facebook is both the curation of materials available for reflective appropriation (notebook) and a tool through which modern subjects:

> make themselves public, work on themselves, talk about their problems and weigh up costs and benefits of future conduct. The possibility for constant real-time updates and instantaneous feedback from multiple fellow users distinguishes modern technologically mediated self-writing from its predecessors.
>
> *(Sauter, 2014: 834)*

This latter 'correspondence' feedback also occurs in blogging.

We bring these understandings to the discussion of our data. We discuss each of our findings in two ways. First, using a phenomenological approach, we report a theme arising from the data; we then offer a re-reading using a Foucauldian lens. We ask: If blogging is a technology of the doctoral self, then what kind of 'PhD-qualified self' is being produced? Our comments are of necessity somewhat speculative, intended to raise questions rather than provide definitive answers.

The survey

Our survey was generated on the Survey Monkey online questionnaire platform (www.surveymonkey.com) with ethical clearance from The University of Nottingham. We solicited responses via social media, as this seemed to be the most likely place to find PhD candidates engaged in blogging. We asked social media users to share the survey with people who might not have seen it. It should be noted, however, that our recruitment method skews respondents towards regular Twitter users, as we promoted most heavily on this platform. The initial call was open for a month and 279 people responded. Of these, we selected 193 respondents who supplied a valid URL to their blog. Our sample was slanted towards a younger age group (over 50% were below the age of 32) and to women (70%).

Our data set was comparatively small, but rich, offering many possibilities for analysis. Much of the survey called for open-ended responses. We concentrated initially on identifying blogging practices reported by participants. We therefore imported our Survey Monkey data into the online qualitative coding tool Dedoose. The data were then coded thematically. Our resulting analysis is reported in the remainder of this chapter.

Blogging repertoires

Our analysis showed four dominant blogging practices:

- creating a scholarly persona;
- 'slow thinking';
- pleasure seeking; and
- knowledge sharing.

Each of these practices brings a different mode of academic self into being. It should not be inferred from our four-part analytic representation that PhD bloggers adhered exclusively to one type of practice or another. Every blogger in our data set combined at least two different practices, and some mentioned all four. We conceived of these four types of practices as constituting a 'repertoire', which each blogger deploys in their own way. While there were some age and gender differences in the data in the way these repertoires seemed to be managed, these were not statistically significant.

It is worth noting at the outset that we found very little evidence of blogging being used as part of a formal research plan. Only one respondent mentioned their supervisor as the impetus for beginning blogging, which suggests that blogging is still not seen as a mainstream research practice. The doctoral researchers exercised freedom, they chose to blog. They elected to write an academic self into being via blogging not because of top-down coercion, but as agents acting in/responding to a particular sociomaterial and discursive environment. This could be seen as the formation of an entrepreneurial self, or a self that makes itself ready for 'governmental rationalities and programmes' (Cannizzo, 2015: 203), but we take the view here that the choice to blog was productive. We do not presume that this was necessarily entrepreneurial, but rather then ask – productive of what?

Creating a scholarly persona

Many PhD bloggers exhibited a high degree of awareness of the affordances of so-called 'Web 2.0 technologies' to create and frame a professional identity. As might be expected, all the PhD bloggers had some knowledge about how their activities create a trace, or signature of their presence on the web and that this presence is multi-layered and complex.

Around 10% of our respondents demonstrated high levels of digital literacy, understanding how webs of influence can be generated and maintained, as can be seen in this quote from participant 165: 'People Google as the first step so an online presence is important. Keywords in the blog will keep the click-fall going.' Although this awareness was widespread, only approximately one in ten PhD bloggers were extremely explicit about their blog being part of an overall career strategy. Some were interested in creating an 'academic' persona, such as participant 249 who said they wanted to 'Raise my profile as a researcher and improve job chances' and participant 247 who said blogging 'creates an image of an active intellectual'. Others were more interested in what the blog could do for them in a particular industry, such as participant 200, who remarked: 'as I am not anticipating an academic career it is also allowing me to build an online reputation and presence in my area for future business opportunities.' Sometimes this awareness of the reputational work that blogging can do seemed to come directly from professional development workshops run by universities, as observed by participant 178: '[I was] persuaded about value of doing so at doctoral development session on social media.'

Not surprisingly, as these were PhD researchers' blogs, there was very little discussion of teaching. The focus was on research. However, it is notable that not one of the survey respondents wanted to generate a large audience for their blogs. Only around 12% of PhD researcher bloggers were specifically writing for non-academic or 'mixed' readers. The overwhelming majority was primarily interested in discussing research and associated ideas with other interested parties. We infer from this that PhD bloggers were more interested in attracting the 'right' kind of audience, than simply a big one. This is a finding which aligns with our earlier study of academic blogging where academics were very concerned to use social media to discuss and debate academic issues (Mewburn and Thomson, 2013). It is not surprising that doctoral researchers seeking to become fully fledged academics see the creation of community as important. Blogging is thus an additional site for the active construction of community/disciplinary/institutional belonging.

The answers to the survey questions additionally demonstrate that blogging afforded the construction of a professional and competent modern academic: expert, authoritative and in charge of their material. This professional self was created through association: by aligning the author with a set of works that reflect their expertise (personality or style was less important). Participant 195 put it most plainly when they said: 'The idea is that if my name is next to something, I want it to reflex [sic] who I am as a person, whether it is a blog, a journal article or a bound thesis.' It seemed that around 16% of our responders set out to intentionally create a blog that could perform a 'professional persona', while around 20% reported recognising this possibility as their blogs evolved into an alternative publishing platform that had unexpected affordances such as sharing, curating, storage, audience reach and interactivity (primarily as a chance to talk with people about what interested them).

Our analysis suggests the presence of a group of doctoral candidate bloggers who not only demonstrate but also act on/out the understanding that the scholarly persona is now distributed across analogue and digital platforms. This persona is manufactured, in the knowledge that multiple invisible viewers, at least some of whom are in positions of power and influence, will look for, and at, their dispersed digital identity. Manufacturing a scholarly self has always been part of the academy, but is now intensified and more high stake than before, given the competition for work, funding and status. Even if blogging does not in itself yield immediate reputational benefits, it can be seen, because of its regularity and frequency, to be producing an academic subjectivity accepting of and familiar with the need for and worth of public self-fabrication – 'personal branding' as it is often named: a distinctive academic self/product for a marketised higher education.

But while blogging was framed by around 10% of respondents as part of what an up-to-date, contemporary academic should be doing, there was also a level of uncertainty about the legitimacy of blogging and whether they were 'academically acceptable'. Sometimes this uncertainty seemed to be a direct result of remarks from others about blogging. Participant 266 reported they were told by their advisory panel: 'You spend too much time seeking attention, focus on research', while participant 46 reported they were told that blogging was '[a] Waste of time, pretentious, etc.'. This uncertainty could suggest: hesitation about the norms governing the scholarly persona (too much public attention is not seemly); concerns about the potential for a highly negative gaze to be directed towards their blog and their self with negative consequences; and/or some discomfort with the exposure that digital blogging platforms bring. Contemporary academics *are* required to make themselves visible to audit and managerial regimes in the modern university, and there may be some of our bloggers who were concerned about the potential for blogs to create academic selves accustomed to, and comfortable with, considerable degrees of surveillance.

Slow thinking

PhD bloggers seemed really interested in using blogs as a way to capture and 'freeze' thinking in action. Blogs enabled PhD candidates to share where they were 'up to', or use them as a record and prompt for private reflection (c.f. Rainford, 2016). Both reflection and pausing to record current ideas can be seen as 'slow thinking'. In slow-thinking practice, the researcher and the research are blurred. Blogging was a way of holding up a mirror to the self to make sense of both the research and the (academic) self. As participant 252 put it: 'The biggest benefit to blogging while I study is that writing teaches me more about what I think, and where I may be wrong.' This strongly resonates with the well-known writing maxim – I write in order to know what I think (variously attributed for example to EM Foster, Flannery O'Connor and Joan Didion).

'Clarity' seemed to be the main aim of the slow-thinking blogging practice; things like 'structure', 'ideas', 'opinions' and 'insights' were written into being. This slow-thinking blog writing could subsequently be treated as a 'seam of knowledge' which could later be mined for thesis nuggets. As participant 203 put it: 'I have a wealth of reflective writing which I am weaving into my thesis and journal articles.' Through this process of mining their blog, PhD candidates could put themselves in the position of knowledge curator, as participant 184 remarked: 'Blogging helps me work out what is connected, which either helps me realise how to put in my own thesis or that actually, it doesn't really fit in my thesis but is interesting anyway.' Externalising this thinking was a way to engage the 'inner critic' (another ubiquitous writing term popularised through social media). As participant 199 put it, blogging had the effect of 'bringing my ideas out of my mind and placing it out in the world which helps me judge and criticise them for enhancing them in quality and logic'.

The sequential nature of blogging as a medium which unfolds over time was valued as a way to see and assess the evolution of ideas. According to participant 187, 'it's a way to see how my reasoning and understanding evolves with time'. In contrast to the sharing/creating knowledge practice, slow thinking is framed as relatively low-stakes writing. As participant 178 commented, bloggers can organise ideas into prose 'without worrying about peer review; it's ok if your thoughts aren't fully developed'.

These sentiments have considerable resonance with the ways in which Foucault describes the self-writing practice of *Hupomnemata*, the process of reflection through which a reasoning self, familiar with relevant literatures and modes of academic debate, is formed. We can see here blogging as a means for forming a scholarly self who values and perhaps desires a 'life of the mind'. While this certainly has a performative function, it is also potentially supportive of a self with an ongoing appetite for practices that run counter to an accelerated academy, allowing for a more contemplative, reclusive intellectual activity.

Pleasure seeking

At the opposite pole from the practices that clustered around constructing a 'scholarly persona' was the blogger who started a PhD blog because they already enjoyed blogging, or discovered that they enjoyed blogging through doing it. Bloggers variously talked about blogging as fun, pleasurable, relaxing, diverting or as a form of cheap therapy. According to participant 245, their blog 'is somewhere to escape to'.

At its simplest, pleasure-seeking blogging enabled a creative outlet that was not related to the thesis work. Blogging could be a way to bring joy. Participant 195 commented that blogging 'makes me happy. Simple as that. I just needed a space to write', while participant 207 said they blogged 'Partly to write about "secondary" interests - my PhD doesn't cover everything I am passionate about, of course'. Some saw blogging for pleasure as another form of academic writing that did not have to be subject to the normal conventions around language and therefore a more relaxing type of writing practice. The pleasure was a source of creative energy that, for some, needed to be carefully guarded. As participant 71 told us:

> it is possible to start putting pressure on yourself to produce blog content. When this happens the blog is no longer my creative outlet but another item on my 'to-do' list. For me, this means forgoing a regular posting schedule to ensure I don't end up resenting the blog for being more work that I imposed on myself!

Blogging for pleasure could also perform a memory function, a way to keep other kinds of 'selves' alive, particularly if that self is not 'academically acceptable'. As participant 193 told us: 'I often feel pressed to hide my faith in my department even though it's a core aspect of who I am. I feel like I cannot include it in what is supposed to be "scientific" research. And so, I blog about it.' At other times, pleasure seeking was a way of providing an emotional 'lift' during what is a long period of study. For participant 147:

> That feeling of accomplishment, of completeness when you finish a blog post, or someone says something nice about it, or someone posts a link of it, is something that feels totally necessary in a long thesis process which never seems to end.

However, we should not be too quick to think that pleasure seeking and more instrumental approaches to blogging need be completely separate. Sometimes this sharing for the sake of another creative outlet could also construct a broader kind of professional self. One participant told us that: 'While my PhD focused largely on applied physiology, people who have visited my blog have also become aware of my interests and skills in other realms such as visual note-taking (sketch notes) and data analytics.'

Foucault (1990) did address the question of pleasure and the ways in which it has become subservient to desire; and it is desire which drives most modern societies, he argues. Arguably, most academic writing is driven by desire, desire to get approval, reputation and so on. It is this desire which drives academics to be self-disciplining, performative producers for audit regimes. On the one hand, taking pleasure in blogging could be seen as producing an academic self that is ready and willing to engage in publication churn. On the other hand, this might not be the case. Foucault addressed the importance of pleasure, positioning it as something different from desire, as something that encouraged more of the same, but not of something else. There may be pleasure in putting ideas down on a page, forming words in an aesthetically pleasing way, and communicating to others. Or there may be pleasure in a 'light-bulb' moment that one can then share. These pleasures blur with knowledge sharing but it is more than this, it is about the *jouissance* of articulating new ideas in a public forum.

Taking pleasure in blogging, therefore, might not be the same as desiring the production of serial journal articles in highly rated publications. It might simply mean taking pleasure in blogging leads to more blogging. We could certainly see a trend towards this in our data through code co-occurrence; those who experienced pleasure were also highly likely to report wanting to continue blogging when their PhD was finished. Our reading of the data related to pleasure is that it seemed more like this latter – the pleasure was in blogging as a distinctive form of writing in and of itself. Blogging is not yet incorporated into audit regimes and it perhaps functions as a more resistant practice for the pleasure bloggers. Are these more resistant academics in formation, we wonder?

Knowledge sharing

The strongest attraction to blogging for our PhD candidates seemed to be the opportunity to connect with various 'publics' such as researchers, practitioners and research participants. These publics included interested non experts and even loved ones. The sharing might be of the content of the research or the experience of study, or both. The practice of sharing and caring exposes an academic self 'in-formation': learning, changing, questioning their knowledge and their ability to express themselves: blogging as thinking aloud and learning in public, as some express it.

There was an explicit recognition by around half of the respondents that the professional academic self was required to communicate with others. Around 20% of the PhD bloggers explicitly recognised blogging as an alternative research dissemination pathway; complementary to conventional academic publishing rather than a replacement for it. As participant 275 put it: 'I wanted to have a professional space online, and my university doesn't provide one, so I started a website. I wanted to include a blog so I could share some thoughts on issues that arise in an easily sharable format.' Blogs were seen by around one-quarter of respondents as one way to make academic knowledge more accessible. Blogs are generally more informal and have less of the formal characteristics of the conventional journal article and are thus easier to read. As participant 261 said: 'I wanted to share research in a format that was easy to read and understand than a journal paper.' Blogging was thus often explicitly an outreach activity, but relatively few PhD bloggers expressed this as clearly as participant 257 who started blogging to 'make linguistics accessible to a wider audience'. Sometimes PhD bloggers were acting as the conduit to other interesting information; participant 251 was engaged in a literal translation project: 'I wanted to share interesting research within my area of study and spread it in an accessible way (and in Swedish, since most research is published in English).' Often the dissemination of research was seen as a way to practise writing in another genre, as participant 248 commented: 'I started blogging to exercise my writing muscle and to communicate weather and climate knowledge from my research group and personal research experiences to the general public.'

Here, then, might be an academic self who is primed and ready for the task of scholarly publication in multiple formats, committed to making global connections, keen to get their work known inside and outside the academy – this is a requirement of current impact agendas. So blogging might be seen as contribution to the production of the impact-disposed academic self. But this readiness might also be seen as a more political academic self, ready and able to communicate in ways that talk back to power, using platforms outside of institutional control.

While research dissemination was a one way 'push out' to readers, around one-quarter of our PhD bloggers saw the act of blogging as a way to get various others to respond, assist or be helped in some way. In other words, some bloggers shared their research as an attempt to create a dialogue. This view was most clearly expressed by participant 202, who remarked that their blog was designed 'To promote my research and thus generate feed-back beyond the strictly academic environment'. Some PhD bloggers seemed comfortable with sharing work in progress as a way to create the opportunity for dialogue, as participant 177 who started blogging 'to get reactions to some of my ideas, to advertise conferences I speak at, to write book reviews and/or annotated books I read'. A few, but not very many (around 5%), were in this position.

This might suggest that the dominant academic self that was in formation via blogging was one committed to one-way rather than two-way communication. This could either be a reflection of a novice who must consolidate their own self before becoming too engaged with others, or the production of a more individualised self that works singly: the lone scholar, a more old-fashioned academic self, constructed through contemporary digital affordances. However, there is a further indication of the importance of connection seen in the responses of those who report not attracting a following to their blog. They were more likely to report being discouraged, or even stopping blogging, because no one else was 'listening'. But the mere act of articulating a developing understanding in a public forum seemed to satisfy some bloggers (around 20%). As participant 261 remarked, 'it's a way to get some of my thoughts and ideas out there, and out of my head, whether people read them or not. But hopefully I can help some by making journal papers more understandable'. There was thus an affective dimension (the 'caring' element) to the sharing: a searching for validation or consolation. As participant 251 explained, blogging helped them to feel that 'I do something meaningful (spreading knowledge) when my research is stalling, or when I feel that my dissertation is uninteresting'.

Sometimes bloggers' efforts to create a dialogue focused on an explicit audience, which might be disciplinary or practice based, but broadly considered. Blogging offered both the opportunity to have a dialogue in a disciplinary community as well as to transcend conventional disciplinary boundaries committed to their conventional academic publishing practices (Hyland, 2000; Thomson and Kamler, 2013). For instance, participant 271 started their blog as a way to make contact with other 'researchers and practioners [sic]' who might be interested in creating 'a space between two fields (education and architecture) that should speak more but tend not to, that can have mutually excluding languages and ways of thinking/doing things'. Similarly, participant 147 was interested in being part of a discussion around a problem, rather than a discipline area: 'Learning about housing (for my PhD) meant I had a lot of opinions on what was happening in [the country] regarding housing, and it felt good to share them, and add my voice to the public debate.' Sometimes this dissemination was practiced with an eye to a goal, as in the case of participant 239, who reported thinking it was 'important to get what I write "out there" as a practice and good publicity ahead of eventually publishing a book'.

This is the aspect of blogging that is most obviously 'correspondence'. Bloggers are pointing to the formation of a self that not only seeks but also anticipates interaction, judgment and potentially also attributions of worth and skill. We also see a desire for interaction that is knowledge building, bloggers who see interaction as potentially forming a community of 'interdisciplinary' selves. This might be seen as becoming a modern academic self competitively positioned to apply for jobs and fellowships, able to respond to research funding calls for interdisciplinary approaches, ready to lead the way in the quest to address 'the big social challenges'. Alternatively, it might equally be the formation of a less-bunkered academic self, willing to explore new ideas and connections for their own intrinsic worth.

We also found two significant issues in the respondents' comments:

(1) Feeling connected

One small subset of PhD bloggers (around 6%) was less interested in sharing the content or findings of their research in preference for sharing the experience of studying for a PhD. Sometimes the practice of sharing the research and the experience were combined. According to participant 260, 'I wanted to have my little space on the internet to communicate my research and hopefully provide others on similar career paths with some helpful tips and advice'. Other bloggers were very interested in sharing their experience of study as a way to help, even warn others. Participant 136 said that they began to blog because '[I] struggled to find the main focus of my research – and how it matches with my passion or true interests. Also because I hated my supervisor and wanted to find a place to rant about him'. More bloggers than we expected (around 10%) explicitly named family members, even their mothers, as an intended audience for their blogging activities. As participant 106 said their blog was designed: 'So family could see what I was up to on the other side of the world. Also a means of explaining what I do so friends / family could have some idea.' This kind of sharing invited significant others (a couple explicitly mentioned their mother) to be engaged with what the blogger was doing in their work and, perhaps, invite support, empathy and engagement in a broader network of others. Blogging, framed this way, was a caring practice that combatted isolation. Participant 197 noted, for example, that 'emotionally, I feel connected and supported. This is important because it is online. I work alone most of the time'.

In these personal affective agendas effected through blogging, we can perhaps see some evidence of resistance to the accelerated 'greedy' (Hochschild, 1983) university demanding emotional commitment only to itself . Blogging maintains personal connection, caring values and practices – care for the self and others. Conversely, it might indicate the formation of an academic self already resigned to ways in which the lines between work and home are continually blurred in time-voracious professional organisations (Hochschild, 1997; Nippert-Eng, 1996). Both readings are possible, and perhaps both exist at the same time in each of the responses.

(2) Managing risk

While the benefits of sharing an academic self in formation were recognised by 'sharing' bloggers, making this evolution of the academic self public was commonly framed as 'risky' by at least one-third of them. Bloggers did not have to have been actively discouraged from blogging to see it as a risky business; many seemed to have been generally influenced by the risk rhetoric about social media which circulates in the academic community and beyond (see Carrigan, 2016 for a discussion of the 'potential pitfalls' of social media).

A strong thread of self-discipline was apparent in the data. PhD bloggers actively shaped their practice in relation to a risk discourse. While we do not have sufficient space to do justice to this aspect of the data, we want to note the idea that blog text is a 'misshapen' academic text which has not had enough time or peer review process and thus is more 'informal' and thus 'not academically acceptable'. This is a highly normative view of what constitutes academic writing; it must be subject to external scrutiny and approval in order to be 'right'. Many bloggers reported feeling that circulating misshapen academic texts would make them vulnerable, now or in the future, to accusations of poor academic conduct. The internalisation of a particular kind of academic gaze is very apparent in these data. This view contrasted starkly with reports of blogging being extremely time-consuming and the seemingly widespread attitude that a good blog post was a high-stakes public document that required a lot of effort to get 'right'. However, the very same sense of a punitive external normalising gaze is common to both, apparently opposed, positions.

It is not terribly surprising that doctoral researchers, about to be or having recently been the subject of an examiner's direct gaze, about to be or in the process of applying for jobs and subject to an employer's gaze, should be so focused on the prospect of academic judgment. Yet we can also understand this concern as the acquisition of self-discipline by newcomers to scholarly communities, and the (re)-production of what counts as normalised right and proper genres of academic text.

Blogging the academic self

We began this chapter arguing that writing was a technology of self-formation. We asked what kinds of academic selves were being created through blogging, mobilising a Foucauldian toolkit in order to help us analyse open-ended questions to an online survey.

In the four blogging practices that we identified – creating a scholarly persona, slow thinking, taking pleasure and sharing knowledge – we can see clear potentials for doctoral researchers to build a blogging repertoire that helps to constitute a self-managing academic, ready, willing and able to function in the modern university. However, we also saw possibilities for other kinds of selves – more contemplative scholars not wedded to writing as a means of gaining individual and institutional approval, scholars keen to act more collectively with others rather than in competition, scholars not prepared to sacrifice family and friends to the call of greedy workplaces. We could see an ethic of self that is compatible with a performative audit-driven academic culture, but also various ethics not entirely assimilated to it (c.f. Carrigan, 2016).

We are not disappointed with this somewhat ambiguous picture. After all, this was simply an online survey, a set of retrospective self-reports, at a particular time, from a very particular group of respondents. Our analysis shows neither a completely gloomy picture of novice scholars already well primed as self-disciplining academic entrepreneurs, nor a picture of politically resistant academic selves committed to the exercise of bottom-up power (as Web 2.0 boosterism suggests). Rather it suggests the potentials for either, and indeed both at the same time. This is congruent we think with the overall positioning of doctoral researchers who have to simultaneously enter the academic world while also acting critically and reflexively. Blogging appears to offer a 'being and becoming' platform for doing both together, retaining possibilities for acting differently, while also offering a technology for entering the current scholarly community.

References

Aitchison C and Guerin C. (2014) *Writing Groups for Doctoral Education and Beyond*. London: Routledge.

Aitchison C, Kamler B and Lee A. (2010) *Writing Pedagogies for the Doctorate and Beyond*. London: Routledge.

Ball S. (2003) The teacher's soul and the terrors of performativity. *Journal of Education Policy* 18: 215–228.

Boklage E. (2014) In defense of narcissism: Blogging as Foucauldian technology of the self. *Reconstruction* 13: 8–27.

Cannizzo F. (2015) Academic subjectivities: Governmentality and self-development in higher education. *Foucault Studies* 20. Available at: http://rauli.cbs.dk/index.php/foucault-studies/article/view/4937 (accessed 19 May 2016).

Carrigan M. (2016) *Social Media for Academics*. London: Sage.

Coverdale A. (2012) Digitally Mediated Doctoral Practices, Identities and Agencies. A Study into How PhD Students are Using Social and Participatory Media. Doctoral thesis submitted to the University of Nottingham.

Drummond J. (2003) Care of the self in a knowledge economy: Higher education, vocation and the ethics of Michel Foucault. *Educational Philosophy and Theory* 35: 57–69.

Du Gay P. (1996) *Consumption and Identity At Work*. London: Sage.

Foucault M. (1978) *The History of Sexuality: An Introduction*. New York: Pantheon Books.

Foucault M. (1988) *Technologies of The Self: A Seminar with Michel Foucault*. London: Tavistock.

Foucault M. (1990) *The History of Sexuality, Volume 2: The Use of Pleasure.* New York: Vintage.

Foucault M. (1997) Self writing. In: Rabinow P (ed) *Ethics: Subjectivity and Truth.* New York: The New Press, 207–222.

Grant B. (1997) Disciplining students: The creation of student subjectivities. In: O'Farrell C (ed) *Foucault: The Legacy.* Brisbane: Queensland University of Technology, 674–684.

Green B. (2005) Unfinished business: Subjectivity and supervision. *Higher Education Research & Development* 24: 151–163.

Harrison JE. (2009) Developing A Doctoral Identity – A Narrative Study in an Autoethnographic Frame. Unpublished Doctoral thesis submitted to the University of KwaZulu-Natal, South Africa.

Hassoun D. (2012) Costly attentions: Governing the media multitaske. *Continuum* 26: 653–664.

Hochschild AR. (1983) *The Managed Heart: Commercialisation of Human Feeling.* Berkeley: University of California Press.

Hochschild AR. (1997) *The Time Bind. When Work Becomes Home and Home Becomes Work.* New York: Metropolitan Books.

Hyland K. (2000) *Disciplinary Discourses: Social Interactions in Academic Writing.* London: Longman.

Ivanic R. (1998) *Writing and Identity: The Discoursal Construction of Identity in Academic Writing.* Amsterdam: John Benjamins.

Kamler B and Thomson P. (2006/2014) *Helping Doctoral Students Write: Pedagogies for Supervision.* London: Routledge.

Mewburn I and Thomson P. (2013) Why do academics blog? An analysis of audiences, purposes and challenges. *Studies in Higher Education* 38: 1105–1119.

Nippert-Eng C. (1996) *Home and Work. Negotiating Boundaries Through Everyday Life.* Chicago: University of Chicago Press.

Paré A. (2011) Speaking of writing: Supervisor feedback and the dissertation. In: McAlpine L and Amundsen C (eds) *Doctoral Education: Research Based Strategies For Doctoral Dtudents, Supervisors and Administrators.* Dordrecht: Springer, 59–74.

Paré A, Starke-Meyerring D and McAlpine L. (2011) Knowledge and identity work in the supervision of doctoral student writing: Shaping rhetorical subjects. In: Starke-Meyerring D, Paré A, Artemeva N, Horne M and Yousoubova L (eds) *Writing (In) Knowledge Societies.* West Lafayette: The WAC Clearinghouse, 215–236.

Peters M and Besley T. (2007) *Subjectivity and Truth: Foucault, Education and The Culture Of The Self.* New York: Peter Lang.

Rainford J. (2016) Making internal conversations public: Reflexivity of the connected doctoral researcher and its transmission beyond the walls of the academy. *Journal of Applied Social Theory* 1: 44–60.

Ransom J. (1997) *Foucault's Discipline. The Politics of Subjectivity.* Durham: Duke University Press.

Rose N. (1999) *Governing The Soul. The Shaping of the Private Self.* London: Free Association Books.

Sauter T. (2014) What's on your mind? Writing on Facebook as a tool for self-formation. *New Media and Society* 16: 823–855.

Thomson P and Kamler B. (2013) *Writing for Peer Reviewed Journals: Strategies for Getting Published.* London: Routledge.

Thomson P and Kamler B. (2016) *Detox Your Writing. Strategies for Doctoral Researchers.* London: Routledge.

Ward MH. (2013) Living in Liminal Space: The PhD as Accidental Pedagogy. Doctoral thesis submitted to The University of Sydney.

Ward MH and West S. (2008) Blogging Phd candidature: Revealing the pedagogy. *International Journal of Emerging Technologies and Society* 6: 60–71.

Weisgerber C and Butler SH. (2016) Curating the soul: Foucault's concept of hupomnemata and the digital technology of self-care. *Information, Communication & Society* 19: 1340–1355.

3

GOING FROM PHD TO PLATFORM

Charlotte Frost

Introduction

The isolation I felt as a PhD student, and then early career academic on the job market, compelled me to find an online community of academics for career growth and support. For over five years I had been professionally researching online art communities and their impact on the emergence of conceptually driven forms of online art. At a personal level, I had also been regularly engaging with the online knitting scene that was partly generated by feminist Debbie Stoller's book *Stitch and Bitch* (2004). I thought there must be equivalent hubs for academics, so when I couldn't find exactly what I was looking for, I decided to start my own. Seeing little value in simply reflecting upon my own (limited) experience, and as my participation in knitting blogging had been about teaching myself new techniques, I recognised the potential for an academic blog to be more of a learning mechanism. I therefore decided to use the blog as a way to publicly teach myself the necessary skill-set for becoming a fully fledged academic.

I set up an independent project called PhD2Published in 2010 as a way to up-skill myself and other early career academics. It was inspired by my very real need to find an academic community and develop professionally after completing my PhD. The results of this project have not only been the creation of a robust community of peers and a website full of advice on academic publishing, but a clear example of what it means to be an academic in the digital age. In this chapter I will provide a history of this ad hoc and DIY platform. I will then discuss the various forms of academic practice it speaks to and moves beyond. Finally, I will argue that it demonstrates a shift in focus from academics being encouraged to publish in legitimised forms of print to producing their own hybrid, online, public platforms.

Origins of PhD2Published

PhD2Published was then launched as a blog-based exploration of academic publishing with several different streams of content. There were posts I specifically prepared on academic book publishing, which were heavily researched and condensed advice given to me in a range of contexts. In particular I was interested in how to select a press by understanding their specialisms and markets (Frost, 2010a). Then I made video blog posts about my own experiences pitching my book to publishing houses. I wrote a set of brief (and social media-friendly) pieces of advice on academic publishing that were posted every Monday under the series title 'Weekly Wisdom' (Frost, 2010b). Again these drew from vast pools of documented and undocumented advice on academic publishing.

I also invited content from published academics and academic presses. These took the form of 'listicles' of five pieces of advice on how to get an academic book published (Frost, 2010c). I also tracked down a variety of guest contributors to tackle various relevant topics. This book-centric line of content was caused by my erroneous belief that first and foremost on my academic 'to do' list was get a book published. I gradually learned that if you are primarily concerned with employability, your safest route – no matter what discipline you belong to – is to get high-impact journal articles written and published as soon as possible. And yet, what I seemed to be discovering was an alternative route to career success through the very production of the website itself.

At roughly the same time I set up the blog, I opened a PhD2Published Twitter account and later a Facebook page. I knew these were key to sharing site content more widely, but they were important for two other reasons. I did not just want contributors in order to expand blog content; I wanted to be part of a community of peers who I could talk to on a regular basis. I was already tweeting through my own personal account and finding Twitter a valuable space for connecting with new people. Unlike my Facebook profile (at the time), which was mostly populated with real-life friends, acquaintances and work contacts, Twitter was regularly putting me in touch with people I had never met. It was like a perpetual coffee break where I was constantly being introduced to new people. Without belonging to a university, having actual colleagues or access to professional development training, I needed to facilitate my own 'outstitutional' framework, and social media seemed to fit with this aim.

After I secured a book contract, I handed the editorship over to someone else so they could use the site for their own publishing research, community building and writing development. Our most successful editor to date, Anna Tarrant, has reported to me how much her PhD2Published experience has helped her career progress. And certainly, under Tarrant's editorship, the site grew to incorporate more guest posts and a particularly valuable series on journal article resubmissions. Meanwhile, as Tarrant was editing PhD2Published, we established an annual event which has grown beyond all initial expectations.

In 2011 I was a post-doctoral research student at the Centre for 21st Century Studies at the University of Wisconsin-Milwaukee. Still interested in building a community and up-skilling, but now with a book to write, I was specifically invested in the development of good academic writing habits. Inspired by local writing groups and the annual NaNoWriMo or National Novel Writing Month, which challenged people to write 50,000 words of fiction in November, I dubbed November Academic Writing Month. Using social media I invited academics all around the world to use the month to work towards particular goal(s) and share their progress and experiences with the group.

The now annual project is facilitated via the PhD2Published website where we announce the event and rules, offer guidelines and advice as well as the infrastructure for people to connect – for example via the hashtag #AcWriMo and in past years through a Google Doc-based 'accountability spreadsheet'. Each year we have around 1000 participants from over 15 different countries and, more recently, institutions like La Trobe University in Australia and the University of Sheffield in the UK facilitating their own in-house AcWriMos.

Following this, and collaborating with a number of other scholars (including Pat Thomson and Rachael Cayley) with experience in academic writing methods, Tarrant began to co-host regular AcWri live chats on Twitter. '#AcWri' is the hashtag the original AcWriMo community elected to use for academic writing discussion year round, and in particular for these types of co-ordinated live discussions. Both of the hashtags originating from AcWriMo have become firm features of the academic social media landscape.

This summary of PhD2Published shows how an independent project about academic professional development was established and grew over the first few years. However, I want to be clear that it was not initiated as part of a legitimised research strategy. Although it is clearly driven by the need to research academic professional practices, it did not begin from a rigorous research question, there was no planned methodology and there was certainly no funding. Neither was it conceived as a radical alternative to academic publishing. I was not positioning the blog as some kind of open access or open peer review journal. And despite being offered as group learning experience, I did not intend to create a massively open online course (MOOC) or any other type of course. Yet this project still resonates with these modes of academic labour.

Creative public research practice

PhD2Published might not immediately look like a research project so much as a blog, although it compares to creative modes of research. Visual arts research is typically divided into two main areas that speak to the concept of practice as research. As Linda Candy (2006) explains in her report 'Practice based research: A guide', 'practice-based' research is where practice is used to conduct research and where the product of that research is a creative work. 'Practice-led' research, on the other hand, involves practice and the production of creative works, but the outcome is usually a model for practice itself. Practice-led and practice-based modes of conducting research are less well accounted for within academia than more traditional methods. Despite many universities having art schools, the frameworks designed to measure academic output (tenure in the US; the Research Excellence Framework in the UK; a mixture of the two in Hong Kong) often struggle with evaluating this type of research. As a result, it is the research framework of the hard sciences and social sciences that provide more legitimised examples of what research should look like.

I believe that PhD2Published is an example of practice-driven research. In particular, I think that a case could be made for it being akin to practice-led research, given that a website is not only produced, but that the website is part of a broader innovation in publishing mechanisms. However, the project does more than simply show a creative approach to research; because it is conducted in public, the project makes research itself more visible as a process.

In general, scholars expect the results of research to be demonstrated in a publication. Even if the publication describes the research methodology, the day-to-day acts of conducting such research are not visible. Academics look to ethnographic methods to help describe what research looks like as it is happening. Yet it is often the case that ethnographic research is presented in print, after the fact. With PhD-2Published, I have demonstrated another take on the presentation of research *as* practice.

Public writing and publishing

Publishing, at its essence, is the act of making something public. While PhD2Published does not directly innovate within the business model of academic publishing, it is my assertion that it does expand the concept of what publishing might be by facilitating the act of being public with research.

Many scholars recognise that digital technologies offer tremendous potential for new systems of research dissemination. One of the first scholars to write substantially on this topic was Gary Hall with his book *Digitize This Book: The Politics of New Media or Why We Need Open Access Now* (2008) which coincided with a project I will describe shortly. He was followed a few years later by Kathleen Fitzpatrick's *Planned Obsolescence: Publishing, Technology and the Future of the Academy* (2011). These books consider how publishing sits at the core of the academic ecosystem and the political implications of both existing and potential future models.

Such research has been accompanied by a number of experiments in academic publishing. For example, the first notable shift occurred when open access journals were introduced. This began mainly in the hard sciences providing literature for free without any reader fees like a subscription or pay-per-view. As early as 1999 the *Journal of Medical Internet Research* launched as an open access online academic journal. The Public Library of Science (PLOS) was established in 2001 to promote open access scientific publishing and provide a system for publishing science journals. It set up the open access journal *PLOS Biology* in 2003 and *PLOS Medicine* in 2004. *PeerJ*'s open access model, founded in 2012, allows scientists to pay a lifetime fee to publish with them for free through two journals: *PeerJ* for biological and medical science and *PeerJ Computer Science*. The differences between open access models can be measured by the Open Access Spectrum Evaluation Tool.

This open access model has begun to take effect in the humanities. In the field of digital humanities, which I will discuss shortly, there is the open access online digital journal *Digital Humanities Quarterly*, which has been published since 2005. By being online it also offers contributors the ability to publish multimodal works containing video for example or comprising of a bespoke website. Open Humanities Press was established in 2008 by Paul Ashton, Gary Hall, Sigi Jöttkandt and David Ottina. Its aim was to create a framework for publishing open access journals and books. Some of their associated journals include *Culture Machine*, *Electronic Book Review* and *Postcolonial Text*. More than an open access journal and books, however, their offshoot project Liquid Books can be considered as an open source because readers can contribute to the text in any way they like. This means they can take a part of an existing online book and use it to develop a new collection of texts. As the project wiki (2010) explains:

> Culture Machine Liquid Books is a series of experimental digital 'books' published under the (gratis/libre) conditions of both open editing and free content. As such, you are free to compose, rewrite, edit, annotate, translate, tag, add to, remix, reformat, reinvent and reuse any of the books in the series, or produce parallel versions of them – and what's more you are expressly invited and encouraged to do so.

Of some relevance to this book chapter, a recent Liquid Book, *Really, We're Helping To Build This . . . Business: The Academia.edu Files*, looks at the history and business models of academic social networking sites such as Academia.edu and Mendeley.

More recently, the Open Library of Humanities (OLH) was established by Caroline Edwards and Martin Eve, both of whom are based at Birkbeck College at the University of London. OLH is a project supported by a group of international university libraries in order to support the open access publishing of humanities research without charging authors publishing fees. Funded largely by Andrew W. Mellon Foundation grants, it provides the infrastructure for journals to solicit, receive, review and publish articles while also publishing its own multidisciplinary journal.

There have also been a number of projects investigating new models for book publishing. The Institute for the Future of the Book, established in 2005 by publishing innovators Bob Stein and Chris Meade, describes itself as a 'think-and-do tank' for multimodal approaches to discourse production and presentation. Their work has spawned several important projects. In particular, they developed the CommentPress plug-in for Wordpress. The blog post format allows for comments only at the end of the posted piece of content, which means that commenters cannot point directly to the sections they wish to refer to and have to summarise the points they want to make. CommentPress allows for paragraph-level commenting that enhances how specific commenters can be.

This system was used in the various versions of Harvard University Press publication *Gamer Theory* by McKenzie Wark (2007). *Gamer Theory* is a hybrid print and digital networked book. Originally published as a blog with CommentPress installed, the text was publicly peer-reviewed before being redrafted and released in a number of formats. *Gamer Theory* was published as a print book, interactive e-book and a new website that was open for comments (rather than peer review) and included a set of data visualisations based on the book's texts. Similarly, in 2011 MIT press (with support from The Andrew W. Mellon Foundation and The National Endowment for the Arts and Vectors) worked with Alexandra Juhasz to produce *Learning from YouTube* (2011). This experimental 'video-book' investigates the impact of YouTube on culture and education. The video-book contains more than 200 modules of content the author describes as 'texteos' (combining video and text) that contain either core content or reader orientation.

There have been so many new forms of academic publishing that the Hybrid Publishing Consortium (HPC) was developed. HPC is a research project investigating models of open source publishing software for factual publications like academic books. It is produced by Leuphana University of Lüneburg Innovations-Inkubator and funded by the European Regional Development Fund and the German federal state of Lower Saxony. In 2014 the project published The Publication Taxonomy, which is an open guide to contemporary (post-internet) academic publication types. Anyone can contribute to the guide, allowing it to keep pace with on-going developments in the field.

Earlier in this chapter, I argued that PhD2Published makes the act of researching more visible. I would like to extend that point by arguing that the project makes such an act visible through a form of web-based public-making, or, rather, publishing. It is a mode of publishing research as it happens in an on-going project that happens to be about publishing. In the next section of this chapter, I explore how being public and collaborative with research mimics the nature of teaching.

Public researching and publishing and/as teaching

Public teaching is at the core of the digital humanities. Although it is a slightly nebulous field – finding its origins in so-called 'humanities computing' practices from the 1980s and 1990s – public teaching broadly involves using computer technology for conducting and disseminating humanities research.

As a recent approach to scholarly practice that is constantly changing thanks to the rapid development of digital technology, the digitising of the humanities has spawned almost a distinct 'genre' (Kirschenbaum, 2010: 196) of self-reflexive literature which attempts to describe the field. As Matthew G. Kirschenbaum (2010: 196) explains:

> Willard McCarty has been contributing papers on the subject for years (a monograph too). Under the earlier appellation, John Unsworth has advised us [about] 'what is humanities computing and what is not.' Most recently, Patrik Svensson has been publishing a series of well-documented articles on multiple aspects of the topic, including the lexical shift from humanities computing to digital humanities.

In his paper 'The landscape of the digital humanities' Patrik Svensson starts by looking at the various ways scholars have defined the field (Svensson, 2010). For example, he describes how Tara McPherson has divided the digital humanities into three different types:

> According to McPherson, the computing humanities focus on building tools, infrastructure standards and collections, whereas the blogging humanities are concerned with the production of networked media and peer-to-peer writing. The multimodal humanities bring together scholarly tools, databases, networked writing and peer-to-peer commentary while also leveraging the potential of the visual and aural media that are part of contemporary life.
>
> *(2010: 14)*

Indeed, digital humanities as a category covers a range of activities that incorporate digital technology into subject, method, publication and even pedagogy. Some digital humanities projects provide tools with which to conduct research. The 2012 Digital Humanities Awards winner in the 'tools' category was Omeka. Created at the Roy Rosenzweig Center for History and New Media, Omeka software provides an online content management system for curators and archivists, allowing them to easily extract material from existing collection databases (at museums and libraries) to create online public collections. It is useful in developing additional online materials to support physical displays or even display materials online that would be difficult to present in a physical space. Another tool that overlaps with the digital publishing work mentioned earlier is Scalar. Scalar is a platform developed by the Alliance for Networking Visual Culture that provides multimodal publishing capabilities. It allows users to combine a range of media (and annotate that media) with written content and design multiple pathways through all of the materials. This means that all kinds of time-based media can be more usefully examined than in print, while the author does not need coding skills.

Other digital humanities projects are focused on how data are presented as a means for conducting further analysis. In 'Jackson Pollock Alchemy in 3D' Roberto Scopigno from the Visual Computing Lab at Istituto di Scienza e Tecnologie dell'Informazione in Pisa has overseen a team to scan Jackson Pollock paintings and model them in 3D so that they can be viewed as a kind of otherworldly physical terrain. The Nagasaki Archive and Hiroshima Archive both offer maps of the terrain affected by the atomic bombs dropped in 1945 as part of the Second World War. The production committee gathered survivor testimonies to show on the map where the survivors were and how they were influenced by the bombs. In a very different vein, novelist Will Self produced a digital essay on Franz Kafka which was commissioned by the *London Review of Books* and funded by The Arts Council England and BBC The Space Arts (Self, no date). The piece can be read in numerous non-linear ways through different associations that the essay interface makes possible. On top of the associative interface, the essay features a wealth of additional content produced by more than 70 people who reflected on Kafka's work in a variety of ways from interviews to music production.

Digital humanities practitioners are also known for running events that help people learn both what the field involves and develop relevant skills or tools. For example, the annual 'Day of Digital Humanities' is an open project inviting digital humanities practitioners from around the world to document their working day and share it with others. It is a large-scale, crowd-sourced community ethnography that makes the work conducted under the title 'digital humanities' uniquely visible. In the 2015 incarnation, Adam Rabinowitz of the University of Texas reflected on the tasks he carries out at spring time such as grading student work rather than conducting research or making something (Rabinowitz, 2015). Sharon Cogdill from Saint Cloud State University, on the other hand, provided an in-depth explanation of meticulous wiki-based archival work she is conducting (Cogdill, 2015). One Week | One Tool, which ran for several years at the Roy Rosenzweig Center for History and New Media at George Mason University, brings a group of people together to collaboratively create an open source digital humanities tool in one week. In 2010 a team built Anthologize, a Wordpress plug-in that allows users to turn blog content into electronic book formats.

Many digital humanities scholars develop and share approaches to public and collaborative teaching, which was important to the conceptualisation of PhD-2Published. In 2011, Professors Zach Whalen, Erin Templeton, Paul Benzon, Mark Sample and Brian Croxall taught the novel *House of Leaves* synchronously across their respective institutions with students taking part in an online discussion forum for part of their grade. In a 2014 incarnation of the networked course, participants collaboratively annotated an online version of the text. Alexis Lothian has produced a project where students investigate how gender is played out in social networking sites. Attached to the course/module 'Gender, Race and Labor in the Digital Worlds', it is a way for students to test out different tools of analysis while also testing the nature of their own online networks. My own Arts Future Classroom platform crowd-sources toolkits for teaching art history using digital tools and ideas. The resource includes the Wikipedia editing class I teach, where students learn how to write artist biographies for Wikipedia as a form of contemporary art history writing. Among the important skills learned are public accountability and referencing.

What is most apparent in such projects is the creation of a learning community or network both within the literal space of the classroom and beyond it, in digital and online environments. The final point I would like to make, therefore, is that PhD2Published provides another example of a networked teaching and learning experience. The website operates as an educational framework, a collection of public researching acts. Rather than creating a one-to-many instruction situation, the site promotes the type of public and collaborative knowledge gathering that is intrinsic to the culture of Web 2.0, where content is user-generated. Specific posts to the site have provided discrete examples of this. For example, a post I co-produced for PhD2Published with Jesse Stommel about using Google Docs for public and collaborative writing (Frost and Stommel, 2013) offered a live public workshop in collaborative writing within a Google Doc itself. The community as a whole can be seen as a live public workshop.

From PhD to platform

My approach in setting up PhD2Published was inspired less by rigorous academic research than the non-profit initiatives of many of the communities I had been engaging with in the arts and crafts field. These were primarily about providing an infrastructure for community building. As a result they could be described as being independent or grassroots, on-going and iterative, not restricted to a particular goal or output and generally allowing for a potentially infinite number or network of contributors. In many ways, such features run counter to (pre-digital) academic research – let alone publishing and teaching – conventions. Academic research is largely conducted from within a hierarchical institution and by a specific set of people who mine defined data sets according to a fixed timeframe to provide instructive published outcomes. PhD2Published, by comparison, provides an example of what academic practice will increasingly look like: where research, writing, publishing and teaching are enfolded in a hybrid, online, public academic practice and platform.

In this sense, PhD2Published indicates the emergence of a new career trajectory. Despite the fact my research specialisation is not academic publishing, what I built over the last five years is a public project that researches, publishes and educates users on academic publishing. Instead of writing a book I built a platform that does many of the same things as an academic book, but in different ways. As the platform came first and heavily contributed to my employability, I went not from PhD to published, but from PhD to platform. Not only that, I have been able to *not* publish and *not* perish; instead I have platformed and flourished. That sounds suspicious given you are reading this chapter right now in a published book, but by comparison to other scholars at my level I have relatively few 'traditional' publications. That will change. At the time of writing, I face a publication bottleneck as I complete my first book, several related papers and write other pieces reflecting on my 'rogue' scholarship. It has taken me longer to legitimately publish because of the time that my online academic life takes, but I have been repeatedly told by employers that a large part of the reason I have been hired is because of my online projects. Not only do they attract attention and make me well known both within and beyond my own field, but departments are often cautiously interested in what new forms of scholarship might look like.

Mine is a career trajectory that I believe we will see with greater frequency in the years to come. It is not that the academic publication will have died, so much as it will mutate into these new forms and measures of impact. As a result, the academic publication (if we can still call it that for now) will be far closer to the continuing academic activities of researching and teaching. Instead, scholars will be able to bring their work to the public as it unfolds, as well as continue to refine findings in a more iterative process. This model will not work for all subject areas: some research pertains to sensitive data and must, by its very nature, be conducted in private. Furthermore, not everyone will feel comfortable with this degree of being public. Yet for those who can work in this way, there remains the opportunity to create interconnected academic platforms with the potential to advance knowledge at a greater pace and with broader impact. That is not to say big and fast are necessarily better, but that we have the chance to explore a wide range of options for academic practice in the digital age.

Bibliography

Academic Writing Month (AcWriMo) (2011) What is AcWriMo? www.phd2published .com/acwri-2/acbowrimo/about/ (accessed 1 June 2016).

Anthologize (2010) http://anthologize.org/ (accessed 1 June 2016).

Arts Future Classroom (2014) www.artsfuture.org/classroom (accessed 1 June 2016).

Candy, L. (2006) Practice based research: A guide. CCS Report: 2006-V1.0 November. University of Technology, Sydney.

Cogdill, S. (2015) Day of DH, step by step. *Day of Digital Humanities 2015*. http://dayofdh2015 .uned.es/scogdill/2015/05/20/day-of-dh-step-by-step/ (accessed 1 June 2016).

Day of Digital Humanities 2015 (2015) http://dayofdh2015.uned.es/ (accessed 1 June 2016).

Digital Humanities Awards (2011) http://dhawards.org/ (accessed 1 June 2016).

Digital Humanities Now (2009) http://digitalhumanitiesnow.org/ (accessed 1 June 2016).

Fitzpatrick, K. (2011) *Planned Obsolescence: Publishing, Technology and the Future of the Academy*. New York and London: New York University Press.

Frost, C. (2010a) The book shelf test or how to research your market Part 1. *PhD2Published*. www.phd2published.com/2010/08/05/the-book-shelf-test-or-how-to-research-your-market-part-i/ (accessed 1 June 2016).

Frost, C. (2010b) Weekly wisdom #1. *PhD2Published*. www.phd2published.com/2010/06/08/weekly-wisdom-1/ (accessed 1 June 2016).

Frost, C. (2010c) Publisher tips: Oxford University Press. *PhD2Published*. www.phd2published. com/2010/07/28/publisher-tips-oxford-university-press/ (accessed 1 June 2016).

Frost, C. and Stommel, J. (2013) Collaborative and public writing techniques for Google Docs by Charlotte Frost and Jesse Stommel. *PhD2Published*. www. phd2published.com/2013/11/27/collaborative-and-public-writing-techniques-for-google-docs-by-charlotte-frost-and-jesse-stommel/ (accessed 1 June 2016).

Hall, G. (2008) *Digitize This Book: The Politics of New Media or Why We Need Open Access Now*. Minneapolis: University of Minnesota Press.

Hiroshima Archive (2010) http://hiroshima.mapping.jp/index_en.html (accessed 1 June 2016).

Hybrid Publishing Consortium (2011) www.consortium.io/ (accessed 1 June 2016).

Institute for the Future of the Book (2005) www.futureofthebook.org/ (accessed 1 June 2016).

Jackson Pollock Alchemy in 3D (2014) http://vcg.isti.cnr.it/alchemy/ (accessed 1 June 2016).

Juhasz, A. (2011) *Learning from YouTube*. Cambridge, Massachusetts: MIT Press.

Kirschenbaum, M. G. (2010) What is digital humanities and what's it doing in English departments? In: Terras, M., Nyhan, J. and Vanhoutte, E. (eds), *Defining Digital Humanities: A Reader*. Farnham, Surrey: Ashgate, 195–204.

Kral, C. (2014) A publication taxonomy: An initial guide to academic publishing types, inside and beyond academe, 10 February. http://hybridpublishing.org/2014/02/a-publication-taxonomy/ (accessed 1 June 2016).

Liquid Books (2010) http://openhumanitiespress.org/liquid-books.html (accessed 1 June 2016).

Liquid Books (wiki) (2010) http://liquidbooks.pbworks.com/w/page/11135951/FrontPage (accessed 1 June 2016).

Liquid Book (wiki) (n.d.) *Really, We're Helping To Build This . . . Business: The Academia. edu Files*, http://liquidbooks.pbworks.com/w/page/106236504/The%20Academia_edu%20Files (accessed 26 May 2017).

Nagasaki Archive (2010) http://e.nagasaki.mapping.jp/ (accessed 1 June 2016).

National Novel Writing Month (NaNoWriMo) (2000) http://nanowrimo.org/ (accessed 1 June 2016).

Omeka (2008) http://omeka.org/ (accessed 1 June 2016).

One Week | One Tool (2010) http://oneweekonetool.org/ (accessed 1 June 2016).

Open Access Spectrum Evaluation Tool (no date) www.oaspectrum.org/ (accessed 1 June 2016).

Open Humanities Press (no date) http://openhumanitiespress.org/ (accessed 1 June 2016).

Open Library of Humanities (2013) www.openlibhums.org/ (accessed 1 June 2016).

PeerJ (2012) https://peerj.com/ (accessed 1 June 2016).

PhD2Published (2010) www.phd2published.com (accessed 1 June 2016).

Rabinowitz, A. (2015) Adam's day of DH: Management vs making. *Day of Digital Humanities 2015.* http://dayofdh2015.uned.es/adamrabinowitz/2015/05/20/adams-day-of-dh-management-vs-making/ (accessed 1 June 2016).

Ramsay, S. (2013) On building. In: Terras, M., Nyhan, J. and Vanhoutte, E. (eds), *Defining Digital Humanities: A Reader*. Farnham, Surrey: Ashgate, 243–254.

Sample, M. (2013) The digital humanities is not about building, it's about sharing. In: Terras, M., Nyhan, J. and Vanhoutte, E. (eds), *Defining Digital Humanities: A Reader*. Farnham, Surrey: Ashgate, 255–257.

Scalar (2013) http://scalar.usc.edu/take-scalar-2-for-a-spin/ (accessed 1 June 2016).

Self, W. (no date) Kafka's wound. *The Space.* http://thespace.lrb.co.uk/ (accessed 1 June 2016).

Stoller, D. (2004) *Stitch and Bitch: The Knitter's Handbook*. New York: Workman Publishing.

Svensson, P. (2010) The landscape of the digital humanities. *Digital Humanities Quarterly* 4(1). http://digitalhumanities.org/dhq/vol/4/1/000080/000080.html (accessed 1 June 2016).

Wark, M. (2007) *Gamer Theory*. Cambridge, Massachusetts: Harvard University Press.

4

ACADEMIC PERSONA

The construction of online reputation in the modern academy

P. David Marshall, Kim Barbour and Christopher Moore

Introduction

Thomson Reuters, one of the largest publishers in the world, has been involved in what it calls the 'Global Institutional Profiles Project', in association with the Times Higher Education World University Rankings. Through its five-stage data collection, the project includes a reputation survey of invited key academics in an array of fields with extensive attention to both region and discipline. The breadth of the survey is impressive, but what is perhaps most interesting is that embedded in the survey is a series of six questions specifically related to online culture and academia. In a series of online screens, participants are asked to rank universities in teaching and research individually in their discipline. The questions on social media use are trawling for a very specific change in the organisation of the knowledge economy at its intellectual apex. Those surveyed were asked to rank their use of social media for academic ends, which are defined in terms of research awareness. Blogs and social media are highlighted in the survey in terms of the blogs participants read in their field, whether they monitor social media activity in their field, and also whether they engage in the use of these forms for the promulgation of their work. The final question of this series asks for their relative connection to publishing in open source journals – a question that in its wording already acknowledges the ubiquity of this form and movement of information in their academic fields.

Thomson Reuters' project is connected to providing comprehensive data in ranking institutions and disciplines within institutions in order to establish that its data are the most reliable for the sector and valuable for those 'using' the sector such as students, corporations and governments who want to know where best practices can be located. They now have what they contend is 'a 360 degree view of the world's leading research institutions', where you can look through the profiles of

769 universities (see Thomson Reuters, 2016). What becomes clear from this effort at surveying individuals is that university reputations are at least partly built from the quality and visibility of their academic faculty.

Building that visibility is a difficult game that universities play as they try to improve their position in the various ranking systems in the world – from the Times Higher Education World Rankings identified here to the now established QS World University Rankings, The Center for World University Rankings (CWUR), the Academic Ranking of World Universities (ARWU) and the country-specific rankings such as US News and World Report ranking of the 1600 colleges and universities in the United States. In addition, there are a number of domestic systems within individual countries, such as the Ivy League in the United States of America, the British Russell Group or the Group of Eight in Australia, which are based on a combination of longevity, prestige and perceived research leadership. Ranking systems can become incredibly granular, determining which departments are the strongest in a country or market based on publications submitted by scholars within that department, judged through journal quality and citation counts (contested and ranked through systems such as Excellence in Research in Australia (ERA) and the Research Excellence Framework (REF) in the United Kingdom). The relative position of universities, and their movement up or down the various national and international rankings from year to year, works to attract the highest calibre school leavers, the most financially valuable industry partnerships, and also drives public and private funding decisions (Pusser and Marginson, 2013: 544–45).

There are several threats to the contemporary academic that are changing what could be described as their relative autonomy and the increased need for them to actively build their reputations. First, universities are increasingly seeing themselves in international competition with other universities as this focus on rankings permeates the sector. Very much connected to this external form of competition is a new anxiety pervading higher education institutions around their purpose and objective in a changed contemporary world. Part of this anxiety is driven by how online culture has progressed in recent years and the availability of information and education via different means. Coursing through the university sector are new techniques of delivery of information beyond lectures and assessment regimes.

For instance, the massive open online course (MOOC) that is no longer wedded to traditional university structures but often connected to the most prestigious universities has been seen as a threat to the organisation of the delivery of higher education in the same way the delivery of news via online sources has produced a sea-change in newspapers. Providers of MOOCs, such as Coursera along with their partners at Harvard, Stanford and MIT, are constructing new hierarchies of where knowledge can be attained and new hierarchies of connecting to the best resources and people for that information. The development of MOOCs over the last half-decade has been major, but less so in terms of the educational impact than how it has facilitated a further heating up of transnational competition amongst universities. One of the ultimate effects on the individual academic is that, because their reputation is partially built on their personal delivery of course content to their students, this potential change to an internationally competitively driven and more centrally delivered content structure downgrades the role and status of the individual academic to 'facilitator' or teacher of centrally produced online content. In addition to these potential changes to what constitutes an academic's work and role, there are also the gradual and advancing moves to eliminate the concept of tenure into structured and limited appointments. In combination, these changes in the higher education sector are producing a kind of instability and insecurity in academics that is very much a push to make their presence and reputation known.

Along with this general higher education-wide professional anxiety, because the academic profession has always operated to a degree in a prestige economy environment, the pressure on academics to build their profile – and particularly their online profile – is growing. A number of scholars have sought to understand the motivations and consequences of adding the additional layer of online labour onto already time-poor academic colleagues. Blogging is a common focus for a number of studies, and Gregg (2009: 474) comments that for junior faculty members, 'blogs give voice to a range of personal and work-related issues that arise for their authors as the reality of professional identity sets in'. However, other than through the practice of being a 'blogger', Gregg's work sees blogging primarily as an expressive, rather than constructive, space. That is, she sees the practice of blogging as a way of performing identity and dealing with workplace frustrations, rather than producing an identity through the blog, although she acknowledges the complexity of the subcultures that surround academic blogging.

Extending Gregg's work on blogging, Mewburn and Thomson (2013) examine the styles seen in different types of academic blogs, coding them according to scholar and content. Discovering a range of stated motivations and types of blog, Mewburn and Thomson complicate prior understandings of why, how and for whom academics blog. Their suggestion to test assumptions against the perspectives of the academics who write the blog – that is, to speak to those academics directly – is one we strongly support, and drives the participatory action research approach we adopted for the pilot research detailed later.

Shifting the focus from blogging, and taking a participatory approach, Stewart (2015) examines the complex strategies academics use in order to determine the influence (or reputation) of another scholar through open networks such as Twitter. Stewart (2015: 306) concludes that engagement with these technologies 'brings into being an alternate but intersecting prestige arena in which credibility is determined by recognizability and commonality rather than credentials, and hierarchies of influence relate to identities and attention, rather than role'.

Veletsianos and Kimmons (2012: 768) examine broader engagement with digital technologies, describing what they dub 'Networked Participatory Scholarship' as 'the emergent practice of scholars' use of participatory technologies and online social networks to share, reflect upon, critique, improve, validate, and further their scholarship'. Although limited by their focus on use of digital technology that is directly related to the scholar's work, Veletsianos and Kimmons do emphasise the importance of engaging with, and influencing the direction of, the role of technological innovation in academic settings. However, Veletsianos' (2013) follow-up study of individual academics' online practices goes further by looking not only at uses of digital media for scholarship, but rather – as with the pilot study reported later – conducts more holistic empirical research into academics' use of social media. He concludes by noting 'it may be worthwhile for future work to further explore how scholars perceive and construct their identity online' (2013: 649).

To this end, the rest of this chapter is a longitudinal study of sixteen academics as they work to present themselves more widely and generally online from 2011 to 2013 in this changing academic environment. What this study reveals are the possibilities and potentials that this presenting oneself more regularly can produce, as well as the pressures and constraints that are placed on these same individuals of building their reputations within the structures and demands of the contemporary university setting.

Concepts and categories of personas

Our work in this area is not without related conceptual work. Collectively, we have been developing the concept of 'persona' and the realisation that much online activity and particularly that related to social media was about producing some sort of public version of the self. Although our own engagement with persona studies has its roots in cultural studies, there is a range of synergies that can be tracked across disciplines. The term 'persona' is used in user experience design (Coorevits et al., 2016) to describe a constructed character or 'ideal customer' for whom a product is designed. In marketing the term can describe an element of a brand encompassing the 'publicly performed persona, not the actual persons who perform them' (Dion and Arnould, 2015: 122) when associated with a particular individual.

The infiltration, importation and colonisation of the workplace by social media, mobile technologies and data metrics represents a shift, and intensification, rather than a break with past experiences of scholarly labour. Our work has collectively advanced the idea that what we are observing in the contemporary moment is a dramatic shift in how we construct our online identities, where each of us, whether academic, celebrity, doctor, electrician or homemaker, is actively producing a public version of ourselves for consumption far beyond our immediate acquaintance. There is a sense of unease in this cultural transformation. Within the academic profession, different sectors and disciplines have dealt with this mediatisation of the self with varying levels of enthusiasm, and these differences in all likelihood parallel the professions outside of universities that most directly relate to the different academic disciplines.

Our research uses the term *persona* to describe a strategic and public identity (see Marshall and Barbour, 2015). Although not always achieving its objective, a persona is the way in which we individually try to move a particular element (or collection of elements) of our sense of self into collective realms and is directly related to Goffman's interactionist approach to the performative presentation of the self (Goffman, 1973). As with a Goffmanian conceptualisation of role play, a persona presented publicly through digital media may be only one of many, and the 'academic persona' may also be nuanced, divided up and performed differently in different contexts. A range of different objectives can drive this strategic deployment of a particular persona. The new layers of what we call the 'intercommunication industries' – that is, those online forms of social media that blend interpersonal communication with a spectrum of mediated communication (Marshall, 2015b) – are the instruments that have led to the expansion of the development of online personas. Parts of our professional academic lives are now circulating in this movement of information, and our activities have become part of other systems of the information economy that work to aggregate and remarket our identities to different products and services.

As our wider research into persona has revealed and the research we explored in this survey has underlined, there is a great need for digital persona literacy. Much of this literacy is a realisation that monitoring ourselves and the data we generate is the fundamental yet onerous starting point in understanding our digital persona (see Marshall, 2015a). Lupton (2015: 79) describes these digital personas as 'constantly changing data doubles' or, drawing on Burrows (2012), 'metric assemblages' (Lupton, 2015: 80). Lupton discusses material created *about* academics (often automatically) such as citation counts, view statistics, download statistics, altmetrics and other tracking tools that could be utilised by academics, administrators, students or the public to determine a sense of a scholar's impact and importance. Along with understanding this type of metric, the study reported later was designed to complement these automated processes of persona production by engaging with the contributions of text, images and so forth that are created and shared online by the academics themselves.

Part of our background research for this study examined what very visible or internationally prominent academics were already doing in online contexts. From that initial research, we developed categories of online identity that served as the guiding structures for how academic personas were forming into patterns. In Barbour and Marshall (2012), we described the categories as:

1. the formal or static online self – an identity derived from a profile page on a university website, for instance, and resembling a static broadcast style, framed by the exigencies of the university or institution where the individual worked;
2. the networked self – in contrast to the formal self, this persona is expressed through a form of narrowcasting to key players and interested colleagues in a discipline; it was extra-institutional, focused on a professional and formal identity and usually relied on a number of platforms for its delivery;
3. the comprehensive self – identified as quite similar to the networked self but included the circulation of what could be seen as private information (hobbies, family lives, friendships, personal interests outside of an academic speciality) embedded within often professionally focused flows of information;

4. the teaching self — a very targeted form of online self that was defined by its collaborative and interactive direction, but also by its constrained and directed professional relationship online. This identity moved generally within a particular institution but much more broadly into related professional industries depending on the goal of the particular academic's teaching objectives;

5. the uncontainable self — this resulted from a general lack of monitoring of or engagement with online identity. The outcome of the lack of participation in social media can see scandal at the extreme level, and a gossip-like persona at the more benign level.

(Derived from Barbour and Marshall, 2012)

Our study

The pilot research project was conducted in the Faculty of Arts at Deakin University in the Australian city of Melbourne. All but one participant was located within the School of Communication and Creative Arts. Participants were recruited via an ALL_STAFF email, and invited to contact the researchers for more information. The initial email also included information about the first session, which was attended by a number of colleagues who chose not to continue with the research project, and whose data are excluded from this report. The project used multiple research methods, including surveys, interviews and workshops. We employed a variation of the Participatory Action Research (PAR) method (see Kemmis, 2006; Townsend, 2013) which situates the researcher in a knowledge-attaining cross-position with the subjects of the pilot study. The participant group following the first meeting (as detailed later) was made up of eight women and eight men, with six post-graduate/early career academics (three of whom were women), five mid-career academics (three of whom were women) and five holding associate professorships or professorships (two of whom were women).

Original survey

Our first task was to determine what the pilot study participants were currently doing to maintain an online presence of some sort, and what they wished to achieve by being a part of this study. To this end, each participant at our first meeting filled in a 'Persona Audit', asking them to identify which social or professional networking platforms they had a presence on, which they used most frequently and how happy they were with their current online persona. They were also asked to identify what they wished to achieve, both in terms of specific goals (increased networking, research funding, student engagement and so on) and in terms of where they wanted to situate themselves in regards to the categories of persona already identified (formal, comprehensive, teaching, networking). Finally, each participant identified their potential time commitment for this project over the initial three-month period.

One-on-one interviews

The original group of sixteen committed participants were each allocated a member of the research team (Marshall, Barbour or Moore) who conducted more detailed follow-up discussions around persona development and planning. These discussions allowed the research team to assist with planning and strategic decisions for each group member, suggest platform choices and gain more specific insights into the training requirements. Additionally, qualitative data around engagement and success with social and professional networking sites were sought, including lurking/ listening behaviour, subjective descriptions of relative happiness and desired outcomes to improve, maintain or consolidate each participant's online persona. As a starting point to allow small changes in behaviour, it was suggested that each participant develop their email signature(s), develop a persona development schedule by making recurring 'appointments' in their calendars, develop links between each online platform related to the persona they wished to develop, update their institutional profile to point to outside presences and to consider developing an Academia.edu profile (if they had not done so already) to connect with others in their department, institution and discipline.

Seminar on social media

Stemming from both the persona audit and the one-on-one meetings, it became clear that almost all of our participants desired a crash course in a range of social media platforms and how these related to their academic positions. To this end, we held a two-hour workshop that covered using Twitter, Facebook, various Google platforms including YouTube and a range of other sites. We also invited the faculty media coordinator to speak on gaining a greater presence through traditional media sites as a response to a number of participants who indicated this is something they sought to achieve. The workshop was an extension of our PAR approach. There is no question the workshop opened up possibilities for the participants and worked to allow them to experiment further in their uses of social media and online platforms for their academic identities. It was also a further opportunity to observe our participants and their capacity to take on and appropriate relatively new ways of expressing their professional academic identity.

Follow-up survey and individual interviews

Between six and twelve months after the first meeting, the research team revisited their allocated participants for a follow-up interview using a similar format to the first one-on-one. This meeting sought a mix of quantitative and qualitative data on changes in behaviour, perceived successes and failures, and satisfaction with persona development. Due to time pressure, role changes and other circumstances, the final cohort of participants for whom we have full data sets is made up of seven people. These people range from full-time professors through to PhD candidates working in casual academic teaching positions, and our findings from their engagement with the project are detailed here.

Findings

The key findings of this pilot study discussed below are taken from the seven participants who completed the full programme of persona audit, one-on-one interview and follow-up interview. Additionally, four of the seven attended the social media workshop. Points of interest within the final data relate to site usage for persona development, the time required to build and maintain a strong online academic persona, successful endeavours relating to students, professional connections and personal development, constraints and problems faced by participants, and an overall consideration of the success of the pilot. Each area is discussed in depth below.

Site usage

The academics who participated in this pilot study were no strangers to presenting themselves online. They all, to varying degrees, participated in a range of professional and/or social networking platforms. On average, they reported using three different platforms, with the heavy users reporting four or more different sites on which they presented a profile. By the close of this pilot project, each participant had a professional profile on LinkedIn, all but one had a Facebook account, and three of the seven had either or both an Academia.edu or Twitter profile. What was interesting was the level of engagement with these different platforms. Despite all being present on LinkedIn, no one actually checked their site or added new information; rather, the LinkedIn profile was dormant, sitting as a placeholder. In contrast, with the exception of one participant who did not have an account, Facebook usage was by far the most frequent of all the reported platforms. Two of the six account holders used Facebook solely for personal networking, and took pains to separate the professional sides of their lives from their personal friend and family networks. Only one used their account solely for professional use.

While Facebook usage tended to be either personal or both personal and professional, the participants who used Academia.edu and Twitter used these solely for professional networking. This is not surprising for Academia.edu, which was set up for this purpose, but is a little more interesting when it comes to Twitter. As a microblogging site made famous by celebrity users such as Ashton Kutcher, and made notorious by other celebrities posting racist, sexist, drunk or derogatory tweets, photos or links, the use of Twitter by academics for professional networking provides a clear counterpoint. However, usage of Twitter can vary in intensity for academics, and one of the participants reported returning to the platform after a long absence, while another reported alternating between Twitter and Facebook rather than engaging with both simultaneously. This predominantly professional adoption of a platform originally designed for entertainment is reflected through the use of YouTube by four of the participants, two of whom started a channel as a result of their participation in the study. The participants reported using YouTube as a way of providing pre-recorded teaching materials for their students, either by making them from scratch or by collecting and linking through to short clips posted by others. Only one participant claimed to use their YouTube account for personal use, but this was likely underreported in terms of using the site as an entertainment forum. However, as this lurking or listening (Crawford, 2009) behaviour does not necessarily add to a persona, watching music videos or funny videos from the privacy of one's computer was not directly investigated.

Our data seem to show a disparity between the participants' reported use in our initial persona audit and their continued use in the follow-up one-on-one interviews. When asked whether they had dropped any platform, not one participant indicated that they had (although they may have stated that they reduced usage), but the platforms listed under current online behaviour do not seem to accurately reflect their current active use when looking at all three sources of information together. Some sites, such as LinkedIn, may be expected to continue to function without input of content or attention, and this neglect, although not surprising, does not make the most of the possibilities offered by the technology.

Time

One clearly reported and often repeated reason for neglecting persona work was time pressure. Although we had expected time to be a constraint for the trial participants, we originally believed that the suggested time allocation each participant made in their persona audit was achievable. In the follow-up interview, however, it quickly became apparent that their initial commitment was harder to fulfil for many of the participants. Additionally, it appeared that none of the participants was able to set aside a set amount of time each week to work on their online persona development and maintenance (particularly those who blogged or were creating teaching materials), which we believed would be the best strategy for the ongoing sustainability of a particular persona type. Rather, the participants reported their time spent as 'sporadic' or they reported spending 'many' hours, while another suggested they spent 'a few hours a week', and a fourth totalled their time expenditure to '2 weeks-ish' over the course of the project. Significant engagement was made by those who were already heavy users of social media, with one stating they spent upwards of 200 hours, of which 'a lot was set up and researching different platforms', while another refused to quantify time spent as her 'whole life was in development right now'. Active users also struggled to separate persona development time from everyday social media usage, something the research team expected and sees reflected in their own behaviour. The queries about time spent on persona development were intended to encourage the participants to think about their usage strategically, rather than continuing to use the sites haphazardly.

Successes

In their follow-up interviews, all participants were asked about what they felt was particularly successful in their engagement with social media for the purposes of building an academic persona. The types of successes varied considerably between participants, but were loosely aligned with their stated aims from the first interview. The aspects of the project of which the participants were most proud relate to student interaction (attraction and retention), professional connections (including speaking opportunities) and professional development (particularly skill development).

Student interaction

Social media engagement developed through this project has led to two PhD student supervision opportunities for participants, which can be seen as an increase in both profile and prestige. A Masters student from another institution contacted one participant due to his profile on Academia.edu, while another was approached by a 'follower' who liked something this participant had tweeted.

An increase in engagement with YouTube proved to be the path to success for another participant. She has filmed and uploaded many instructional videos that her students are able to access. She states that she has received a positive response from students and also seen a decline in the number of queries from students about how to use equipment as a direct result of uploading these particular videos. Although the process of filming and editing the clips was time consuming, the end result has proven very successful. This participant stated she had met her goal of YouTube being an 'effective and useful space for students and grads to talk and network', and feels very 'smug' about the way that this project panned out. In addition to her use of YouTube as a host site for her teaching materials, the same participant also increased the accessibility of her 'alumni' Facebook group. This is a private group to which she has invited students who have graduated from her courses. After starting this project, she opened the invitation to third-year students as well, allowing them to use the group to make connections with and gain experience from others already in the workforce, and giving her graduated students a great source of cheap or volunteer labour for their projects. Although the group was still building at the time of the last interview, this participant felt that it was becoming self-sustaining, although she still contributed to the discussion and would work to include new members when necessary.

Professional connections

Given that the majority of the participants in this pilot project chose to focus their efforts on developing a comprehensive professional persona, the success of their endeavours is particularly heartening. Having taken the time to develop their profiles on Academia.edu, be more consistent and provide more value from their Twitter usage, and become more active in using Facebook for professional networking, these participants were able to see a reward for their labour.

One participant who spent some time developing a more up-to-date and comprehensive profile on Academia.edu, cited this updating as helping to receive more searches/hits on the site. After the update, he saw a corresponding increase in enquiries and requests for help, along with an invitation to give a presentation to senior secondary school students in Sydney. The speaking opportunity came after the organisers found his name via a journal article, and were able to find more information about him via Academia.edu (and an older LiveJournal account) to determine that he was the right person for the job.

Twitter led not only to enquiries about PhD supervision, but one participant found that it allowed her to connect to others at conferences more easily by starting a conversation on a digital platform which could be translated into a physical meet-up later in the day. She also used Twitter to comment and make notes on papers during conference sessions, and access them to write up later on. Another successful use of the microblogging platform was to publicise her long-form blog writing, increasing and diversifying its readership, while also finding it a good research site, participating in the exchange of links and material. This contribution to the online debate has resulted in her becoming a book reviewer for an important domestic journal, and has led to the development of two conference papers.

Another participant used this project as the impetus needed to set up his blog. He spent a considerable amount of time planning and designing the site, aiming to move beyond the basics and create something that was as close to a commercial site as he could manage. This formed the majority of the persona work that this participant did during the course of the project, but he acknowledged the set-up period was necessary, and having put the work in, the process of promoting and developing his online persona would be more manageable.

The capacity of Facebook, or 'email on steroids' as one participant characterised it, to construct a dialogue or train of comments relating to an image (this participant is an artist) was used to good effect. By widening his professional connections on Facebook, and trying to deliberately engage in critical debate, the participant continues to develop his use of the platform for debate and personal development. Although he has used Facebook intermittently in the past, he used his involvement with this pilot persona development project to further his use and sees the development of his persona on the site as an ongoing project.

Personal development

A key aim of the pilot project was to give the participants access to and information about a wide range of possible platforms that can be used in the development of an academic persona. Learning about what tools are available around social media opened up new possibilities for a number of the participants who are now looking to learn about and experiment with Prezi for sharing lectures and presentations, Zotero for both citation management and sharing of sources, Moodle and MOOCs for examples of online teaching and ways to increase student engagement, and even to develop their more practical skills in areas such as image manipulation and digital file management. A number of participants took part in technical workshops in order to improve their skill sets to allow them to achieve the goals they had set as a part of this pilot project.

Problems and constraints

Participants were asked also to note and report parts of the process that were less successful, and to consider why these problems occurred. One participant found the constant upgrading of the university's online teaching and learning systems a real frustration. Shortly after completing a personal development session relating to the online teaching site, and planning his course materials accordingly, the platform received a complete upgrade which rendered what he had learned redundant.

A similar complaint came from a participant who was employed to teach at the university in a series of fixed-term contracts rather than in an ongoing position. Upon the completion of each contract when her staff access lapsed, it was necessary to 'eliminate yourself from Deakin', which had run-on effects, affecting personal profiles on sites such as Academia.edu. The casualisation of the academic workforce has a considerable effect on the way that this particular academic worked to develop an online persona, not only meaning it was difficult for her to claim continued allegiance with the university sites designed specifically for academics, but also impacts on her borrowing and database privileges at the library, meaning that it is more difficult for her to maintain a research and publication record. For example, each time an institutional email account was closed down, she would need to update a number of sites to reflect the changing ways in which she could be contacted. Given she was rehired at the beginning of the next teaching semester, with the same email address, this caused significant frustration. Having an .edu or an .ac email address is also a requirement for access to the student and teacher editions of some online software such as Prezi, and the loss of that email address can lead to the necessity to purchase additional storage space for a public account in which to archive teaching or conference presentations.

Time commitments elsewhere (both work and family), were most often cited as reasons for lack of success in achieving their persona-related goals. One participant cited his three-year-old child as the key reason why he had not made more progress, along with the need to keep his large semi-rural property under control. The cyclical nature of the academic year, marked by intensive work during assessment periods, was another common (if expected) complaint. The recommendation to devote a set period of time to persona development was not taken up by many within the pilot, which may have contributed to the sense of 'not having time', as this project was an extra thing to do for already overloaded staff.

Technical issues were another reason cited for lack of success. One particularly technology-savvy participant described the technology itself as limiting and therefore a cause of frustration. She was grappling with how a site that she establishes about herself and her own research could be different from her profile on Academia.edu, her university website or even Wikipedia. Other participants struggled with their own capacity to use existing platforms, including completing tasks such as uploading high-resolution photos correctly. Another saw her own technical prowess as directly relating to her success with regard to her use of YouTube to engage her students. It was due largely to her knowledge of filming, editing and being able to upload the clips directly into the Deakin system that the endeavour was successful, as opposed to the capacities of the technology itself. Without her prior knowledge, she would have struggled to complete the task, especially when the university's system wouldn't allow her to upload her videos onto YouTube on campus, a task she had to perform at home.

Positive outcomes

Despite a range of problems and challenges to the process of developing an online academic persona, most participants were positive about their experiences as a part of this pilot project. One participant said she felt her involvement as giving her a necessary push to do the things she's been putting off, while having someone to bounce ideas off helped her to clarify her aims and gave her new ways of thinking about what had worked or not in the past. Another felt that the project allowed her the space to consider in a collective manner the way that she presented herself online, and believes that her continued and extensive engagement with social media has made her more positive as a person, stating 'the sheer weight of social media that I engage in is forcing me to be a glass half-full person'. Throughout the project, participants were asked to rate their 'happiness' with their online persona on a scale from 1 (not happy) to 5 (very happy). The happiness rating of six of the seven participants increased by at least 0.5 over the course of the project, and one participant shifted their rating from a 2 at the first meeting to a 5 at the final interview. The one participant who did not increase their happiness rating remained steady at a 4, claiming that there was still work to be done as persona creation is an ongoing process.

Conclusion

This pilot project provides insight into the complexity of producing and maintaining an online academic persona. The range of platforms used for persona development, even within the small number of participants who saw this project through to the end, demonstrates that academics are willing and able to seek solutions they need for presentational requirements well outside of their institutional platforms. However, the constraints of time and resources to fully engage with social media, especially when starting a new profile from scratch, makes it difficult to deal with the diverse content each platform requires. Sites such as Academia.edu and Twitter appear to be popular because of their relatively intuitive systems. Academia.edu has a relatively involved initial set-up process. However, the site has also automated the fields that academics are likely to require, particularly in terms of locating and uploading publications that are online elsewhere. Additionally, the integration of

Facebook and Google means that it is possible to use personal details already shared on those sites to build the basis of the Academia.edu public details. The aggregation features of Academia.edu suit the time constraints of academic lifestyle: for example, sharing posts to other social media sites when new content is published. Twitter requires minimal time, effort and information to set up, providing a less significant barrier to entry. Academics can focus instead on making connections, following colleagues and contributing to discussions. Twitter reduces the requirement of biometric information in the user profile and therefore provides opportunities to maintain a professional and purely work-related persona.

What has become evident in our pilot project is the changing workscape of contemporary academia as it is reconfigured into an array of online places and spaces. We discovered that our former categories did not match the reported experience of the users' relationships to technologies and applications. The results showed that a messier constitution of online public identity is at play, without clear distinctions between and amongst the categories of static; networked; comprehensive; and teaching persona. This was not unexpected – our initial exploration of online academic persona was not only deliberately limited in scope, but also based solely on observational data. The much richer quality of the data collected through the pilot study, reported in this chapter, was sought in order to flesh out our initial categories, and to test their broader applicability. Our participants were clearly motivated to engage in producing these categories of persona, but their relationship to the patterns of academic work often led to moments of increased and decreased online activities. Also, the lack of tools and techniques to observe the relative effectiveness of their persona work was quite evident at this stage in the development of online academic persona theory.

Our work developing methods in studying persona (Marshall, Moore and Barbour, 2015) demonstrates that the capacity to visualise social media data helps to provide insight into how we are networking ourselves into various communities. This recognises the growing trend for users to access and review their own data using the analytics and visualisation tools provided by social media sites and other online services. There are still elements of digital persona literacy that need to be advanced further, including how we characterise the relative values of imagining, presenting and regulating our public selves via networks. Tracking the impact of online 'engagement' is possible to an extent, but many of the tools available are complex or distributed (lacking a consistent front-end interface for example, or only tracking a single platform). This additional layer of persona data analysis may simply be a step too far for already time-poor academics struggling with the ongoing impacts of an 'increasingly managerial approach to higher education' (Lupton, 2015). This study has pointed to the movement beyond the established schema of academic persona, which parallels a much wider cultural transformation (Marshall, 2016). The results indicate the emergence of new and hybrid patterns of digital academic persona, that will serve as a way to negotiate the dramatically changed, data-driven university landscape. The task ahead is to expand this approach to consider the relationship between academic and non-academic persona, beyond the exigencies of an increasingly reputation- and ranking-driven university culture.

Acknowledgements

We would like to thank the participants in the pilot project entitled 'Operationalising Academic Persona'. We would also like to acknowledge the supportive research work that Tamara Heaney conducted on the second round of interviews to help us complete the project.

References

Barbour, K and Marshall, P D. (2012) The academic online constructing persona. *First Mondays* 17. Available at: http://firstmonday.org/ojs/index.php/fm/article/viewArticle/3969/3292 (accessed 11 April 2017).

Burrows, R. (2012) Living with the h-index? Metric assemblages in the contemporary academy. *The Sociological Review* 60: 355–372.

Coorevits, L, Schuurman, D, Oelbrandt, K and Logghe, S. (2016) Bringing personas to life: User experience design through interactive coupled open innovation. *Persona Studies* 2: 97–114.

Crawford, K. (2009) Following you: Disciplines of listening in social media. *Continuum* 23: 525–535.

Dion, D and Arnould, E. (2015) Persona-fied brands: Managing branded persons through persona. *Journal of Marketing Management* 32: 121–148.

Goffman, E. (1973) *The Presentation of Self in Everyday Life*. Woodstock, New York: The Overlook Press.

Gregg, M. (2009) Banal bohemia blogging from the ivory tower hot-desk. *Convergence* 15: 470–483.

Kemmis, S. (2006) Participatory action research and the public sphere. *Educational Action Research* 14: 459–476.

Lupton, D. (2015) *Digital Sociology*. New York: Routledge.

Marshall, P D. (2015a) Intercommunication and persona: Intercommunicative public self. *International Journal of Interdisciplinary Studies in Communication* 10: 23–31.

Marshall, P D. (2015b) Monitoring persona: Mediatized identity and the edited public self. *Frame: Journal of Literary Studies* 28: 115–133.

Marshall, P D. (2016) *Persona in Formation*. Minneapolis: University of Minnesota Press.

Marshall, P D and Barbour, K. (2015) Making intellectual room for persona studies. *Persona Studies* 1. Available at: https://ojs.deakin.edu.au/index.php/ps/article/view/464/489 (accessed 10 February 2017).

Marshall, P D, Moore, C and Barbour, K. (2015) Persona as method: Exploring celebrity and the public self through persona studies. *Celebrity Studies* 6: 288–305.

Mewburn, I and Thomson, P. (2013) Why do academics blog? An analysis of audiences, purposes and challenges. *Studies in Higher Education* 38: 1105–1119.

Pusser, B and Marginson, S. (2013) University rankings in critical perspective. *The Journal of Higher Education* 84: 544–568.

Stewart, B. (2015) Open to influence: What counts as academic influence in scholarly networked Twitter participation. *Learning, Media and Technology* 40: 287–309.

62 Marshall, Barbour and Moore

Thomson Reuters. (2016) Institutional profiles: A 360 degree view of the world's leading research institutions. Thomson Reuters. Available at: http://researchanalytics.thomson reuters.com/institutionalprofiles/ (accessed 6 June 2016).

Townsend, A. (2013) *Action Research: The Challenges of Understanding and Changing Practice*. Maidenhead, Berkshire: McGraw-Hill/Open University Press.

Veletsianos, G. (2013) Open practices and identity: Evidence from researchers and educators' social media participation. *British Journal of Educational Technology* 44: 639–651.

Veletsianos, G and Kimmons, R. (2012) Networked participatory scholarship: Emergent techno-cultural pressures toward open and digital scholarship in online networks. *Computers & Education* 58: 766–774.

5

ACADEMIC TWITTER AND ACADEMIC CAPITAL

Collapsing orality and literacy in scholarly publics

Bonnie Stewart

Introduction: The Twitter watershed of 2014

When I was doing my doctoral research in 2013–14, I took perverse pleasure in telling people – from all walks of life, in the academy and beyond – that I was studying scholarship and Twitter. Their first responses tended to posit social media and scholarship as an incongruous combination. Some did meet the news with enthusiasm and interest, but many expressed incredulity at the topic, in the vein of 'but Twitter's where people talk about what they had for lunch!' Non-academics sometimes received the information with an amused 'wow, they study *everything* at universities these days!' A number of higher education professionals expressed discomfort with the topic, disavowing any relationship between the academy and the world of social media, at least in their own practices.

I saw the scepticism and dismissal not as personal, but as part of the backdrop to my study: an articulation of the broader culture and contexts whose changes I was investigating. I wanted to explore the forms of scholarly expression, connection and influence that circulated on Twitter, and make them legible to those for whom they were unfamiliar. People's responses to my research told me a great deal about the work my dissertation would need to do to communicate its findings beyond the 'choir' who already understood the implications of networked communications, as exemplified by the microcosm of Twitter, for scholarship and knowledge.

However, as 2013 wore into 2014 and beyond and I prepared to defend and disseminate my dissertation, I noticed a broad shift in the way individuals responded to the story of my research topic. Increasingly, mention of Twitter generated a new reaction, one that differed from the vague 'Twitter is what people had for lunch' and 'Twitter is unrelated to academia' positions I'd originally encountered. By late 2014, Twitter had become a topic that generated a new intensity. People increasingly began to say things like 'oh, Twitter? I heard Twitter is failing', or 'Twitter is abusive', or

'Twitter can get you fired'. Inside and outside of higher education, my research topic had crossed a watershed, shifting from a not-really-new novelty to an apparent political and professional threat, one on which just about everybody had an opinion.

This shift reflected the increasing tactical and institutional usages of the platform (Meyer, 2015), as well as scrutiny of Twitter's first year as a publicly traded company (Twitter went public on 7 November 2013 and published its first results on 5 February 2014), all of which were visible in 2014's dominant media narratives surrounding Twitter. The December 2013 Justine Sacco case, in which the global head of communications for a digital media company posted 'Going to Africa. Hope I don't get AIDS. Just kidding. I'm white!' to her hundred or so Twitter followers before getting on a plane to Johannesburg, brought Twitter's 'call-out culture' into mainstream media. Sacco's tweet, which she claims was ironic and intended to skewer the ways that many perceive the ongoing AIDS epidemic in South Africa, was picked up and retweeted at face value by a senior writer for *Gawker* with a sizeable following (Biddle, 2014). The tweet went viral. When Sacco's plane landed in South Africa she found herself the object of international outrage, a trending hashtag and out of a job. The way in which Sacco was catapulted to notoriety and professional rejection demonstrated the capacity of mass Twitter outrage to generate swift real-world effects (Ronson, 2015), and made evident Twitter's potential material and professional consequences.

Tactical Twitter use continued to emerge in the public consciousness throughout 2014. The hashtag #gamergate erupted in the spring of that year, generating public discussion of Twitter as a space for gendered abuse and harassment. Then, in August, the police shooting of black teenager Michael Brown in Ferguson, Missouri sparked the hashtag #Ferguson and prompted unprecedented discussion in the USA on extrajudicial killing and race. The discussion stemmed primarily from Twitter, whereas on Facebook's more heavily filtered algorithmic feed, the discussion remained hidden from view far longer (Tufecki, 2014). Activism around #Ferguson eventually led to the birth of the ongoing #blacklivesmatter movement (Solomon, 2014). In academic circles during that same summer of 2014, news also spread of the University of Illinois Urbana-Champaign's revocation of newly appointed professor Steven Salaita's tenured position due to his outspoken public tweets in opposition to Israeli military operations (Jaschik, 2014). As my research wrapped up, mainstream media articles began to emerge with analysis, backlash and eulogies for Twitter itself (Cooper, 2014; LaFrance and Meyer, 2014; Yang, 2014).

In September 2014, in the wake of both the #Ferguson protests and Twitter's almost immediate announcement that feeds would become more algorithmically determined, I publicly fretted on my blog '[W]ill my dissertation end up being about the Twitter that *was*, rather than whatever it is in the process of becoming? Can a person become an historian by accident?' (Stewart, 2014: para. 4). Since my study emphasised academic Twitter as a socio-material and cultural space for knowledge creation and dissemination (Stewart, 2015a), I had expected the social norms and memes that constitute in-group behaviour within academic

Twitter and Twitter more broadly to shift, but not as dramatically as they appeared to in 2014.

A couple of years later, with Twitter still a relatively viable social platform in spite of regular media pronouncements of its imminent death, I conclude that what became visible in 2014 was a logical – if problematic – manifestation of the platform's socio-material and cultural constitution. Specifically, as this chapter will examine, Twitter's collapse of oral and literate practices and expectations makes it a particularly fraught type of scholarly public, but one with a great deal to teach us about the status quo of scholarship and where change may be desirable.

Conceptual frameworks

The substantive goal of my dissertation research was to create an ethnographic portrait of how scholarly engagement and influence operate within the open, participatory, networked spaces at the boundaries of the official cultural unit of the academy. Twitter was the primary site and topic of my investigation (Stewart, 2017), though all of the 13 participants in the daily ethnographic observation process also blogged and used other social networking sites (SNS) in addition to Twitter. I engaged in daily participant observation on Twitter and any other platforms volunteers identified, in addition to conducting extensive interviews and collecting reflective and analytic written information on participants' daily social media use and their perceptions of other volunteers' academic Twitter profiles. Participants and volunteer profiles were recruited through my blog and social media channels, and were selected for maximal diversity of geographic locales, identity markers and academic positions within English-speaking academic Twitter. Nine were female, four were male; four identified as gay or queer. Their ages ranged from twenties through fifties, and their Twitter followers ranged from a few hundred through 15,000.

The emphasis on Twitter was due to its dominance as the platform of choice for networked scholars: Lupton's (2014: 14) study of 711 academics using social media found that 90% reported using Twitter for professional purposes, while nearly 50% used Academia.edu, 40% Facebook and over 30% used personal blogs. However, just as 'the academy' refers, imperfectly, to a broadly understood confluence of practices, norms and outlooks as well as to the historical public concept of the university, so a participatory subculture of scholarly networks – referred to as 'academic Twitter' – was invoked in my research to identify both a conceptual space and the practices that distinguish it. Neither term was intended to refer to any single representative entity but rather to a particular form of social imaginary, or what Taylor (2003: 23) called 'that common understanding that makes possible common practices and a widely-shared sense of legitimacy'.

In order to frame the social imaginary of academic Twitter, my study drew on three key concepts related to digitally networked practice. The first was networked publics, which are both 'the space constructed through networked technologies, and the imagined collective that emerges as a result of the intersection of people, technology, and practice' (boyd, 2011: 39). Both material and conceptual, networked publics are enacted via blogs and public social networking platforms such as Twitter, Facebook and Instagram. The second concept was what Veletsianos and Kimmons (2012: 773) call networked participatory scholarship (NPS), or the 'complex techno-cultural system' by which academic communications and dissemination take place within networked publics. The connections, identities and reputations formed via NPS do not, of course, remain confined to online spaces, but intersect with the material prestige arena of academia via keynote invitations and media mentions (Stewart, 2015a), among other things. This can sometimes create institutional tension for highly successful networked scholars whose paths may not be considered legitimate by more traditional peers. Although social media participation has been demonstrated to increase scholarly visibility and academic citations (Terras, 2012; Mewburn and Thomson, 2013), networked practices have thus far largely remained on the margins of the tenure and promotions systems that mark academia (Ellison and Eatman, 2008; Gruzd, Staves and Wilk, 2012).

The third framing concept was White and LeCornu's (2011) visitors and residents continuum of digital engagement. Drawing on visitors and residents as a core concept enabled me to consider networked participation qualitatively without relying on numeric metrics, such as how many followers a participant had or how many times they had tweeted, in order to determine their eligibility for the study. Developed as a counter-typology to Prensky's (2001) generational 'digital natives/ digital immigrants' conceptualisation of web use, the visitors and residents continuum posits that visitors to a particular digital environment will tend to approach it in tool-oriented or instrumental terms: as a task-oriented space. Residents, on the other hand, are framed as users who conceive – and engage – given platforms as relational and social spaces, and thus will approach those platforms for connection rather than specific instrumental purposes. I chose to study academic Twitter users whose approach to networked participatory scholarship and to Twitter reflected the resident side of the continuum. As I was investigating scholarly connection and influence in social media spaces, I needed to access users who perceived these spaces as social, relational environments rather than merely tools.

The study investigated the practices and perceptions of participants who approached Twitter and networked participatory scholarship as a collegial, social endeavour, and who integrated the networked public of academic Twitter into their scholarly identities. In that sense, the three framing concepts taken together serve to delineate the limits of the study, in that they emphasise and centre the relational, social practices being explored as a collapse of oral and literate traditions within digital and networked scholarship.

Orality, literacy and academic Twitter

Together these practices also suggest the emergence of a new kind of public within contemporary scholarship, one that involves less gatekeeping than conventional academia and operates more like an oral culture, rather than one that is literate or print based. In my analysis, I delved briefly into Walter Ong's (1982) foundational work in media and communications, specifically on orality, literacy and the later mediated phenomena Ong calls secondary orality (1982) and secondary literacy (Kleine and Gale, 1996). At the core of this work is the premise of a meaningful relationship between forms of human communications and societal characteristics and interactions. The final paper to emerge from my dissertation posits academic Twitter as a phenomenon in which oral and literate traditions and expectations become collapsed, creating a scholarly public that opens participants to very specific risks, vulnerabilities and experiences of connection and care (Stewart, 2016). In this chapter, I delve more deeply into this idea of academic Twitter as a collapsed public, framing Twitter as an intersection of oral and literate cultural traditions within the context of knowledge production and scholarship.

Ong's (1982) seminal text, *Orality and Literacy: The Technologizing of the Word*, focuses on how the shift from orality to literacy creates new forms of identity and thought, reflected in resulting social structures. His work characterises human interaction within primary oral cultures – those with no knowledge of writing – as situational, participatory and empathetic, polarised by conflict-based or agonistic forms of engagement and by fulsome, rhetorical praise. In orality, Ong notes that words cannot operate as labels or tags because they are ephemeral and contextual. In literate, typographic cultures, on the other hand, words operate as 'written or printed tags imaginatively affixed to an object named' (Ong, 1982: 34). Literacy therefore introduces a capacity for abstraction, separating 'the knower from the known' (Ong, 1982: 45) and setting up the conditions for what academia often calls objectivity.

According to Ong, literate cultures are marked by distanced, innovative discourse in which thought is interiorised and direct interpersonal struggle is less central. While memory plays a core role in orality, as demonstrated in the agile feats of bards and oral poets (Ong, 1982: 58–9), oral cultures are homeostatic, focused on the present and maintaining equilibrium 'by sloughing off memories which no longer have present relevance' (Ong, 1982: 46). Literacy effectively freezes thoughts out of context, fixing ideas for as long as the technology used – be it stone tablet, scroll, newspaper or floppy disk – remains functional and decipherable.

In developing this capacity to communicate across time and context, literate cultures also develop the capacity for the precise, indexical analysis foundational to academia. Lists, as Ong points out, have no oral equivalent, and eventually printed typographic indexes fully disengage words from their contexts, making post-manuscript print books 'less like an utterance and more like a thing' (1982: 123). Ong posits modern science as a consequence of the exact replication that print made conceptually possible, and to the emphasis on visuals and exactness that it normalised. As he frames it, literacy is 'necessary for the development not only of science, philosophy, explicative understanding of literature and any art, and indeed for the explanation of language (including oral speech) itself' (1982: 14).

Academia can be seen as an instantiation of what Ong (1982: 38) calls 'high literacy', with its 'different contours from those of orally sustained thought'. In both form and symbolism, the academic curriculum vitae (CV), in which scholars list publications and other expressions of what Bourdieu (1984) called academic capital, is emblematic of high literacy and its emphasis on indexical thinking and representation of the past as 'itemized terrain' (Ong, 1982: 96). Bourdieu (1986: 241) defined capital as 'accumulated labour... which, when appropriated on a private, i.e., exclusive, basis by agents or groups of agents, enables them to appropriate social energy in the form of reified or living Labor'. For Bourdieu, the assumption that all capital can be reduced to economics or mercantile exchange is a mistaken one which fails to account for the functioning of what he calls the social world. In the academy, academic capital functions to imbue prestige and status upon scholars based on indexical listings of publications and institutionally sanctioned awards and achievements.

Twitter is different. There are audible echoes of Ong's characterisation of oral cultures in the ways in which Twitter operates, particularly since the watershed of 2014. While Twitter does occasionally play host to extensive public lists, these tend towards the rhetorical and the agonistic: a litany of points or grievances, rather than a detailing of achievements. The widespread tactical use of Twitter hashtags by marginalised groups, as well as the tactical amplification or citation of tweets with the aim of having people removed from non-Twitter-related jobs, reflect participatory, conflict-based and agonistic forms of engagement. In the course of my study, I observed parallel agonistic interactions within academic Twitter (Stewart, 2015b), but also hallmarks of orality such as relational empathic engagement and rhetorical praise, both of which were reported by participants as exceeding their experiences of care and praise within academia (Stewart, 2016).

These differences in techno-cultural systems and social realities, both of which are inhabited by self-identified scholars, are meaningful distinctions. Academia's conflation of high literacy with academic capital and professional influence denotes scholarship – and cultural capital generally – as belonging to the territory of literacy, thus rendering spaces like academic Twitter inherently marginal or illegitimate. The use of high-status higher education platforms to decry social media use as a narcissistic waste of time (Egan, 2016), or as antithetical to being a 'serious academic' (Anonymous, 2016), has accompanied the watershed of awareness around Twitter and other scholarly social media spaces. However, in-depth examinations of the ways in which Twitter and other SNS platforms represent alternate forms of scholarly influence, capital and knowledge structures are only beginning to emerge. This consideration of Twitter as a collapsed public, combining orality and literacy and thus representing a threat to traditional forms of academic capital, is one contribution to that emerging realm of study.

Secondary orality/literacy and collapsed publics

My claims in this chapter about Twitter and orality are not meant to indicate a space or scholarship truly separate from literacy. Ong's work makes clear that societies built on the typographical thinking that literacy makes possible are different from primary oral cultures, even if the spoken word gets re-centred through technologies such as radio and television. In positing academic Twitter as an intersection of orality and literacy, I am not suggesting that the hallmarks of orality visible in scholars' Twitter engagement come from any residual proto-oral culture, but rather that the affordances and social norms of Twitter and academic Twitter specifically reintroduce meaningful elements of orality back into the high literacy culture of academia.

Ong himself explores different ways in which technologised communications shape cultural practices. With the rise of electronic media and communications, Ong identifies a phenomenon he called secondary orality, which generates communal, rhetorical performances of orality and its 'participatory mystique' (1982: 136), though with less of the redundant, agonistic emphasis that marks oral engagement. The re-emergence of orality that Ong identifies as secondary orality is an effect of the communications medium and its operations, even on already-literate subjects acculturated to typographic thinking.

Bounegru (2008) appears to have been the first scholar to connect Twitter to secondary orality. She identifies its participatory structure, wherein the 'text' of Twitter (as with other SNS platforms) is contributed entirely by users, as a hallmark of orality. She suggests that Twitter users may identify with the broad audience group that the medium generates, as oral listeners would around a campfire, but that as individuals Twitter users nonetheless possess the interiorised sense of self fostered in print culture, and thus remain self-conscious in regards to the permanence of text.

Ong himself offers an additional framing for understanding the reintroduction of hallmarks of orality into literate cultures, long before Twitter existed. In a 1996 interview, he clarified that while he saw radio and television producing a particular type of technologised orality, he felt that text-based electronic communications are experienced with the immediacy of orality, but might be better represented by the term 'secondary literacy':

> I have also heard the term 'secondary orality' lately applied by some to other sorts of electronic verbalization which are really not oral at all—to the Internet and similar computerized creations for text... the network message from one person to another or others is very rapid and can in effect be in the present. Computerized communication can thus suggest the immediate experience of direct sound. I believe that is why computerized verbalization has been assimilated to secondary 'orality,' even when it comes not in oral-aural format but through the eye, and thus is not directly oral at all. Here textualized verbal exchange registers psychologically as having the temporal immediacy of oral exchange. To handle such technologizing of the textualized word, I have tried occasionally to introduce the term 'secondary literacy'.
>
> *(Ong in Kleine and Gale, 1996: 80–1)*

Ong died in 2003, and so never saw the rise of social media. However, his work offers an important conceptual apparatus for grappling with the challenges of networked publics, NPS and resident digital scholarship. Ong's extensive detailing of orality, literacy and the cultural implications of the continuum between the two allows for an analytic lens on Twitter and networked scholarly practice that de-naturalises the connection between high literacy and legitimate forms of knowledge, and instead posits a broad, more contingent historical frame that, to an extent, collapses orality and literacy and their attendant practices into a new form of academic public.

The ways in which Twitter and other SNS collapse audiences and contexts has been well documented by Wesch (2009) and boyd (2011) in a phenomenon they call 'context collapse'. In instances of context collapse, personal connections tied to separate aspects of an individual's identity, such as familial, social and professional ties, are all present in a single communicative space and common audience. This collapse of disparate audiences challenges people's capacity to direct their self-presentation and communications, forcing an individual to anticipate the 'nearly infinite possible contexts he or she might be entering' (Wesch, 2009: 23) before engaging.

The idea of context collapse does not necessarily fully address the issues that literate persons – and certainly scholars, whose professional status is dependent on particular forms of high literacy behaviour – face when confronted with SNS as social spaces for public engagement. The issue is not only the presence or potential presence of audiences for whom a given communication may not be legible, but that resident networked publics do not operate – as social spaces – on the communicative terms of high literacy. I posit cultural spaces like academic Twitter as 'collapsed publics' (Stewart, 2016) comprised of highly literate subjects interacting socially according to the participatory and sometimes agonistic tenets of orality, but with the digital capacity to capture, circulate and make viral the contributions of others, regardless of their intended contexts and audiences.

As Ong (1982: 132), following in the steps of McLuhan (1962), notes, the sense of closure and fixed point of view that print make possible creates the distancing and consistency of tone required for a 'reading public' to come into being. This reading public, according to Ong (1982: 132), is 'a sizeable clientele of readers unknown personally to the author but able to deal with certain more or less established points of view'. This view differed from the pre-existing necessity of addressing an audience directly and adapting performatively to their sensibilities. Similarly, with the rise of academic Twitter and networked scholarship, I suggest that a new, networked scholarly public, unknown personally to the author but potentially open to establishing relational connections, is emerging. Not only is that public able to deal with established points of view, but to infer identity and positionality from fragmented and sometimes decontextualised communications.

This new public collapses the oral practices of Twitter and networked engagement with the high literacy practices of academia, bringing greater responsive, performative demands into the writer–readership relationship than many writers have been accustomed to, and blurring the boundaries between writer and reader. Whereas reading publics tend to remain largely unknown and impersonal (except in rare instances), readerships and publics in networked environments, with their capacity for immediate response and virality, can challenge fixed points of view instantaneously. This can turn what were once soapboxes into conversations and potential collegial relationships relatively quickly, but it can also devolve into the mob responses that marks Twitter's call-out culture at its worst.

Collapsed publics and orality in academia

What 'counts' as influence or academic capital in a collapsed scholarly public cannot, by definition, be the same as what counts within the high literacy confines of academia. My study examined how networked scholars signal their influence on Twitter and in NPS more broadly, and the ways in which they interpret the influence or academic capital signalled by peers (Stewart, 2015a). I found that within the alternate public sphere of Twitter, ideas and resources often get shared either without or in advance of formal peer review and publication. For this reason, the influence or status that is conventionally conferred by affiliation with recognisable publishers – an indexical, high literacy form of academic capital – carries significantly less status and importance in NPS practices, even among scholars who fully understand and deploy these signals in more formal contexts or for non-networked publics. What networked scholars highlight on CVs and tenure applications is seldom what they highlight on Twitter bios or in their relational interactions with network peers.

This collapsed public has significance for scholarship and academic practice because it overtly introduces qualities that Ong would call oral into what has traditionally been a bastion of high literacy. The immediacy of social media communications – especially as compared to the academic publishing cycle as a core driver of professional communications and dissemination – brings elements of orality into academic practice for those who engage as NPS residents. This contributes to the challenge the existing system of peer review and academic publishing faces from open access advocates and from that system's own increasingly recognised profit monopoly (Fox, 2015; Schmitt, 2015) and backlog (Morrison, 2012).

However, the fact that alternate channels exist for sharing academic knowledge does not necessarily mean that all scholars are interested in using networked channels such as blogs or even pre-print sites to disseminate their work. The social imaginary of academia, with its tradition of precise and analytic abstract thought, embodies Ong's high literacy, which can render Twitter's contextualised, immersive, performative and often-mundane stream of expression foreign and illegitimate by professional standards cultivated in the distanced register of high literacy.

NPS and academic Twitter foster participatory and relational rather than indexical means of acquiring influence or academic capital with scholarly peers (Stewart, 2015a). These 'collapsed publics' make communications immediate, personal and performative, and create social norms that value humour, hyperpersonal expressions of connection and capacity for rhetorical emphasis (Stewart, 2016). Successful long-term engagement in these collapsed publics therefore tends to favour individuals who present with the 'fluency, fulsomeness, volubility' (Ong, 1982: 40) of highly skilled oral performances. While my dissertation research concluded that networked scholarship did indeed align with all four of Boyer's (1990) components of scholarship (Stewart, 2015c), these components are expressed differently in NPS. On Twitter, for example, a self-identified scholar's contributions are as likely to be valued based on their content and on the scale and visibility of those who share them as they are on any institutional or journal status, outside of those most widely recognised.

In academia, on the other hand, gatekeeping is central to the social imaginary – and the prestige economy – that the academy embodies. Scholars are deeply acculturated to a system that is exclusive by design; the persistent mythology of academia as a meritocracy in which failure to complete a PhD or win tenure is a sign of individual rather than structural deficit continues to inform a great many contemporary comments in *The Chronicle of Higher Education*. Journals, schools and academic roles are all part of complex status hierarchies signalled through indexical, externally referenceable means. This close affiliation between markers of literacy and academia's sense of itself means that the value of both PhDs and peer review can be perceived as under threat from the open circulation of knowledge and influence that academic Twitter generates. This reality may address part of the reason my announcement of Twitter as a research topic was received by many non-networked colleagues with discomfort, even when their work contexts placed value on social media.

However, my research indicates that scholars who are resident on Twitter are not simply replacing one set of academic capital criteria with another, but rather navigating a collapsed social imaginary that incorporates both versions of prestige or capital simultaneously. A hallmark of the academic Twitter users I studied was a sort of double-consciousness, wherein they were able to engage in playful and/or agonistic in-the-moment manners, while nonetheless recognising that all tweets leave a potential long-term trace or searchable, scalable artefact that can be taken out of context. In addition to being conscious and discerning regarding both oral and literate forms of engagement, participants in my study were equally conscious of their institutional status – or lack thereof, in some cases – as well as of their relative reach and reputation on Twitter. They simultaneously inhabited both sites of scholarship and understood quite well the differential ways in which they were perceived in each. For some, there was dissonance between the influence wielded in the two spaces: those who were graduate students and early career scholars in particular tended to note that Twitter and NPS had often afforded a sense of opportunity to contribute in a way that the academic hierarchy had not, at least to date (Stewart, 2015a). But even those who saw themselves as having more parallel status positions in both sites of scholarship were clear that the terms by which the two operated were different.

The collapsed publics of academic Twitter also foster a particular performative register that academia does not tend to reward a voice of the collapse's double-consciousness, in a sense. Distinct from more formal, depersonalised academic communications, this voice tended to straddle the personal and professional, and to generate far more signals of attention in terms of likes and retweets than strictly formal or high literate forms of communications did on the networked platforms I observed. Participants and exemplar identities in my study who used this register tended to be perceived by peers as having higher status or belonging within the academic Twitter environment. Many but not all of the active and high-status users in the academic Twitter-sphere are therefore scholars, professors or PhD students who can be assumed to communicate relatively effectively on the academy's high literacy terms. Some even list tenured positions in their Twitter bios. But most also have a corpus of searchable, replicable tweets available under their names and public identities wherein they crack jokes, contribute to conversations and share mundane stories from their daily lives. This body of what might not formally be called 'work' represents the emotional labour and presence which the hierarchy of conventional academia tends to negate or make invisible when counting academic influence or capital. Thus, the fact that a space like Twitter is not only inhabited by a broad constellation of professionals and scholars but is used and valued as a scholarly network (Stewart, 2015c) by many participants does pose a genuine and important challenge to the status quo of higher education practices.

Sometimes this double-consciousness of mixed oral and literate performativity can make it difficult for scholars to reconcile the conflicting interests of the collapsed publics they navigate. In the Twitter watershed of 2014, institutional observation of Twitter and tactical and agonistic uses of the platform to achieve visibility all became more mainstream within a brief span of time. Data collection for my study was taking place during this period, and a number of participants referenced that they had learned – both personally and from observation of others – that casual tweets or NPS exchanges can be interpreted with a gravitas usually culturally reserved for the written word. Codeswitching – or addressing networked communications to different registers depending on topic and audience – was common among participants (Stewart, 2015a) throughout the study; day-to-day interactions were often casual and reflective of oral cultural norms, while public tweets sharing research or educational resources were more likely to include formal signals of scholarly or high literate practice. But as Twitter became more visibly and overtly an agonistic and conflict-based space, and Steven Salaita's loss of a tenured position became a widely reported cautionary tale, participants' concerns reflected Costa's (2014) assertion that digital scholarship is often perceived, institutionally, as a trajectory of deviance. They were able to adeptly navigate two separate registers of speech and forms of academic capital, but addressing searchable, replicable, scalable digital speech to the collapsed public of academic Twitter became harder for many as that public became increasingly broad and unknown.

Nonetheless, the majority of participants asserted that resident networked practices – including oral, relational approaches to the development of capital and connection with geographically diverse colleagues – were important to their own sense of themselves as scholars and contributing members of scholarly communities. Twitter's asynchronous and profile-based structure enabled them to connect with unknown peers on the basis of shared attributes or interests. Most expressed significant appreciation for the care and community they'd found as a result of these connections. In an era when the increasingly rationalised, managerial and precarious professional culture within higher education (Clawson, 2009; MacFarlane, 2011) enables fewer and fewer to find belonging or even job security in academia's hallowed halls, the belonging experienced in networked publics and NPS can make a difference. Quinn (2016: para. 4) calls belonging 'a domain where definitions are generally agreed upon, with a stable if evolving framework of relations between people and things, and a means of negotiating them'. The 'stable if evolving' framework of relationality and oral and literate collapse that academic Twitter and other NPS platforms enable offers networked scholars a geographically diverse, relatively heterarchical collection of colleagues with whom they can explore ideas and build ties, academic capital and care (Stewart, 2016). This can have professional and personal benefits: the media exposure and connections that can come from developing a trusted scholarly voice via blogging, Twitter or other visible, public NPS participation can open professional doors and offer support and a sense of community.

Conclusion

If academic Twitter and NPS bring a semblance of orality into the sanctuary of academia and scholarship via new collapsed publics and forms of academic capital, what does this really mean for the academy and higher education? Two years after the watershed of 2014, which made academic Twitter look like a quick way to get fired, reactions to my area of research are muted once again. While I still encounter educators and academics who are convinced that Twitter is a space for harassment or a litany of what people had for lunch – both of which carry elements of truth[1] – increasing numbers of colleagues perceive Twitter as an informal, ongoing professional development space where they can, at least, stay up to date on higher education news and developments.

This development is interesting, as the social imaginary that is academia does not truly have a communications platform or channel by which its many diverse and often-opposed epistemological camps can establish any version of the 'stable if evolving' framework for belonging described by Quinn (2016) earlier. If academic Twitter or NPS gained enough ground among mainstream higher education professionals, the disciplinary silos that are (in part) enforced by the lack of broad, cross-disciplinary communications and vision could potentially be undermined. This might actually be a positive development for innovation and the creation of new knowledge; Parise, Whelan and Todd (2015) found that when Twitter users actively fostered diverse professional networks and sought out ideas and experts outside their comfort zone, they generated higher-quality ideas in a series of anonymous experiments.

While I don't anticipate the complete normalisation of resident NPS practices into institutional scholarship over the short term, the ongoing increase of orality's relationality and performativity into academic circles and publics certainly warrants ongoing observation and analysis. The ways in which academic Twitter cultivates forms of expression and academic capital that differ from conventional institutional practices points out to everyone invested in higher education that many of the traditions and outlooks we – or our colleagues or students – may take for granted are not inherent to the pursuit of knowledge, but are products of print and its assumptions and limitations. As digital and networked practices enable us to expand scholarship beyond those limitations, my study offers a portrait of new, more relational publics for knowledge production and scholarly engagement, with what Ong would call a distinct oral residue in its otherwise highly literate terms of engagement.

Note

1 Twitter has been repeatedly charged with failing to address abuse and harassment, as well as with building the capacity for abusive trolling behaviour into its design (Warzel, 2016).

References

Anonymous. (2016) I'm a serious academic, not a professional instagrammer. *The Guardian Higher Education Network*. Available at: www.theguardian.com/higher-education-network/2016/aug/05/im-a-serious-academic-not-a-professional-instagrammer (accessed 2 November 2016).

Biddle, S. (2014) Justine Sacco is good at her job, and how I came to peace with her. *Gawker*. Available at: http://gawker.com/justine-sacco-is-good-at-her-job-and-how-i-came-to-pea-1653022326 (accessed 2 November 2016).

Bounegru, L. (2008) Secondary orality in microblogging. *Masters of Media*. Available at: http://mastersofmedia.hum.uva.nl/blog/2008/10/13/secondary-orality-in-microblogging/ (accessed 30 July 2015).

Bourdieu, P. (1984) *Distinction: A Social Judgement of the Critique of Taste*. Cambridge, MA: Harvard University Press.

Bourdieu, P. (1986) The forms of capital. In: J Richardson (ed) *Handbook of Theory and Research for the Sociology of Education*. New York, NY: Greenwood, 241–258.

boyd, D. (2011) Social network sites as networked publics: Affordances, dynamics, and implications. In: Z Papcharissi (ed) *A Networked Self*. New York, NY: Routledge, 39–58.

Boyer, E. (1990) *Scholarship Reconsidered: Priorities of the Professoriate*. Princeton, NJ: The Carnegie Foundation for the Advancement of Teaching.

Clawson, D. (2009) Tenure and the future of the university. *Science* 324: 1147–1148.

Cooper, B. (2014) In support of #CancelColbert: Why Stephen Colbert needs to make this right. *Salon*. Available at: www.salon.com/2014/03/28/in_support_of_cancelcolbert_why_stephen_colbert_needs_to_make_this_right/ (accessed 12 October 2016).

Costa, C. (2014) Outcasts on the inside: Academics reinventing themselves online. *International Journal of Lifelong Education* 34: 1–17.

Egan, G. (2016) Why academics should NOT make time for social media. *Times Higher Education*. Available at: www.timeshighereducation.com/blog/why-academics-should-not-make-time-social-media (accessed 5 January 2017).

Ellison, J and Eatman, T K. (2008) Scholarship in public: Knowledge creation and tenure policy in the engaged university. *Imagining America: A Resource on Promotions and Tenure in the Arts, Humanities, and Design*. Available at: www.rackham.umich.edu/publicscholarship/documents/TTI_FINAL.pdf (accessed 28 September 2016).

Fox, J. (2015) Academic publishing can't remain such a great business. *Bloomberg View*. Available at: www.bloomberg.com/view/articles/2015-11-03/academic-publishing-can-t-remain-such-a-great-business (accessed 3 November 2015).

Gruzd, A, Staves, K and Wilk, A. (2012) Connected scholars: Examining the role of social media in research practices of faculty using the UTAUT model. *Computers in Human Behavior* 28: 2340–2350.

Jaschik, S. (2014) Out of a job. *Inside HigherEd*. Available at: www.insidehighered.com/news/2014/08/06/u-illinois-apparently-revokes-job-offer-controversial-scholar#ixzz-39gASNRzT (accessed 5 February 2017).

Kleine, M and Gale, F. (1996) The elusive presence of the word: An interview with Walter Ong. *Composition FORUM* 7: 65–86.

LaFrance, A and Meyer, R. (2014) A eulogy for Twitter: The beloved social publishing platform enters its twilight. *The Atlantic*. Available at: www.theatlantic.com/technology/archive/2014/04/a-eulogy-for-twitter/361339/ (accessed 15 December 2016).

Lupton, D A. (2014) *'Feeling Better Connected': Academics' Use of Social Media*. Canberra: News & Media Research Centre, University of Canberra. Available at: www.canberra.edu.au/about-uc/faculties/arts-design/attachments2/pdf/n-and-mrc/Feeling-Better-Connected-report-final.pdf (accessed 12 April 2017).

MacFarlane, B. (2011) The morphing of academic practice: Unbundling and the rise of the para-academic. *Higher Education Quarterly* 65: 59–73.

McLuhan, M. (1962) *Gutenberg Galaxy*. Toronto, ON: University of Toronto Press.

Mewburn, I and Thomson, P. (2013) Academic blogging is part of a complex online academic attention economy, leading to unprecedented readership. *LSE Impact Blog*. Available at: http://blogs.lse.ac.uk/impactofsocialsciences/2013/12/12/academic-attention-economy/ (accessed 22 November 2016).

Meyer, R. (2015) The decay of Twitter. *The Atlantic*. Available at: www.theatlantic.com/technology/archive/2015/11/conversationsmoosh-twitter-decay/412867/?utm_source=SFG+ (accessed 10 February 2017).

Morrison, A. (2012) Scholarly publishing is broken: Is it time to consider guerrilla self-publishing? *LSE Impact Blog*. Available at: http://blogs.lse.ac.uk/impactofsocial-sciences/2012/07/11/scholarly-publishing-broken-guerrilla-self-publishing/ (accessed 22 November 2016).

Ong, W. (1982) *Orality and Literacy: The Technologizing of the Word*. London, UK: Methuen.

Parise, S, Whelan, E and Todd, S. (2015) How Twitter users can generate better ideas. *MIT Sloan Management Review*. Available at: http://sloanreview.mit.edu/article/how-twitter-users-can-generate-better-ideas/?utm_source=twitter&utm_medium=social&utm_campaign=featmay15 (accessed 7 February 2017).

Prensky, M. (2001) Digital natives, digital immigrants. *On the Horizon* 9: 1–6.

Quinn, J. (2016) Technologies of belonging in an era of precarity. *Cyborgology*. Available at: https://thesocietypages.org/cyborgology/2016/08/29/technologies-of-belonging-in-an-era-of-precarity/?utm_content=bufferd6914&utm_medium=social&utm_source=twitter.com&utm_campaign=buffer (accessed 7 February 2017).

Ronson, J. (2015) How one stupid tweet blew up Justine Sacco's life. *The New York Times*. Available at: www.nytimes.com/2015/02/15/magazine/how-one-stupid-tweet-ruined-justine-saccos-life.html (accessed 20 December 2015).

Schmitt, J. (2015) Can't disrupt this: Elsevier and the 25.2 billion dollar a year academic publishing business. *Medium*. Available at: https://medium.com/@jasonschmitt/can-t-disrupt-this-elsevier-and-the-25-2-billion-dollar-a-year-academic-publishing-business-aa3b9618d40a#.3g5y89rsb (accessed 20 December 2015).

Solomon, A. (2014) Get on the bus: Inside the black life matters 'freedom ride' to Ferguson. *Colorlines*. Available at: www.colorlines.com/articles/get-bus-inside-black-life-matters-freedom-ride-ferguson (accessed 6 February 2017).

Stewart, B. (2014) Something is rotten in the state of… Twitter. *The Theory Blog*. Available at: http://theory.cribchronicles.com/2014/09/02/something-is-rotten-in-the-state-of-twitter/ (accessed 6 February 2017).

Stewart, B. (2015a) Open to influence: What counts as academic influence in scholarly networked Twitter participation. *Learning, Media, and Technology* 40: 287–309.

Stewart, B. (2015b) In public: The shifting consequences of Twitter scholarship. *Hybrid Pedagogy*. Available at: www.digitalpedagogylab.com/hybridped/in-public-the-shifting-consequences-of-twitter-scholarship/ (accessed 4 February 2017).

Stewart, B. (2015c) In abundance: Networked participatory practices as scholarship. *International Review of Research in Open & Distributed Learning* 16. Available at: www.irrodl.org/index.php/irrodl/article/view/2158/3343?utm_content=buffer4b8c7&utm_medium=social&utm_source=twitter.com&utm_campaign=buffer (accessed 4 February 2017).

Stewart, B. (2016) Collapsed publics: Orality, literacy, and vulnerability in academic Twitter. *Journal of Applied Social Theory* 1. Available at: http://socialtheoryapplied.com/journal/jast/article/view/33 (accessed 5 February 2017).

Stewart, B. (2017) Twitter as method: Using Twitter as a tool to conduct research. In: A Quan-Haase and L Sloan (eds) *SAGE Handbook of Social Media Research*. London: SAGE, 251–265.

Taylor, C. (2003) *Modern Social Imaginaries*. Durham, NC: Duke University Press.

Terras, M. (2012) The verdict: Is blogging or tweeting about research papers worth it? *LSE Impact Blog*. Available at: http://blogs.lse.ac.uk/impactofsocialsciences/2012/04/19/blog-tweeting-papers-worth-it/ (accessed 20 March 2015).

Tufecki, Z. (2014) What happens to #Ferguson affects Ferguson: Net neutrality, algorithmic filtering and Ferguson. *Medium*. Available at: https://medium.com/message/ferguson-is-also-a-net-neutrality-issue-6d2f3db51eb0 (accessed 28 March 2015).

Veletsianos, G and Kimmons, R. (2012) Networked participatory scholarship: Emergent techno-cultural pressures toward open and digital scholarship in online networks. *Computers & Education* 58: 766–774.

Warzel, C. (2016) A honeypot for assholes: Inside Twitter's 10-year failure to stop harassment. *BuzzfeedNews*. Available at: www.buzzfeed.com/charliewarzel/a-honeypot-for-assholes-inside-twitters-10-year-failure-to-s?utm_term=.dgWEE82wZ9#.ggaBBW7V3M (accessed 5 February 2017).

Wesch, M. (2009) Youtube and you: Experiences of self-awareness in the context collapse of the recording webcam. *Explorations in Media Ecology* 8: 19–34. Available at: https://krex.k-state.edu/dspace/bitstream/handle/2097/6302/WeschEME2009.pdf?sequence=1 (accessed 15 January 2017).

White, D S and LeCornu, A. (2011) Visitors and residents: A new typology for online engagement. *First Monday* 16. Available at: http://firstmonday.org/article/view/3171/3049 (accessed 22 May 2016).

Yang, J. (2014) Stephen Colbert, racism, and the weaponized hashtag. *Wall Street Journal*. Available at: http://blogs.wsj.com/speakeasy/2014/03/29/stephen-colbert-racism-and-the-weaponized-hashtag/ (accessed 5 February 2017).

6

INTERSECTIONS ONLINE

Academics who tweet

Narelle Lemon and Megan McPherson

Introduction

Social media platforms such Twitter are shaping scholars' practices of organising and disseminating information (Li and Greenhow, 2015; Pearce et al., 2010; Veletsianos and Kimmons, 2012). As more academics engage with this technology for professional engagement associated to research, learning and teaching, and establishing a community of practice, more understanding of engagement and participation is required. In this chapter, we discuss some of the findings from a research project called *Academics Who Tweet*, involving qualitative interviews with academics. In these interviews, we concentrated on how academics applied Twitter as a research tool, to develop and maintain research networks and for professional development. We investigated how academics are conducting their scholarly lives on social media in ways that make relations with others, their practices and the university more visible.

In this chapter, we discuss our findings critically framing the notion of digital interaction through Ingold's (2005) concepts of lines, intersections and meshworks. In so doing, we theorise Twitter as a place that is borderless and points to insights and knowledge of social relations enacted by academics. We position Twitter and contemporary academic practices as enactments of entangled lines whereby complex and layered weaving of ideas is carried out. The work of social geographer Doreen Massey reminds us to think:

> of places as areas with boundaries around, they can be imagined as articulated moments in networks of social relations and understandings, but where a larger proportion of those relations, experiences and understandings are constructed on a far larger scale than what we happen to define for that moment as the place itself, whether that be a street, or a region or even a continent.

And this in turn allows a sense of place which is extroverted, which includes a consciousness of its links with the wider world, which integrates in a positive way the global and the local.

(Massey, 1994: 6)

In referring to Twitter as a place, consideration of the spatiality of knowledge requires us (the academic participants or observers/readers) to suspend judgment of online environments. We refer to online media as personal learning environments, thus drawing attention to their pedagogical function. Participating in Twitter from the perspective of an academic illuminates how 'moments in networks of social relations and understandings' (Massey, 1994: 6) can be explored. After Ingold, we think of these moments as the construction of learning lines. As he puts it:

it takes only a moment's reflection to recognise that lines are everywhere. As walking, talking and gesticulating creatures, human beings generate lines wherever they go. It is not just that line-making is as ubiquitous as the use of the voice, hands and feet — respectively in speaking, gesturing and moving around — but rather that it subsumes all these aspects of everyday human activity and, in so doing, brings them together into a single field of inquiry.

(Ingold, 2007: 1)

In response to Ingold's concept of line-making through speaking, gesturing and moving around, we argue that we can view Twitter use as an everyday human activity that happens to make lines, that is a complex and layered weaving of ideas or lines, or meshwork, as Ingold (2011) puts it. Lines run through space as lines of movement and growth as real lines of life, where they meet and sometimes are bound together (or meshed), 're-imagined as sites of external contact or adjacency' (Ingold, 2011: 63). This is a different conceptualisation of a network of drawn lines with intersections at point A and B. Instead, meshwork is an *inversion* (Ingold, 2011: 63) of thinking about interaction as a simple meeting of lines of flight (Ingold, 2010). Ingold is describing a complexity that is layered, both connecting and adjacent, and involving external meeting and intersecting 'behind the conventional image of a network of interacting entities' (2011: 63). In some ways, a visual of a spider's web, where lines intersect, overlay, join together but are not always reliant on one another provide a metaphor for Ingold's notion of meshworks.

Using the notion of meshwork, we can conceptualise the online practices in academic life as movement and growth with complex, layered spatial weavings. We can further incorporate Doreen Massey's (1994) conceptualisation of space as dynamic and emergent rather than inert and flat. To bring in yet another metaphor, she describes this dynamic space as 'like a pincushion of a million stories' (Social Science Bites, 2013). She describes space as 'the dimension of things being, existing at the same time: of simultaneity. It's the dimension of multiplicity. . . space that presents us with the question of the social' (Social Science Bites, 2013). Time and line-making are interwoven in space, generating situated meshworks. In the following sections of this chapter we demonstrate how meshwork and emergent space can be used to situate the 'lines', or our themes, from narratives in interviews conducted with academic Twitter users.

Twitter and academics

Most people in the academic world are now familiar with Twitter due to its growing popularity in the mainstream community as a social media platform (Li and Greenhow, 2015; Veletsianos and Kimmons, 2012). Understanding this way of communicating, collaborating and co-curating as a scholarly practice requires new research. As more academics use social media in a variety of visible and public ways, it is important to identify aspects of their practices such as possible conflict with the social media policies and values and behavioural expectations of the universities in which they work, and how social media use contributes to the dissemination of both information about researchers and their scholarly outputs.

There is an emerging research literature on academics and their use of Twitter. In a study of academics and Twitter, Fransman (2013) and her colleagues at the Open University in the UK identified a number of ways in which academics interact with Twitter (or not). They concluded that 'developing a strong "digital footprint" will enhance an individual's influence in academic networks' (Fransman, 2013: 33), use of Twitter is linked to 'strong "digital scholarship" practices and better networking' (34), Twitter use is 'distinctly social' (35) and confidence in engaging in this social realm develops over time. Other studies have identified academics' use of Twitter in relation to promotion of their work/research (Lupton, 2014; Priem et al., 2012), as a medium to source up-to-date information (Li and Greenhow, 2015; Pearce et al., 2010), to participate as a networked scholar (Stewart, 2015), communicate with others in their fields or across academia (boyd et al., 2010; Lupton, 2014; Pearce et al., 2010), to use as a way to collaborate with people they may never have had the opportunity to meet in person (Stewart, 2015) and as an access point to link with other social platforms (Fransman, 2013; Lupton, 2014).

In our study, we were interested in what it is that academics 'do' when they use Twitter: how they define or brand themselves, for what purpose they use the platform, how they engage with others, what are their philosophies of use and how this engagement contributes to their identities as scholars. In this chapter we unpack five of these identified academic activities and label them as the following lines: 'noticing', 'research inquiry', 'digital becoming', 'visibility' and 'hooking up'. These themes are not independent, rather interweaving into meshwork. Before we move into the next section of the chapter that highlights the methodology and the narratives, it is important that we define these themes as they are identified in previous studies.

Lines by noticing

In deciding to engage with Twitter as an academic, lines by noticing emerge. Observing and 'doing' on Twitter, such as sending a tweet and watching a conversation grow are ways to learn how to use the platform. In some cases a strategic approach is required, whereby watching how others engage in order to work with an imagined audience is enacted (Burr, 2015; Mazuro and Rao, 2011). This can also be called 'elegant lurking' (White, 2015). Trial and error, or evolutionary, iterative practices are especially important in the change of enacting scholarly work and establishing academic identity. Marwick and boyd (2011: 121) suggest that individuals using social media platforms like Twitter operate as micro-celebrities who 'have an audience that they can strategically maintain through ongoing communication and interaction'. This aligns to the work of Satchwell et al. (2013) who have found that online social media profiles can change as one imagines their future and connects with experiences.

Lines by research inquiry

In the contemporary interdisciplinary academy, Manathunga and Brew (2012: 53) describe a knowledge creation that is 'more holistic, life-affirming and respectful', challenging and disrupting a 'tribal' view of the disciplinary approach in the historical academy (Becher and Trowler, 1989). This post-colonial critique gives insight into the ways academia has changed through a metaphor of fluidity as a constantly moving ocean. Manathunga and Brew outline that '[a]cademics both individually and collectively bring together disciplinary spaces converging, merging, changing and challenging previous structures' (2012: 53). In the academic networks on Twitter, nodes of influence (Stewart, 2015) work in similar ways, amplifying and dispersing information. Using these networks is a way to keep in touch with streams of knowledge, finding similar and disparate voices and points of view which can then be retweeted, and engaged with in discussion individually and collectively. This is no longer dependant on location or time as Twitter hashtags can converge the conversation with active participation of scholarly networks. This visible conversation is then also merged into other network structures, as the academic network as a leaky dispersive model is tangled in other networks.

Lines by digital becoming

Online communities are 'characterised as groups of people who share similar backgrounds, values, or interests and meet regularly' (Gruzd, 2014: 1171), or as 'networked publics', 'the space constructed through networked technologies, and the imagined collective that emerges as a result of the intersection of people, technology, and practice' (boyd, 2010: 39). Academics utilising Twitter change how scholarly work is enacted and thus is in states of becoming (Lemon et al., 2015; Lupton,

2014; McPherson et al., 2015; Stewart, 2015). We argue in our thinking about this theme that new ways of working are underpinned by: a) openness; b) sharing/reciprocity; and c) networking and extending connections. An openness to share and work in different ways is promoted in the online sphere and used for multiple purposes, including the establishment of networks locally and globally, working across boundaries beyond the physical, formation of connections, promotion of openness and sharing of information, development and broadcasting of research, and support (Lupton, 2014; Stewart, 2015; Veletsianos, 2012). In this new way of working, a 'digital becoming' is enacted by academics who are using Twitter to build ties (Stewart, 2015) while also accessing other social networks to 'cultivate and reinforce a nuance of understanding and scale' (Stewart, 2015: 306).

Lines by visibility

Related to the notion of digital becoming, lines by visibility are the ways we make apparent the work of becoming an academic (Lemon et al., 2015; Lupton; 2014; McPherson et al., 2015; Stewart, 2015). Academics have multiple roles of teaching and supervision, research and its incumbent scholarly writing, and service to the university and community. On Twitter, hashtags draw attention to the activities of the role. These include practices that define the hierarchical institutional structure, and identify activities that individuals define and differentiate for themselves (Stewart, 2016) in their academic practices. These hashtags include, for example, #acwri (academic writing), #marking (marking assessments of students) and #ecrchat (early career researcher). The #marking hashtag, especially prevalent at the end of term or semester, draws attention to the academic work of assessment of school and higher education sectors. Twitter makes practices of academic writing visible through #acwri. In the process, writing is positioned as asynchronous, networkable and connected to available others, sometimes without a direct conversation. It places the practice of academic writing into a space where it is a recognisable activity that is both a part of the work of being an academic and academic identity. As such, Twitter is a way for users to codify their activities, make them visible and recognise and support others' academic practices.

Lines by hooking up

Profiles or biographical notes are 'not unique to social network sites, but they are central to them ... and reflects their engagement with the site' (boyd, 2010: 43). This activity is closely connected to identity, and indeed new academic identities linked to a type of self-branding (Lemon et al., 2015). The core of identity production via social media occurs via profiles (boyd and Heer, 2006) whereby 'bios' provide identifying information or link to the individual's social network profiles. Identity can 'change according to imagined future and experienced presents' (Satchwell et al., 2013: 44). When working with social media platforms such as Twitter, we are reminded that the creation of profiles and 'bios' highlights that 'literacies of the digital are directly related to individual identity, in particular an individual's stance towards knowledge in digital forms' (Littlejohn et al., 2013: 131). The profile enables a 'hooking up', a point whereby like-minded people or academics who are interested in similar research areas can form a relationship or interconnection.

Method

Our own use of Twitter has informed this study (Budge et al., 2016; Lemon et al., 2015; McPherson et al., 2015). We have moved from a reflexive study of our own practices into investigating what others 'do' in order to understand how Twitter can support professional engagement. By following and engaging with academics active on Twitter, our links expanded outwards. Our interactions enabled us to use a modified snowball recruitment method (Mewburn and Thomson, 2013) using our Twitter accounts to begin the process. This enabled us to find connected Twitter users and assisted us to quickly build up a participant sample of 34, with a breakdown of 35% male and 65% female. We stopped recruiting once we realised that data saturation was being reached, with few new observations emerging in the interviews. Gender and academic position were uncounted for in the selection of participants. Participants identified themselves in regards to the work they do in academia as academics (53%), scholars (20%), researchers (9%), academic and PhD students (6%), academic development (3%), research news (3%), university administration (3%) and research fellows (3%). In these roles, different descriptions of what is work in academia came to fore. We believe this represents a window into how academic work informs identity in the university.

We designed this project[1] using a qualitative methodology to enable us to investigate the complexities of life and living, to explore people and social processes and capture the rich experiences held within these (Mason, 2011; Denzin and Lincoln, 2008). The principal method for data collection was semi-structured, one-to-one interviews with the participants, to explore questions pertaining to the overarching research question: *By participating in the use of social media sites such as Twitter, are academics transforming what it means to be an academic?* The majority of participants were interviewed by a research assistant and in the case of two interviews, by one of the researchers. Interviews were conducted face-to-face, by phone or via video technology such as Skype, and then transcribed. If an interview was not possible due to logistical reasons, we asked participants to provide a written response to the interview questions.

The interview data generated through the project were analysed using a thematic approach. We explored data for patterns and relationships, to 'find explanations for what is observed' (Boeije, 2010: 76) through segmenting and reassembling. We coded, themed and analysed the interview transcripts' data using a combination of inductive and deductive approaches guided by previously published academic literature, research questions and our own personal use of Twitter as academics. In asking academics about what they do on Twitter, we gathered information about what they *think* they are doing. These data constitute reflections and memories of practices. In this examination of three interviews, we want to make visible the way that Nicole, Louise and Conrad use Twitter to support their role as academics in the contemporary university. We do this through the meshworks and entanglement of lines by noticing, research inquiry, digital becoming, visibility and hooking up.

Louise

Louise is an example of an academic who has carefully constructed her professional online identity (boyd and Heer, 2006; Satchwell et al., 2013). She explored various social media platforms personally before she moved into her now-established professional online profile. Trial and error or evolutionary practices were especially important in the change of enacting scholarly work and establishing academic identity. Louise is very much aware of how her becoming on Twitter connects to her identity and her becoming as she recalls, 'I try to be very aware of the fine line between being personable and showing the human side and how much is too much to share'.

As noticing became an inherent way to develop her professional digital identity, Louise shares how she developed her voice: 'I would tell people who are starting out you don't have to do everything, you try it out and you see how it is.' She goes on to note that: 'assume that everything is public – I try to keep that as my golden rule and that's why I went from not identifying myself in my Twitter bio to using my full name. I thought eventually an employer is going to see it. If they really wanted to find me, they would find me so I decided to just embrace it'. A similar approach was identified in the work of Satchwell et al. (2013), who have found that online social media profiles can change as people imagine their future and connect with experiences. As Louise embraced her digital becoming, she found 'for academics who are starting, just assume that it's public and so be aware of what you're saying, and would you say that in public'. She further elaborates that:

> At the beginning, I think I was – trying to find out what to use Twitter for. I probably tweeted a bunch of things that had nothing to do with my work or with academia. Over the years, I became a little more comfortable talking about my work, reaching out to people. I know that there was a moment where I really opened up about, say, struggles I was having with the dissertation, or questions I had about where I'm going with my academic career; or struggles about being an adjunct, where I wondered, I don't know if I feel comfortable going further in this job. So there was a time where I talked a little more, where I opened the door to people, and I was a little more personal, not personable, but a little more personal on Twitter.

In this way, Louise's academic identity and becoming are forming specifically the online presence to engage an appropriate scholarly audience (Fransman, 2013; Stewart, 2015). There is a sense of transforming academia and creating new identities that specifically brand oneself with considered purpose (Marwick and boyd, 2011).

Enacting a professional identity through Twitter is an evolving practice (Stewart, 2015). Louise reminds us that her lines of noticing, becoming, research inquiry, visibility and hooking up mesh as she continues her participation:

> So I don't have a strategy per se or I don't have a strategy in general but I did see a boost in my numbers [followers] when the [online higher education blog] posted an article about four tweeters who were going to be at the [discipline conference] in January. I was one of the people they highlighted and I was very humbled by that. My numbers went up after that because people were looking. I thought, 'I'm not sure what they're going to find here.' ... I'd say especially in the past year, I'm a little more conscious of I don't want to bore people or say that might be a little too personal. I'm a little more cautious now about what I post on Twitter. I try to think what I tweet as would this be something that I want to have a conversation about.

Nicole

Nicole's lines of noticing and lines of becoming have been ongoing. She noted that:

> my role has really been that of more of a digital coach in the online world, but I also try to encourage people to set up communities and to help them see how the social media and social networking tools can really augment their work and make their work easier and more effective.

Nicole came to Twitter as an academic by trying to create conversations. This was underpinned by noticing how she wanted to engage. She reflects on how a conference can be a starting point to notice and identify audiences which are relevant to research professional areas of interest:

> The power of Twitter is that you're going to find conversations that are of interest to you and you can set up basically a personal filter for conversations. So you start following people who have shared interests with you. Through that, they will become your filter to the fire hose of the internet. That's how you're going to find out what is actually current and what is happening in your field. Starting at a conference is always really good because you follow the conference hashtag. It means that you're in conversations that are pertinent to what you are experiencing at that moment. But at the same time, the people who are at that conference are very likely to have shared interests with you beyond the conference. You make those connections and they are like the root of your personal learning network. They become the base and then from there it can grow.

In describing her digital becoming, Nicole illuminates how she presents herself: 'I think in a way I've had it easy, because my digital identity is very much a reflection of how I am in real life.' Nicole's growth in use and profile on Twitter was linked closely to self-branding as an academic (Fransman, 2013; Satchwell et al., 2013; Stewart, 2015). Her intersections with lines of visibility, digital becoming and noticing are entangled:

> When I teach or when I present – I once said to someone I teach by force of personality. You just get there and you just dial it up to ten and blah. With Twitter I had no qualms about that, I was ready to do that and I was ready to chat. I think most people actually do that. I'm talking about the people in our kind of communities, most people, when you meet them, they're exactly how you thought they were going to be.

As Stewart (2015) reminds us, being an open scholar requires an openness that addresses material as well as social realities different from more traditional ways of being an academic. There is a tension between being in and a part of open networks and past practices 'to develop new and conventional forms of academic influence' (Stewart, 2015: 5). Nicole highlights how connections online help one in face-to-face academia – for example shifting institutions or roles – illuminate the meshwork of lines of digital becoming, visibility and hooking up:

> How I use Twitter is that I use it as a broadcast channel to share, as part of my curation process, to share interesting links that I find. That is my contribution to my posse, my community. My posse and community changes, I've got several. Mostly it used to be to do with Moodle and eLearning. Then, as my interests have shifted, it has gone to networked learning, social media learning etc. etc. Obviously last year there was a huge time when it was around crowdfunding and what crowdfunding could do. Then ever since I've made the move to the start-up scene that has also become one of the topics I curate on. In a way, it's an example of that shifting, how you can embed yourself in a community and how you can create new relationships.

Conrad

Twitter is a platform and way of being that has supported Conrad to explore his own career path within academia. As he outlines, his lines of digital becoming and visibility have been varied:

> I engaged with Twitter in the first place as part of a support network while I was doing my PhD. I developed quite a strong group of people with similar interests [who] were tweeting about either doing their PhD or doing research that I was interested in. I started to realise that it could build a stronger academic network around that as well. So over time, I suppose my user case for Twitter has changed as my career path has changed. I think of the building as having an impact on that, but that's only one part of the impact

on my pedagogy. And so in the course that I teach I also use social media as a way of gathering information and then sharing that information back to the students.

Conrad observes that in exploring Twitter professionally:

> I initially first saw Twitter as a way of capturing those kind of random [PhD] student thoughts. So you're just starting to engage with the topic and you're walking to the train or something like that. And so, for me now that I really think about it, what I was doing was I was hash tagging as a way of coding my thoughts so that I could then go back and look at those hashtags and see a connected train of thought.

As his digital becoming emerged, so did his lines of noticing in regards to profile use:

> You kind of get on there, you whack up a profile and you forget about it for six months, and then you go back and you look at it again and you kind of think no, that really doesn't sort of capture what I'm about.

He reflects that:

> when it came to putting my professional profile up, that photo [sand dune], it's a useful metaphor for the kind of research that I do, because I do research in [discipline] as practice and I'm looking at the micro practices. So I'm looking at the very, very fine detail of what [practitioners] do and trying to infer out of that how practices of [the discipline] develop. So I'm very much in my research practice looking at the individual grains of sand, but together they form kind of these beaches and these sand dunes … I'm trying to make those linkages together. No one else would probably understand that, but when I show it to them and then I explain it in that kind of term, it's a nice way for me to be able to explain what I do.

This is a demonstration of how the meshworks of lines by noticing, research inquiry, digital becoming, visibility and hooking up are intrinsic to academic professional Twitter use. Highlighted is a conscious approach to building scalability in order to broaden distribution of ideas while being an open scholar. Conrad comments how he sees Twitter as being 'really, really valuable. You can easily get into networks'. He goes on further to say:

> I engage back with those people in the way in which they engage with Twitter. One of the guys that I follow, he put a piece of research out. He's published it, he put a link out and it's great for my teaching, and so I tweeted him and said, 'Look, this is great, can I use this in my class?' and you know,

underneath that, 'It's a [discipline] class,' sort of thing. He wrote back and said 'Yes, that's great, no worries, feel free to do that.' Subsequently after that I made sure that most of the tweets that came out on my timeline were really [discipline]-related tweets, and that ended up in him following back. It took about a week or so, but I made sure that I entered in – for that little period of time, I made sure that I entered into that conversation that he was having, and it was very much a professional conversation about [our discipline]. It's nice now, I'm connected there, and I wouldn't feel uncomfortable now about moving that connection to the next level by emailing him and saying, 'You know what? The stuff that you're doing is really interesting and I really like it, and it's useful for my class but I also find your research really interesting. Let's chat.' Otherwise I would have to cold-call this guy, and he doesn't know who I am or why would he bother talking to me, and he's in London.

This is an example of broadcasting and amplifying using Twitter with a perceived audience in mind (Marwick and boyd, 2011; Stewart, 2015). It allows the Twitter user to be a curator of information by following up on leads, examining the authenticity of sources and the currency of the information. This reveals some of the many different ways in which academics use Twitter and how these uses develop by observing and engaging in others' practices.

Conclusion

In our study, we followed the lines of individual practices of using social media to gain knowledge about how academics connect with each other on Twitter and talk about their academic work. These individual practices give insights into ways of becoming and doing academia. We have looked at academics' Twitter conversations around their everyday practices of research and teaching, and positioned these as a complex meshwork. It is in these intersections, divergent, overlapping and connecting lines that we can get an idea of the complexity of practices that enables a rethinking about how to practice in the contemporary academy that encompasses multiple places, not just in the lecture hall or tutorial rooms. The mundane nature of the practices of academics using Twitter gives insight into how emplaced use becomes lines. These lines become visible, sliding together and apart, intersecting and moving parallel, and become active from use by academics. It is this activity and movement that shifts the focus from the artefacts of Twitter (that is, a tweet) to the qualities of the embodied and social processes such as the conversations and the relationships generated online.

In thinking about Twitter as a place, the intersection between academics and how they think that they relate to others goes some way to illustrate the idea of meshworks. We make lines, and this line-making on Twitter makes the speaking, gesturing and travelling that Ingold writes about. It is the meshwork of these conversations, gestures and movements that places academics into a meshwork that is able to be noticed, by ourselves and others, and makes relations with others that support our research endeavours. For some like Conrad, it makes available to him the roles and identity work (Stewart, 2016) of becoming an academic, showing his interests to others makes him a part of the discipline conversation. For Nicole, using Twitter shows open scholarship, a digital becoming and a way to be academic. Louise has attended to the ways she has conducted her conversations that make relations. It is in these activities that academics who use Twitter have ways to make conversation, gesture to others and move along, through and intersect lines that place them inside, outside and between the academy and people in this meshwork.

Note

1 You can read more about the methodology on https://meganmcpherson.com.au/projects/academics-who-tweet/ or http://chatwithrellypops.wordpress.com/academic-who-tweet-2014-2015/.

References

Becher, T and Trowler, P. (1989) *Academic Tribes and Territories: Intellectual Inquiry and the Cultures of Disciplines*. Buckingham UK: SRHE and Open University.

Boeije, H. (2010) *Analysis in Qualitative Research*. London: Sage.

boyd, D. (2010) Social network sites as networked publics: Affordances, dynamics, and implications. In: Z Papacharissi (ed.), *Networked Self: Identity, Community, and Culture on Social Network Sites,* New York, NY: Routledge, 39–58.

boyd, D and Heer, J. (2006) Profiles as conversation: Networked identity performance on Friendster. Paper presented at the *Annual Hawaii International Conference on System Sciences*, Hawaii.

boyd, D, Golder, S and Lotan, G. (2010) Tweet, tweet, retweet: Conversational aspects of retweeting on Twitter. Paper presented at the *Hawaii International Conference on System Sciences,* Hawaii.

Budge, K, Lemon, N and McPherson, M. (2016) Academics who tweet: 'Messy' identities in academia. *Journal of Applied Research in Higher Education* 8: 210–221.

Burr, S. (2015) The value of lurking. Available at: https://blogs.jobs.ac.uk/the-digital-academic/2015/08/17/value-lurking/ (accessed 13 November 2015).

Denzin, NK and Lincoln, YS. (2008) *Strategies of Qualitative Inquiry.* Thousand Oaks, CA: Sage.

Fransman, J. (2013) Researching academic literacy practices around Twitter: Performative methods and their onto-ethical implications. In: R Goodfellow and MR Lea (eds), *Literacy in the Digital University: Learning as Social Practice in a Digital World,* London: Routledge, 27–41.

Gruzd, A. (2014) Online communities. In: R Alhajj and J Rokne (eds), *Encyclopedia of Social Network Analysis and Mining*, New York, NY: Springer, 1171–1181.

Ingold, T. (2005) Epilogue: Towards a politics of dwelling. *Conservation and Society* 3: 501–508.

Ingold, T. (2007) *Lines: A Brief History*. Abingdon, Oxon: Routledge.

Ingold, T. (2010) *Bringing Things to Life: Creative Entanglements in a World of Materials*. Manchester: ESRC National Centre for Research Methods.

Ingold, T. (2011) *Being Alive: Essays on Movement, Knowledge and Description*. London: Routledge.

Lemon, N, McPherson, M and Budge, K. (2015) Academics doing it differently: Wooing, hooking up and spinning stories. *Journal of Perspectives in Applied Academic Practice*. Available at: http://jpaap.napier.ac.uk/index.php/JPAAP/article/view/129 (accessed 15 April 2016).

Li, J and Greenhow, C. (2015) Scholars and social media: Tweeting in the conference backchannel for professional learning. *Educational Media International* 52: 1–14.

Littlejohn, A, Beetham, H and McGill, L. (2013) Digital literacies as situated knowledge practices: Academics' influence on learners' behaviours. In: R Goodfellow and MR Lea (eds), *Literacy in the Digital University: Critical Perspectives on Learning, Scholarship, and Technology,* London: Routledge, 126–136.

Lupton, D. (2014) '*Feeling Better Connected': Academics' Use of Social Media.* Canberra: News & Media Research Centre, University of Canberra.

Manathunga, C and Brew, A. (2012) Beyond tribes and territories: New metaphors for new times. In: P Trowler, M Saunders and V Bamber (eds), *Tribes and Territories in the 21st Century: Rethinking the Significance of Disciplines in Higher Education,* London: Routledge, 44–56.

Marwick, A and boyd, D. (2011) I tweet honestly, I tweet passionately: Twitter users, context collapse, and the imagined audience. *New Media Society* 131: 114–133.

Mason, J. (2011) *Qualitative Researching* (2nd ed.). London, England: Sage.

Massey, D. (1994) *Space, Place, and Gender.* Minneapolis: University of Minnesota Press.

Mazuro, C and Rao, N. (2011) Online discussion forums in higher education: Is 'lurking' working? *International Journal for Cross-Disciplinary Subjects in Education* 2: 364–371.

McPherson, M, Budge, K and Lemon, N. (2015) New practices in doing academic development: Twitter as an informal learning space. *International Journal for Academic Development* 20: 126–136.

Mewburn, I and Thomson, P. (2013) Why do academics blog? An analysis of audiences, purposes and challenges. *Studies in Higher Education* 38: 1105–1119.

Pearce, N, Weller, M, Scanlon, E and Kinsley, S. (2010) Digital scholarship considered: How new technologies could transform academic work. *In Education* 16: 16–29.

Priem, J, Costello, K and Dzuba, T. (2012) Prevalence and use of Twitter among scholars. Available at: http://figshare.com/articles/Prevalence_and_use_of_Twitter_among_scholars/104629 (accessed 13 January 2016).

Satchwell, C, Bartone, D and Hamilton, M. (2013) Crossing boundaries: Digital and on-digital literacy practices in formal and informal contexts in further and higher education. In: R Goodfellow and MR Lea (eds), *Literacy in the Digital University: Critical Perspectives on Learning, Scholarship, and Technology,* London: Routledge, 42–55.

Social Science Bites. (2013) Doreen Massey on space. Available at: www.socialsciencespace.com/2013/02/podcastdoreen-massey-on-space/ (accessed 29 April 2016).

Stewart, B. (2015) Open to influence: What counts as academic influence in scholarly networked Twitter participation. *Learning, Media, and Technology* 40: 287–309.

Stewart, B. (2016) Tower of song. Available at: http://theory.cribchronicles.com/2016/03/04/tower-of-song/ (accessed 29 April 2016).

Veletsianos, G. (2012) Higher education scholars' participation and practices on Twitter. *Journal of Computer Assisted Learning* 28: 336–349.

Veletsianos, G and Kimmons, R. (2012) Networked participatory scholarship: Emergent techno-cultural pressures toward open and digital scholarship in online networks. *Computers and Education* 58: 766–774.

White, D. (2015) Elegant lurking. Available at: http://daveowhite.com/elegant-lurking/ (accessed 13 December 2015).

7

SUSTAINING ASIAN AUSTRALIAN SCHOLARLY ACTIVISM ONLINE

Tseen Khoo

Introduction

Recent controversies around digital activism and its reception within the academy showcase the continuing, fraught nature of involvement by scholars in social and political movements. The high-profile case of Steven Salaita and his 'de-hiring' by the University of Illinois Board of Trustees demonstrates the punitive consequences that politically outspoken academics can engender. Salaita's case made headlines when the university reportedly withdrew its offer of employment because of his anti-Israeli opinions on social media and his outspoken scholarly persona more generally. The Salaita case generated international debate about academic freedoms, identities and roles; what constituted scholarly 'civility'; and the institutional consequences of political participation (Abraham, 2015; *Journal of Asian American Studies*, 2016; Perry, 2014).

Salaita's and other academics' experiences are instructive when it comes to examining the figure of the scholar activist in contemporary higher education. The heightened public attention afforded by social media platforms and their ability to amplify audiences and public sentiments brings to a head the standing tension between being a scholar and an activist that is long held within the academy (Cancian, 1993; Hartsock, 1987; Shayne, 2014; Taylor and Raeburn, 1995). Paul Walsh states that the 'age-old dichotomy of activism versus academia is sterile – no longer generative – and should be transcended', that the focus should be on 'extending the spaces from which scholarship can emerge and extend the production of knowledge to new agents' (Walsh, 2016). In his call for a 'porous, committed scholarship' that can take place outside the university, Walsh foregrounds an activism that resides already in digital spaces.

That said, persistent academic/activist tensions now play out on digital platforms, with particular difficulties faced by scholars in these environments when their institutions increasingly invest in building digital profiles that depend on harnessing their academics' reputations as part of their 'brand'. These same institutions often do not inform and protect their staff with nuanced and supportive social media policies, or scholarly solidarity in the face of public controversy (Cook, 2016; Gelber, 2016; Neylon, 2015). Cassidy Sugimoto (2016) argues that '[t]he distinction between on- and off-campus has dissolved—the professor's podium has expanded and so too must our policies on science communication and academic freedom'.

In this chapter, I focus on the context of Asian Australian Studies and its activist practices in this higher education context of digital scholarship and politicised engagement. It examines the negotiated tensions between traditional components of academic networks and the advent of digital scholarship in a field characterised by diasporic flows. For example, Asian Australian Studies researchers contribute to debates and conversations surrounding diasporic Asian anti-racist campaigns, including recent instances that influenced perception, analysis and activity locally and elsewhere.[1] What can this mean, then, for Asian Australian activist scholar networks that form, and perform, overwhelmingly in unbound digital spaces yet agitate for crucially local anti-racist and social inclusive change and action?

I examine in particular the academic activism associated with the Asian Australian Studies Research Network (AASRN). It traces the creation of what was a relatively traditional, and always already diasporic academic network, on online platforms and its development through digital modes of engagement. The focus is on the particular tensions between the open, aspirational spaces of digital scholarly activism and the texture of everyday, localised scholar–community interactions. This work analyses the research network's digital history, using critical race theories as applied to the higher education context in Australia, and elements of diasporic Asian and transnational community activist frameworks. It also draws on my critical perspectives over the last ten years on the development and directions for the AASRN, as a co-founder and convenor. This chapter, then, presents an 'autoethnography otherwise' (Lai, 2008), or layered account (Ellis et al., 2011), that combines my experiences in leading the academic research network, discussing research on activism and public scholarship and examining diasporic Asian community politics.

Applying Lai's definition in this instance, my work aims to be concerned with more than the immediate research network and its activities. The digital development and actions of the network exist at the crossroads of critical race communities online, Asian diaspora studies and critical academic cultures. Similarly, while it is a major focus, the chapter cannot *only* be about how the AASRN functions in digital spaces as so much of the anti-racist work supported by the AASRN and its members enables transition through online platforms from debate, to mobilisation, to material spaces of action.

The latter part of this chapter focuses on the AASRN's intersections and enmeshment with cultural activist work through the example of *Peril,* a digital Asian Australian arts and culture magazine. Through *Peril,* I discuss the ways that collaborative scholarly activist and creative community initiatives are perceived, valued and can be sustained.

The network and its digital enmeshment

The AASRN is an organisation generated from distinctly activist imperatives. Its earliest research clusters formed in 1999, alongside a watershed series of academic events.[2] The formal network was founded in 2006 with funding provided by the International Centre of Excellence in Asia Pacific Studies (ICEAPS) at The Australian National University. Many of its founding (and still current) members are visual artists, writers, performers and cultural workers, as well as university scholars and community researchers. The network sought to consolidate and support the research being done on Asian Australian communities, politics and cultures, and to provide a counterpoint to the more established fields of Asian Studies (that had strong regionalist foci) and Australian Studies (that had a strong nation–state focus). Asian Australian Studies work was already being done prior to the founding of the AASRN, and the network sought to bring together existing work in the field across scholarly, community and creative contexts. It made manifest this particular niche of research and brought new momentum to the area.

For me, founding and further developing the network fulfilled key academic and personal political needs. These aspects came to the fore when the network recently published the '10 x 10' special issue of *Peril* to mark AASRN's tenth birthday. I proposed and guest-edited the issue. In their pieces, many of the authors traced their activist and intellectual journeys through the lens of engagement with the network and its activities. In my editorial, I stated that finding Asian Australian Studies peers in academia allowed me to have 'close conversations with people who were similarly interested in the intersections of Asian diaspora, racialisation, politics, society, and culture' (Khoo, 2016). For others, the network offered a promise of political and intellectual solidarity, and long-time members, such as Japanese Australian artist Mayu Kanamori, describe 'no longer feeling so small, isolated and up against a large wall, looking up at an unbreakable ceiling on my own' (Kanamori, 2016). In academia, as in society, the work that needed to be done reflected 'the constant challenge of finding and making space for ourselves in a nation that is very good at dismissing and denigrating groups that don't align neatly with its dominant discourses' (Khoo, 2016).

Online community-building and mobilisation characterises the network's operations since the AASRN's informal beginnings as an email list, Yahoo discussion group and a Blogger news blog. For the majority of its life, the network has existed as a digital entity that hosts occasional face-to-face events, including biennial network conferences, monthly social meetups in various cities and events when area-relevant international visitors are in town. The formal founding of the network with the ICEAPS grant has been the only time the organisation has had any stand-alone funding.

Since its creation then, the AASRN established and grew its membership base primarily through online channels. With little resourcing through the years, and particularly without the leverage traditionally afforded to more established areas that had institutional traction, the AASRN capitalised on the highly flexible and open opportunities for collaboration and discussion afforded by digital spaces. Early iterations of the network's discussion groups were closed, members-only spaces. This was for several reasons; a key one being that the group felt they were building a community that was vulnerable to racial abuse and trolling. Many of the original network's members were known to each other and we depended on word-of-mouth and collegial advocacy to grow our numbers.

Being an emerging field of research, and with many members in short- or fixed-term positions, the AASRN remained deliberately unaffiliated with any institution so it could retain its independence and agility in badging events that aligned with its aims. These events did not always produce traditionally recognised academic outputs such as scholarly publications or funding applications. They produced instead collaborative performance programmes, niche exhibitions and non-academic writing as collections or stand-alone contributions. The compromise for maintaining this choice for non-affiliation, however, is that the network has no sustained institutional funding or resource (for example, administrative assistance), is heavily dependent on volunteers within its ranks and the dominance of its online activities has only increased over the years.

The AASRN made a concerted move to Facebook and Twitter platforms in 2010, both to streamline communications (moderated Facebook group: www.facebook.com/groups/4665717569) and to open up network channels to public streams (Twitter: @aasrn). Along with a Wordpress website and news blog (to which members are strongly encouraged to subscribe), these social channels became the means through which the research network mobilised members for events and actions, shared information and debated relevant issues. There is no network mailing list and, if members are not accessing network information through one of the social channels, they will receive nothing to indicate network activity. Put another way, if members are not present on at least one of the network's social media platforms, they are not engaged in the network and its potential activities.

This move to social media platforms marked a major shift away from email lists or static forums that were the standard way the AASRN operated previously. The network alienated and lost some longer-term members who were not familiar with social media (or willing to become so). Many of them still indicated a desire to remain as members of the network, but their failure to be present on any of the available channels for network communication excluded them from being current, or particularly invested, members. Despite this, the shift in network communications granted the AASRN an 'immediacy and constancy of contact through social media [that] has served the network well, allowing us to cultivate a sense of momentum and breadth of membership' (Willing and Khoo, 2011). The lightly moderated Facebook group was now open to anyone who was interested in Asian Australian Studies issues, and its members did not have to be formal members of the AASRN.

Since broadening its channels beyond formal members, this Facebook group has grown from a starting core (of formal members, transferred from the previous Yahoo group) of approximately 70 members to almost 900. It appears to be an excellent example of Kathleen Fitzpatrick's argument that 'the value of joining a scholarly society in the age of the network is less in getting access to content the society produces (the convention, the journal) than in the ability to participate' (Fitzpatrick, 2015). The majority of activity on the AASRN Facebook page is scholarly resource-sharing, members' activities and news and occasional discussions about current affairs. This proliferation of Facebook group members appears to be Australia-based, but the numbers of international scholar activists (particularly from North America) is notable. A key element of the AASRN is its engagement from the start with diasporic Asian Studies scholars and their work, particularly from North America.

Asian Australian Studies and the myths of digital diaspora

The AASRN has had an enmeshed relationship with diasporic scholar activists that began, and further developed, primarily through its earliest online platforms. The reach of Asian Australian Studies scholars and their digital projects is global and generates significant links with the UK, North America, Europe and South East Asia. Asian Australian scholar activists enjoy a constructive friction in learning and sharing about building cultures of critique within their communities with their North American peers. They have done this while being aware that the North American context – particularly the US experience – is not necessarily an ideal or given developmental trajectory for Asian Australian Studies to follow (Khoo and Lo, 2008; Lo, 2006; Nakanishi, 2010; Yu, 2013). Distinct differences in population, types of community groups and socio-political histories render unconstructive any attempts to map North American experiences onto that of Australia. Numerous scholars caution against an uncritical embrace of globalised or transnational community connections (Chow, 1993; Lipsitz, 2001), and this caution appeals directly to the accelerated models of activist community-building and individual affirmation that occur online.

The field's complementary connections with Asian American and Asian Canadian Studies, namely in terms of theoretical frameworks of diaspora and transnational community-building, includes a constant interrogation of the narrative of disciplinary progress. Jacqueline Lo wrote on 'Disciplining Asian Australian Studies' in 2006, and much of her nuanced insight into how the scholar activist field was formed remains relevant today. Her call for the field to be 'more attentive to the ways in which it negotiates between community interests and intellectual objectives to ensure that the tensions between the community and the academy are productive, rather than debilitating' (Lo, 2006: 23) has particular resonance for a higher education context that increasingly prioritises and rewards certain kinds of external collaborations and engagement. The terrain of collaboration between the academy and the community stays fraught if viewed only in terms of functionality and funding. That said, I want to focus here more on Lo's call for tensions between community and intellectual priorities to be productive, and argue for scholars to give due consideration to local environments while staying informed of the larger diasporic Asian Studies world.

The tensions between the need to gain momentum and capacity for local activities (online and on-site) and a dispersed online community that is interested but not necessarily able to contribute constructively on a local level are long-standing. Diversely located Asian Australian Studies activists have differing levels of identification with other Asian diasporic groups. Some identifications can over-estimate the relevance of the diasporic in local contexts and lay claim to a solidarity or connections that may not be present. Lisa Nakamura, writing on racialisation in online gaming communities, has described this dynamic as an 'ambient awareness between users that many experience as community' (Nakamura, 2010: 337). Experiencing the online space as a community, and having those same networks perform particular forms of on-site activist work locally, are very different situations.

The limits of diasporic identification in these online communities, and how they can progress an activist agenda, then, remain open to question. A new Sydney-based group called the Asian Australian Alliance (AAA), which launched an 'academic' arm in January 2016, is a good example of this issue. Part of the AAA launch involved bringing in an Asian American speaker who was tasked with telling Asian Australian groups how to follow the Asian American model. This new arm of the AAA, led by an academic with few ties to existing Asian Australian Studies scholars and networks, declared that there were no networks or organisations in Australia that undertook this work (SBS Radio, 2016), and functioned on the presumption that the initiatives and models of activism formed within the Asian American Studies movement could be transplanted seamlessly in Australia. In doing this, the new group failed to acknowledge the substantially different formations of Asian American history, scholarship and activist struggle. David Parker and Miri Song (2006: 591) argue that '[t]he transnational fixation of much literature on the Internet overlooks the local and national involvements that continue to shape everyday lives'. The new AAA academic group's actions reflect this elision, and there is little acknowledgement that the scholarly activist agendas of Asian Americans and Asian Australians may be markedly different in aim and scope.

Diasporic identification is a fraught issue for Asian Australian Studies. Ien Ang (2003: 142) cautions that 'it can be the site of both support and oppression, emancipation and confinement, solidarity and division'. For digital academic activism, these complexities of diasporic identification online are complicated by our transmediated selves where 'the anytime connection of an online identity to a "real" person is a valuable, if not necessary, social and economic premium' (Elwell, 2013: 236). Attending to the contextual terrain – the *local* terrain – for scholarly activist projects, then, is paramount when undertaking critical academic work in comparative frames. Digital scholarly activism and internet mobilisation has the 'potential to both destabilise and reinforce existing mimic forms of representations…and they are able to renegotiate, re-represent and reconstruct offline identities' (Marotta, 2011: 551). To do so, however, requires sophisticated engagement with the politics of positioning, a robust critique of collaborations, and where (and by whom) authority is claimed. Jen Tsen Kwok's research on Asian Australian political and community leaders and their particular investments in representational roles demonstrates how crucial it is for researchers to consider these elements, and to never presume Asian Australian groups are united in political or social opinion (Khoo et al., 2004; Kwok, 2008; Kwok, 2011).

Forms of Asian Australian digital scholarly activism

Asian Australian digital scholarly activism takes many forms, and engages in different ways with existing markers of academic value. The clusters of researchers who became the AASRN came together in the late 1990s, almost a generation before scholarship marked by 'fast academy' imperatives (such as directed numbers of publications in stated quality journal rankings and competitive funding quotas for individual researchers) gained traction (Chubb and Watermeyer, 2016). The network featured traditional benchmarks of academic status and output (formal membership, scholarly publications, conferences and symposiums, collaborations with a view to gaining project funding) while occupying digital space that, as yet, had little recognition in terms of academic value or prestige. Its awkward positioning as an emerging area between established Studies fields – namely, Australian Studies and Asian Studies – meant that Asian Australian Studies had novelty value and some profile in each, but little institutional leverage overall.

What this has meant is that Asian Australian Studies scholars have chosen to invest in building their own channels of research dissemination, debate and collaboration. With no consistent funding stream and a membership that has depended for the most part on emerging scholars, many of the field's digital projects and key political mobilisations were as much a response to scarce resources as they were to taking a proactive stance on creating fresh cultural scholarly and community models that invited different groups' participation. The flat and open structure of the AASRN exemplifies 'the emergence of an academic subculture firmly grounded on participatory ideals' (Veletsianos, 2013: 646).

The AASRN remains a network that constantly negotiates the tension between offering normative indicators of academic success and value, and pursuing relatively unrecognised activist projects – in higher education terms – among its academic, creative and community members. For Asian Australian Studies scholar activists, these bifurcated priorities generate what amounts to a form of 'DIY scholarly citizenship', to paraphrase Matt Ratto and Megan Boler (2014), a form of working in academia that requires constant, active negotiation of professional and political ends. Issues of job protection and career progression (and what the external face of academia could and should be) versus activist initiatives that expose scholars and their potentially 'unprofessional' actions in particular ways, are long-standing tensions for scholar activists. These forms of activism within the academy itself can be varied (for example, transform the curriculum, address lack of diverse representation and undertake research in traditionally overlooked or dismissed fields). They can often involve threats to professional life and prospects (Flood et al., 2013).

Despite these negative associations with scholarly activism, many highly politicised activist projects have been established by AASRN members and their associates. Several cultural and political groups with a strong (if not exclusive) online presence have emerged that focus on screen cultures, political participation and creative cultural activism. These include *Peril* (a digital magazine of Asian Australian arts and culture; since 2006), the Asian Australian Film Forum and Network (AAFFN; since 2011), the Asian Australian Democracy Caucus (AADC; since 2014), and *Southern Crossings* (the online publication of a South Asian writers' collective; since 2015). Long-time AASRN collaborators and fellow activists in critical Asian Australian cultural and social work, with more than ten years of interwoven scholarly and practitioner activity, include Performance 4A (founded in 2004) and the 4A Centre for Contemporary Asian Art (founded in 1996). Particularly for these latter organisations, cultural activist actions in recent times have culminated in building infrastructure for formal capacity-building and international linkages for Asian Australian creatives.

Alongside this growth of groups engaged in socio-political and cultural Asian Australian activism, Asian Australian history and heritage has had a prominent scholarly face and distinct online presence. In particular, groups and projects focused on Chinese Australian history have proliferated,[3] and the concomitant development of open digital historical resources affords a broad overview of the focus and priorities of the archival activism (Flinn, 2011; Yaco and Hardy, 2013) undertaken in this research. The influence of the National Library of Australia's massive resource digitisation and open access database, Trove Australia (trove.nla.gov.au), is undeniable in the growing porosity of scholarship and momentum in the area. Specific Chinese Australian research projects based on Trove material include the *Tung Wah Times* archive (key Chinese-language Australian newspaper: resources.chineseaustralia.org/tungwah), *Invisible Australians* (a project that presents archival evidence that White Australia was not as White as traditional accounts say: invisibleaustralians.org) and *The Tiger's Mouth* (Kate Bagnall's research blog: chineseaustralia.org).[4]

Many Asian Australian Studies projects have a deeply embedded awareness of work being done in and for the community. With her ethnographic research on Chinese Australian dance and debutante culture, Grace Edwards states that her 'major challenge will be to create a community history that is recognisable to members of the Chinese Australian community and contributes significantly to global scholarship' (Edwards, 2013: 111). Given the professional and often restrictive modes of working within the academy, however, many Asian Australian Studies scholars feel the need to create their own organisations and projects. By establishing projects that do not operate under the aegis of universities, but which can avail themselves of scholarly expertise and resources, these cultural activists (many of whom are university-educated and have taken, or are undertaking, higher degrees) create organic, responsive and sector-relevant organisations.

Peril, an Asian Australian magazine of arts and culture

One of the most successful of these in terms of profile, sustained scholarly and cultural community collaboration and adeptness across sector forums is *Peril. Peril*, an online publication founded in 2006, demonstrates how cultural activist initiatives can effectively generate rhizomatic groups and projects (Lacey, 2005; Viviani, 2014), while maintaining complementary scholarly and activist threads within it. *Peril* publishes a blend of arts, culture and politics articles from an extremely broad range of Asian Australian writers. Its founding aim is to support and encourage a broad range of Asian Australian creative artists, writers and other cultural workers, and provide a community and platform for their work. For much of its existence, it has secured funding from the Australia Council, and expanded its editorial team to cover various streams of creative arts (particularly writing, with editors in poetry and prose), politics, popular culture and cultural reviews.

In late 2015, with major cuts to Australia's arts and culture sector, *Peril* did not gain funding and faces an uncertain future. That said, under the editorship of Elea-nor Jackson, the publication is celebrating its tenth birthday in 2016, like AASRN, with major publication plus events and projects. Two of these events are in collab-oration with the AASRN (Melbourne, 16 November 2016) and the 4A Centre for Contemporary Asian Art (Sydney, 4 November 2016). *Peril* was founded as an online publication, and exists for the most part as an online magazine, Twitter account (@PerilMag) and Facebook page. It has hosted occasional events, and its editors and key contributors are often invited to speak on panels for creative writ-ing, academic and/or community festival panels. They are approached to speak on issues as broad as multiculturalism, queer cultures, emerging writers and artists, racism and diversity in the arts, and diasporic identities. The publication's profile is significant on the Australian literary scene and is known for its contribution to discussions around Asian Australian cultural production (Graham, 2013).

In its earlier years, *Peril* included an academic member in its editorial advisory team or within its committee. The initial rationale for this was that *Peril* aimed to maintain connections between scholars, creative producers and their cultural com-munities, and to make interventions (via these scholars) into the circuits of higher education such that a broader range of Asian Australian texts could be read, taught and circulated. Many of the founding editorial and advisory team held, or have worked towards, doctorates, including myself, Hoa Pham and Tom Cho; poetry edi-tors Lucy Van and Miriam Lo; and visual arts editor Owen Leong. Other editorial team members and contributors are recognised Australian writers and entertainers, including Alice Pung, Benjamin Law and Kamahl.

The intellectual traffic between *Peril* and the AASRN is significant, with many editors and contributors to the magazine being members of AASRN and published in consequent academic publications led by AASRN. The associations between *Peril* and the research network have been consistent, supportive and collabora-tive. The perceived need for *Peril* to maintain a stated academic presence receded as the publication and its surrounding community established and grew stronger. I say 'stated academic presence' because very few of the academic representatives associated with *Peril* have disassociated from that creative activist community. They remain within it, and many are still keen participants in projects and events.

The way in which *Peril* has developed is interesting for its shift away from the more direct scholarly activist impulse that started it. While the intellectual politics of the publication remain consistent, the sources and authors of critique have broadened to include more journalistic and immediate content (for example, event reports, blogging). Part of this is due to the growth in the publication's profile, and the growing number of people identifying with the project and wanting to contribute. Part of it is also an organic differentiation from the more formal strictures of literary or cultural studies journals and their perceived hierarchies. *Peril* demonstrates a deliberate embrace of the diverse politics and identities within the Asian Australian creative cultural community (Pallota-Chiarolli and Low, 2015), and resulted in no small part in response to the narrow, circumscribed range of ways to read and make meaning from Asian Australian texts in established cultural structures of production and criticism (Bobis, 2008; Cho, 2008; Khoo, 2003; Lazaroo, 2008). *Peril* has led in sharing digital space (literally, giving space on its website) with newer Asian Australian activist groups such as the AAFFN (for whom *Peril* published a double-issue in 2012) and the AADC.

Conclusion

Asian Australian scholarly activism today happens across multiple platforms and with an increasingly diverse range of intellectual actors. The AASRN, which began life with a relatively conservative and traditional set of academic aims, has established a significant international profile as the peak body for Asian Australian Studies. Much of this work and its continuing growth occur online through its social channels and associations with online publications and projects (including *Peril*). Increasingly, digital scholarship in Asian Australian Studies is leading to a more diverse blend of intellectual and community collaborations that circumvent the traditional hold that institutional structures have over their scholar activists. This liberation from the university processes, however, can come at the cost of recognised academic output, which is essential for scholarly career progression.

This is a long-held tension in academia, however, and the more open approach to research and consequent community-building priorities could also be a more recognised – that is, rewarded – endeavour in contemporary academe. Particularly for Australia, base institutional funding is now heavily skewed towards research system inputs (for example, research funding gained, particularly from/with external partners). This results in a scholarly environment that is even more risk-averse and progressively values only the measurable (for example, see Wang et al., 2016). While there is growing discussion around digital activist initiatives and networks being counted in the service of 'research impact', as part of a suite of figures in alternative metrics (altmetrics), this may only replace one set of measures for another without moving away from the stultifying numbers game.

The ease and openness of creating digital connections for Asian Australian activism has led, in some instances, to complex issues around transplanting models from elsewhere and the elision of contextualised, nuanced histories. With the rapid spread of ideas and anti-racist actions comes the need for activist groups to recognise that corrective or mimic representations, as flagged by Marotta (2011), are not transformative. They function within the same discriminatory hegemonic structures that give rise to racism in the first instance.

Part of the essential work for building a strong critical community around providing counter-narratives and alternative cultural views is developing broader intellectual and political literacy for these issues. Kwok argues in 'Community building as political act' that 'we cannot and should not be bogged down in the histories of other movements or fields. The history we make must be our own' (Kwok, 2016). With a complementary view, US academic Anita Mannur (2016) states: 'I had come back "home" to Oz to find a community, and decentre the growing monolith of the US centrism of my thought. I left with a sense of the power of what the small can effect.' Mannur's use of Arjun Appaudrai's concept of the small and its power to challenge and reconceive captures well the nature of the digital activist scholarship that is created and sustained by the AASRN and its allies. Though the AASRN began its life online from necessity rather than design, its longevity resides in supporting and developing its 'small' presence on these platforms.

Notes

1 Good examples of key anti-racist 'hashtivism' that engendered persistent discussion in Asian Australian scholar activist circles include #NotyourAsiansidekick (in 2013) and #Oscarssowhite (in 2016). It is worth noting that both of these tags originated in North America.
2 These 1999 events include the AASRN's inaugural Asian Australian Identities conference (The Australian National University, ACT) and the Alter/Asians conference (Sydney, NSW). Both events produced highly influential publications in the field of Asian Australian Studies (Gilbert et al., 2000; Ang et al., 2000).
3 This momentum was arguably activated by the signal Chinese Heritage of Australian Federation (CHAF) project (2004), and the activities of the Chinese Australian Historical Society (CAHS; Sydney-based), Chinese Australian Family Historians of Victoria (CAFHOV), Chinese Heritage in Northern Australia (CHINA Inc; national group) and Chinese Heritage Association of Australia (CHAA; Sydney-based), to name but a few of the more well-known organisations.
4 It should be noted that the key researchers behind many of the initiatives in Chinese Australian history are the digital historians and historian/curators Kate Bagnall, Sophie Couchman and Tim Sherratt.

References

Abraham M. (2015) Conceptualizing academic freedom after the Salaita affair. *First Amendment Studies* 49: 8–12.

Ang I. (2003) Together-in-difference: Beyond diaspora, into hybridity. *Asian Studies Review* 27: 141–154.

Ang I, Chalmers S, Law L, and Thomas M. (eds) (2000) *Alter/Asians: Asian-Australian Identities in Art, Media and Popular Culture.* Annandale, NSW: Pluto Press.

Bobis M. (2008) 'Voice-Niche-Brand': Marketing Asian-Australianness. *Australian Humanities Review* 45: 119–125.

Cancian FM. (1993) Conflicts between activist research and academic success: Participatory research and alternative strategies. *The American Sociologist* Spring: 92–106.

Cho T. (2008) 'No one puts baby in a corner': Inserting my self into the text. *Australian Humanities Review* 45: 101–107.

Chow R. (1993) *Writing Diaspora: Tactics of Intervention in Contemporary Cultural Studies.* Bloomington and Indianapolis: Indiana University Press.

Chubb J and Watermeyer R. (2016) Artifice or integrity in the marketization of research impact? Investigating the moral economy of (pathways to) impact statements within research funding proposals in the UK and Australia. *Studies in Higher Education* 41: 50–79.

Cook H. (2016) University suspends Safe Schools cofounder Roz Ward over Facebook post. *The Age Online.* Available at: www.theage.com.au/victoria/university-suspends-safe-schools-cofounder-roz-ward-over-facebook-post-20160601-gp9ezu.html (accessed 11 December 2016).

Edwards G. (2013) Dancing dragons: Reflections on creating a cultural history of the Chinese Australian community. *Chinese Southern Diaspora Studies* 1: 102–111.

Ellis C, Adams TE, and Bochner AP. (2011) Forum qualitative sozialforschung / Forum: qualitative social. *History of Autoethnography* 12: 1–23.

Elwell JS. (2013) The transmediated self: Life between the digital and the analog. *Convergence: The International Journal of Research into New Media Technologies* 20: 233–249.

Fitzpatrick K. (2015) Scholarly communities face crucial social challenges in maintaining digital networks that can sustain participation. *LSE Impact Blog.* Available at: http://blogs.lse.ac.uk/impactofsocialsciences/2015/01/06/scholarly_communities_digital-networks/ (accessed 11 November 2016).

Flinn A. (2011) Archival activism: Independent and community-led archives, radical public history and the heritage professions. *InterActions: UCLA Journal of Education and Information Studies* 7. Available at: http://escholarship.org/uc/item/9pt2490x (accessed 11 February 2017).

Flood MG, Martin B, and Dreher T. (2013) Combining academia and activism: Common obstacles and useful tools. *Australian Universities Review* 55: 17–26.

Gelber K. (2016) University changes to academic contracts are threatening freedom of speech. *The Conversation.* Available at: https://theconversation.com/university-changes-to-academic-contracts-are-threatening-freedom-of-speech-66207 (accessed 7 February 2017).

Gilbert H, Khoo T, and Lo J. (eds) (2000) *Diaspora: Negotiating Asian Australia.* St Lucia, Qld: University of Queensland Press.

Graham P. (2013) Alice Pung's *Growing Up Asian in Australia*: The cultural work of anthologized Asian-Australian narratives of childhood. *Prose Studies* 35: 67–83.

Hartsock N. (1987) Rethinking modernism: Minority vs. majority theories. *Cultural Critique* 7: 187–206.

Journal of Asian American Studies. (2016) Academic freedom, publishing, and the future of Asian American Studies. *Journal of Asian American Studies* 19: 101–126.

Kanamori M. (2016) Don't mention the war? *Peril* '10 x 10' issue. Available at: http://peril.com.au/topics/dont-mention-the-war/ (accessed 7 February 2017).

Khoo T. (2003) *Banana Bending: Asian-Australian and Asian-Canadian Literatures.* Montreal: McGill-Queen's University Press.

Khoo T. (2016) Then we were ten. *Peril* '10 x 10' issue. Available at: http://peril.com.au/back-editions/then-we-were-ten/ (accessed 7 February 2017).

Khoo T and Lo J. (2008) Introduction to Asia@Home: New directions in Asian Australian Studies. *Journal of Australian Studies* 32: 425–432.

Khoo T, Kwok JT, and Ling C. (2004) Chinese voices: Dialogue. *Meanjin* 63: 149–159.

Kwok JT. (2008) Clientelism in the ethnopolis: Ethnic contribution networks and political fundraising under late multiculturalism. *Journal of Australian Studies* 32: 467–479.

Kwok JT. (2011) Chinese Australian urban politics in the context of globalisation. *Cosmopolitan Civil Societies Journal* 3: 86–102.

Kwok JT. (2016) Community building as political act: A tribute to Don Nakanishi. *Peril* '10 x 10' issue. Available at: http://peril.com.au/topics/community-building-as-political-act-a-tribute-to-don-nakanishi/ (accessed 7 February 2017).

Lacey A. (2005) Networked communities: Social centers and activist spaces in contemporary Britain. *Space and Culture* 8: 286–301.

Lai P. (2008) Autoethnography otherwise. In: Ty E and Verduyn C (eds) *Asian Canadian Writing Beyond Autoethnography*. Waterloo, Ontario: Wilfred Laurier University Press, 55–70.

Lazaroo S. (2008) Not just another migrant story. *Australian Humanities Review* 45: 109–118.

Lipsitz G. (2001) 'To tell the truth and not get trapped': Why interethnic antiracism matters now. In: Chuh K and Shimakawa K (eds) *Orientations: Mapping Studies in the Asian Diaspora*. Durham and London: Duke University Press, 296–309.

Lo J. (2006). Disciplining Asian Australian studies: Projections and introjections. *Journal of Intercultural Studies* 27: 11–27.

Mannur A. (2016) To Melbourne, with love. *Peril* '10 x 10' issue. Available at: http://peril.com.au/topics/to-melbourne-with-love/ (accessed 7 February 2017).

Marotta V. (2011) New online ethnicities and the politics of representation. *Journal of Intercultural Studies* 32: 539–553.

Nakamura L. (2010) Race and identity in digital media. In: Curran J (ed) *Mass Media and Society*. London: Bloomsbury Academic, 336–347.

Nakanishi D. (2010) Lessons from Asian Australia. *Amerasia* 36: v–xii.

Neylon C. (2015) Academic freedom and authority are fundamentally about responsibilities and public scholars must navigate with care. *LSE Impact Blog*. Available at: http://blogs.lse.ac.uk/impactofsocialsciences/2015/06/29/academic-freedom-authority-responsibility-neylon/ (accessed 18 March 2016).

Pallota-Chiarolli M and Low L. (2015) 'And yet we are still excluded': Reclaiming multicultural queer histories and engaging with contemporary multicultural queer realities. In: Mansouri F (ed) *Cultural, Religious and Political Contestations: The Multicultural Challenge*. New York: Springer, 169–184.

Parker D and Song M. (2006) New ethnicities online: Reflexive racialisation and the internet. *Sociological Review* 54: 575–594.

Perry DM. (2014) Don't speak out: The message of the Salaita affair. *The Chronical of Higher Education*. Available at: www.chronicle.com/article/Dont-Speak-Out-The-Message/148393 (accessed 18 March 2016).

Ratto M and Boler M. (2014) Introduction to DIY citizenship: Critical making and social media. In: Ratto M and Boler M (eds) *DIY Citizenship: Critical Making and Social Media*. Cambridge, MA, and London: MIT Press, 1–22.

SBS Radio. (2016) Asian Aussie academe unites to call for more research, 12 January.

Shayne J. (2014) *Taking Risks: Feminist Activism and Research in the Americas*. Albany, New York: State University of New York Press.

Sugimoto CR. (2016) 'Tenure can withstand Twitter': We need policies that promote science communication and protect those who engage. *LSE Impact Blog*. Available at: http://blogs.lse.ac.uk/impactofsocialsciences/2016/04/11/tenure-can-withstand-twitter-thoughts-on-social-media-and-academic-freedom/ (accessed 11 April 2016).

Taylor V and Raeburn NC. (1995) Identity politics as high-risk activism: Career consequences for lesbian, gay, and bisexual sociologists. *Social Problems* 42: 252–273.

Veletsianos G. (2013) Open practices and identity: Evidence from researchers and educators' social media participation. *British Journal of Educational Technology* 44: 639–651.

Viviani M. (2014) Chinese independent documentary films: Alternative media, public spheres and the emergence of the citizen activist. *Asian Studies Review* 38: 107–123.

Walsh P. (2016) From under the volcano. *Hybrid Pedagogy*, 13 April. Available at: www.digitalpedagogylab.com/hybridped/from-under-volcano/ (accessed 7 February 2017).

Wang J, Veugelers R, and Stephan P. (2016) Bias against novelty in science: A cautionary tale for users of bibliometric indicators. *LSE Impact Blog*. Available at: http://blogs.lse.ac.uk/impactofsocialsciences/2016/08/23/bias-against-novelty-in-science-a-cautionary-tale-for-users-of-bibliometric-indicators/ (accessed 15 December 2016).

Willing I and Khoo T. (2011) Visionary or 'slackademic': Social media's role in tomorrow's academia. *The Social Interface*. Available at: http://socialinterface.blogspot.com.au/2011/11/visionary-or-slackademic-social-medias.html (accessed 15 December 2016).

Yaco S and Hardy BB. (2013) Historians, archivists, and social activism: Benefits and costs. *Archival Science* 13: 253–272.

Yu T. (2013) On Asian Australian poetry. *Southerly* 73: 75–88.

8

DIGITAL BACKGROUNDS, ACTIVE FOREGROUNDS

Student and teacher experiences with 'flipping the classroom'

Martin Forsey and Sara Page

Introduction: Pushing for disruptive change?

At a crucial time in the writing of this chapter, an email popped into our inbox declaring the following:

> A truly remarkable college or university is more than classrooms, students and academics. A modern, dynamic institution also provides the tools and technology for its constituents to excel at teaching, learning and working. It's a thriving community with the ability to leverage technology to help change the world. Institutions that fail to keep up with mobile or cloud technology will fall behind. Those that ignore technology designed to assist students and teaching staff face the prospect of becoming inefficient with poor reputations, and additionally, those that fail to secure data will risk considerable financial damage.

The email was sent from the headquarters of the Australian higher education news provider, *Campus Review,* and is a crypto-advertisement for a company that provides software and services for educational institutions. It carries an easy and all too familiar message about universities being out of touch with the realities of the broader community, strongly hinting at the need for administrators to catch up and keep up or run the risk of losing competitive advantage. The message moves in an opposite direction to the one pursued here. We argue that it is not enough to be digitally sophisticated in the learning and teaching spaces of universities; academic staff also need to be socially, culturally and pedagogically adept to ensure that the variety of technologies in and around the classroom can be used effectively. Clearly there is a dialogical relationship between the two impulses between technological development and socio-cultural change. Neither is sufficient by itself to improve student learning, or more broadly the 'student experience', which has become a keen focus of so many universities in recent years. It is helpful, we believe, to acknowledge that in entering into the digital classroom more fully, academic staff are not only part of a process of social change, but we are also shaping these changes.

Clicking back into the *Campus Review* website to read what the producers of the news have to say about themselves and their advertising strategies led us to an article that captures a key debate pursued here about embracing digital technologies in and for the classroom (Wells, 2016). The journalist cites Brenda Frisk, head of learning technology at Open Universities Australia, arguing that a broad range of university staff are ready to take up the challenge of 'digital disruption' but are held back by 'cumbersome university infrastructure that slows the pace of change to a crawl' (Wells, 2016). In the same article the journalist picks up a counter-view emanating from Simon Eassom, an Executive from IBM, who identifies a key issue lying with 'recalcitrant academics'. He adds an obvious provocative claim that 'the people who are employed by universities don't want to change, they're in the most sheltered workshop on the planet'. We will return to this matter a little later, with a view to occupying some of the wide spaces existing between the poles re-presented by Wells (via Frisk) and Eassom.

Amidst occasional apocalyptic rendering of the effects of digital technology in neoliberal times (see Feenberg, 2015; Inglis, 2011; Noble, 1998; Olsenn and Peters, 2005; Selwyn, 2014) we concur with Selwyn's (2014: 9) focus on the mundane, everyday realities of university life. Beyond the hype and fears surrounding notions of the 'virtual' university and 'massive open online courses' (MOOCs), Selwyn makes the telling point that the main work of university educators remains very much concerned with 'classroom-bound courses delivered on bricks and mortar campuses'. Things may change much more dramatically in the coming years, but we'll leave speculation to the futurists; our job here is to work with what we have.

Disruption is a term often associated with the digital classroom (Archer et al., 1999; Conole et al., 2008; Sharples, 2003). Defined by Blin and Munro (2008) as a serious transformation of teaching and learning in formal education arising from the deployment of e-learning technologies, we suggest that disruption is often in the beholding eye and the imaginaries this apprehension helps create. That said, we agree with Feenberg's (2015) assertion that three decades of computer technology use in universities has had little to no 'disruptive consequences'. Interestingly for someone who is so critical of the not-so-hidden hand of neoliberal markets in tertiary institutions, Feenberg is sanguine about the effects of the internet on higher education. Highlighting the three main areas where digitisation has affected the delivery of knowledge, he suggests that: distance learning has benefitted greatly from the continuing developments of the internet; MOOCs have offered more hype than disruptive reality – but are interesting because of the software innovation they are yielding; and the effects of digital technologies on regular university education have been rather modest in most instances.

Our attention turns swiftly then towards the regular university activities of classroom-bound courses delivered on bricks and mortar campuses, but not before pointing to the rarity of course delivery that is confined simply to the concrete spaces of universities. Centralised recording and streaming of lectures is now commonplace (see Brown, 2016;[1] Crook, 2015; Lorenzetti, 2014), offering students opportunities to engage with unit material through a digital interface should they choose to do so. In other words, many a class is now blended with digital technology to at least a minimum degree. An indeterminate number are also 'flipped', a verb signifying a dramatic move away from traditional modes of face-to face (F2F) teaching. Abeysekera and Dawson (2015: 3) offer a useful definition, portraying current flipped classrooms as based on pedagogical approaches that: move most of the *information-transmission* of teaching out of the face-to-face class (our emphasis); use class time for learning activities that are active and social; and require students to complete pre- and/or post-class activities to fully benefit from in-class work.

Flipping units of university study does not necessarily rely on the uptake of digital technology; indeed, insofar as students have long been required to complete some form of preparatory work prior to attending face-to-face classes in which they are expected to discuss concepts at a deeper level, the flipped classroom preceded digital technology (Strayer, 2012). That said, it is clear that the contemporary flipped classroom is typified by 'computer based individual instruction occurring outside the classroom' (McNally et al., 2017: 282). It is a mode of teaching that challenges some long-held views about the most efficient ways to deliver educational content to a large audience.

Thinking about uptake of new models of teaching, we were intrigued to read in a very recent report presenting what is an annual *Technology Outlook for Australian Tertiary Education* (Adams Becker et al., 2016: 4) that the various panels of experts canvassed expressed the view that 'flipped classrooms are on the cusp of widespread adoption': so much so, the organising body plans to remove the category of flipped classroom from future panels for consideration: 'a step taken when developments and accompanying practices become commonplace' (Adams Becker et al., 2016: 4). From where we sit, in one of Australia's leading research universities, it certainly does not appear as though we are located on this particular cusp. Our 'grassroots perception' may arise from the lack of consensus regarding the definition of a flipped classroom, or perhaps it comes from a lack of experience with distance education in our workplace that has resulted in slower uptake of the approach than is evident in other institutions (Faculty Focus, 2015; McNally et al., 2017). However, if we think broadly of the flipped classroom as a model committed to shifting the face-to-face engagement between student and teacher away from lectures to various forms of active learning symposia (Forsey et al., 2013; Strayer, 2012), we do not see this as commonplace. Hamilton (2012) suggests that up to 75% of university instruction in the USA is still delivered through lectures. While this is a highly dynamic space and set of practices marked by swift change, we have no reason to believe the situation in the USA, or other parts of the world, is very much changed.

In the absence of evidence of massive uptake of flipped classroom models of teaching and learning, perhaps it is more helpful to contemplate the flipped classroom as 'a quiet revolution' (Crossley, 2016), reflecting the commonplace aspiration of those persons located in tertiary institutions leading changes in teaching practices. In this vein, it is worth remembering the observation by one of these leaders, physicist Eric Mazur (cited in Lambert, 2012), that the real flip to which we should aspire is from teaching to learning. There are two authors for this chapter, and you are about to hear from one of them as Page outlines her recent experiences in entering into a fully flipped classroom for the first time as an undergraduate student. As her comments help show, in shifting emphasis towards active learning, the unit of study (that was developed and delivered by Forsey, 2010) centred on a qualitative research project that formed the major assessment item of the unit. The unit introduces students to the sociology of Australian society, placing particular emphasis on the experiences of young Australians in a 'second modernity' in which the apparent certainties and securities of initial modernity – collective patterns of life, progress and controllability, full employment – have given way to globalisation, increased individualisation, underemployment and global risks (Beck and Lau, 2005: 526). The research assignment requires students to interview a young Australian and to write a sociological biography of that person. Forsey's (2010) main aim in shifting his pedagogical emphasis away from formal lectures towards extended tutorial time in the form of workshops was to allow greater training of students in qualitative research methods and sociological writing, particularly in relation to connecting social theory to lived experience.[2]

Connecting the lived experience of teaching in contemporary universities to the realities we all face in a neoliberal modernity is a major aim of this paper. The extent to which the flipped classroom fits with the individualising imperatives of 'the now' is important to contemplate; not simply because of the critical purchase this allows, but also as a means of focusing on the pedagogical advantages offered by a late modern call to a student-centred, more individualised curriculum that can flip our priorities from teaching to learning. In keeping with ongoing commitments to practice theory, understanding everyday action as cultured, structured agency, this paper draws out insights into the cultural and institutional drivers of a pedagogical practice that emerges simultaneously from the depths and breadths of the self (see Forsey, 2010). We can start to see some of this practice in Page's description of her transition into the digital classroom offered below.

Stepping into the digital classroom

When I first signed up for the Australian Society unit in 2015, I was expecting the usual sort of thing: a two-hour lecture followed by a 45-minute tutorial. Given the lecturer was someone who is usually very enthusiastic, with an interesting enough lecturing style, I was excited to be taking a new unit of study. However, at the first lecture we were informed that this would be the only lecture and for the rest of the semester we would have a two-hour workshop/tutorial space instead. The learning material was to be presented online. Apprehension set in.

The changed format was surprising. It is fair to say that initially I was disappointed with the change: I had always enjoyed lectures and wondered how this was really going to work. I am not really 'into' digital tools, so it is fair to say that I was apprehensive about what was to come and nervous that more work was required of me. The idea that I would need to learn the material online and in my own time as opposed to learning in the face-to-face lecture space was intimidating.

The introduction to the Australian Society unit was indeed confronting in that it required immediate engagement and seemed to call us to 'get the work done'. It was outlined to us that around eight to ten hours work per week is expected outside of the tutorial/workshop time and the self-directed nature of this unit was becoming apparent. In these initial stages I was hesitant about my ability to do this. At the same time, knowing my character as a self-driven, fairly disciplined and conscientious individual I felt like I could take up this challenge.

The next phase to understanding the structure of this unit was learning to navigate the online work space; it quickly became less intimidating than I had first anticipated. The Learning Management System (LMS) program was well organised with each weekly module set out in a methodical order with specific instructions on what was required of students.

I was surprised at how easy it was to navigate the LMS, and, yes it was exciting to engage in a range of different learning modalities set out into weekly modules or topics. The work for each week would go something like: a short introductory lecture, highlighting the main theories, the aims for the week, and asking relevant questions to get us thinking about the topic at hand. This would be followed by an article or two to read, a short video to watch, a website to visit, something to go and research, and so on, followed usually by a lecture, often from the unit coordinator, and sometimes from guests, including interviews the lecturer conducted with one of the authors of the paper we had just read and at one point with one of the authors of the set textbook.

Each module would finish with tutorial preparation work which was clearly explained and was directly related to the information we had just covered. Completing these tasks really consolidated my understanding of the week's topic and prepared me well for the collaborative workshop space. My attitude towards this new learning structure shifted as I became aware that this was me actively engaging in the material and it was actually fun and seemed more meaningful than other university learning experiences.

I felt that there was a real purpose in the process of learning; a sense of the self-making meaning of the material as opposed to a more familiar experience of hearing and accepting content for what it is and remembering it for assessment. We really had to be active in the learning and grapple with the ideas and information ourselves – this served the foundations for our assessment projects.

Page's reflections are offered as a coherent illustration of what is a common-enough student experience of the Australian Society unit, at least among those who found the educational approach amenable to their needs and perhaps also their personality. Such students are good examples of what McNally et al. (2017: 289) describe as 'flip endorsers'. Based on a survey of 563 individuals based in an Australian university, they suggest that these endorsers come to view university education with expectations of active class participation and of teaching based on techniques and class activities compatible with more active forms of learning. The endorsers are also open to interacting with their fellow students and comfortable that their success in class has some reliance on this interaction.

Forsey has commissioned a social researcher to survey the students taking the Australian Society unit twice, in 2013 and 2015. On both occasions the students were invited to reflect upon their experiences of what was for the vast majority of students a new experience in a class that had shifted away from F2F lectures, towards a two-hour tutorial–workshop as the main focal point for learning. The survey conducted among the students in 2015 suggests that about two-thirds of the group could be described as flip endorsers, albeit with different degrees of enthusiasm. The survey consisted of a variety of questions, firstly seeking broad demographic information: gender, age, faculty and major of enrolment. We then asked about study habits (how often do you attend face-to-face lectures?) and invited students to describe the unit experience (what three words or phrases spring to mind when you think of the format of this unit?). The survey also included 16 items to be responded to using a five-level Likert scale (from 'strongly disagree' to 'strongly agree'). The statements sought to capture a sense of the learners' practices and preferences. For example, the question we most associate with 'flip endorsement' invited a response to the proposition that 'the mix of online delivery and face-to-face sessions suited my learning'. Most respondents were positive in their response, with 23% 'strongly agreeing' and 40% agreeing.[3]

The word cloud derives from responses to one item in a survey inviting student responses to being involved in a flipped classroom. The item requested 'three words or phrases that spring to mind when you think of the format of this unit'. Of the 62 students who completed the survey, eight reported phrases, seven reported nothing, while the remaining 47 students reported three words. The word cloud was created in order to capture these reflections and present the themes which emerged from this question. It reflects the relative popularity of responses by proportionately enlarging those that were most regularly expressed (see Forsey and Low, 2014). In preparing the data for generating the cloud, long phrases of five words or more were not included. Words with no analytical relevance were removed (teacher's name and props used in videos, for example), while others were grouped into categories allowing for a stronger capture of particular concepts expressed slightly differently. As can be seen, some of the most common reflections are that the unit format was 'engaging', 'interactive' and 'interesting'. Tellingly, for those who argue we are on the cusp of a flipped educational world, five students described it as 'new', while others commented on how it was 'challenging' ($n=4$) and had a 'heavy workload' ($n=7$).[4]

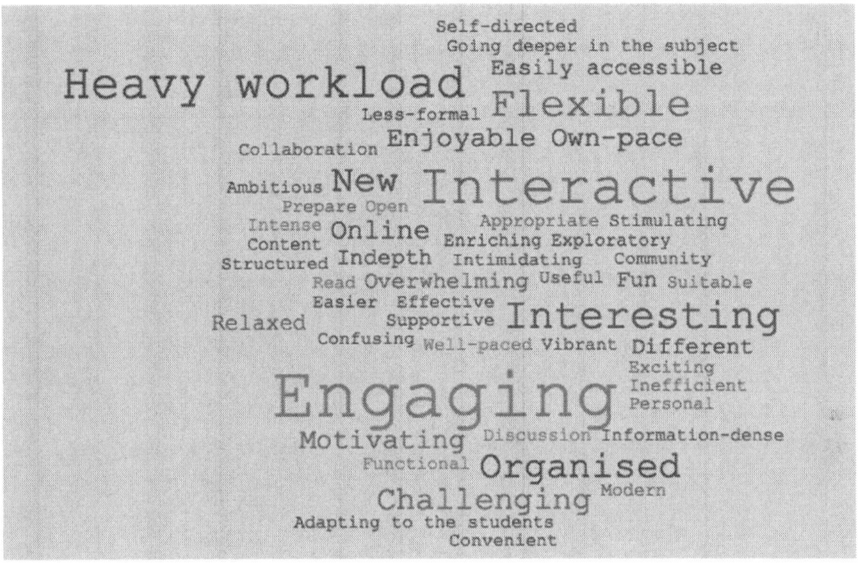

FIGURE 8.1   Word cloud depicting student responses to survey question: 'What three words or phrases spring to mind when you think of the format of this unit?' (*n*=47)

Building upon the 2015 survey data reported above Page's research commenced in 2016. Her brief was to get underneath the survey questions through a series of interviews, for which seven students from a class of 46 volunteered to participate. Three sets of interviews were conducted over the course of the semester. The first were conducted in week two of the semester and sought to capture the initial response to being in a flipped class; students were asked about how they were feeling towards the proposed structure of the unit and how this differed from other units they were doing. Secondary interviews were carried out around the middle of the semester to gauge the progress of the unit experience. The students were asked to reflect on their initial responses to the unit and how the process had actually been for them – what they liked/did not like. They were also asked about what they thought is important in making this kind of structure work. Finally, end-of-semester interviews invited the students to reflect on the unit experience as a whole and to describe the learning they had engaged in. Four of the seven made it to this final interview. Following up on their overall experiences, they were also asked what it was like to be in a 'digital classroom' and what they imagined learning at university to be like in 20 years' time. We will draw on some of this interview data to illustrate the points we are about to make.

In working with these various forms of data, we want to address concerns raised by O'Flaherty and Phillips (2015) in their recent scoping review of the flipped classroom. Their initial systematic trawl of the literature yielded 1084 results, from which O'Flaherty and Phillips filtered out just 28 papers that focused simultaneously on undergraduate teaching in higher education and research in the flipped classroom. Raising concerns about flipped classroom curriculum approaches 'withering on the vine' due to a 'lack of pedagogical integrity' (p.94), they point to a lack of robust evidence supporting the efficacy of flipped learning approaches when compared with more conventional teaching methods. While O'Flaherty and Phillips suspect that the majority of authors arguing that flipped methods deliver more effective outcomes are correct, they worry about the systematic nature of these findings (see also Abeysekera and Dawson, 2015).

Two of the issues raised by O'Flaherty and Phillips are of particular interest to us: pedagogical design and the time required to develop interactive materials. O'Flaherty and Phillips are concerned with teachers in both instances but, as we are about to show, these issues matter to students also. The word cloud presented in Figure 8.1 indicates quite strong concern about the heavy workload involved. As we are about to suggest, for those who maintained their enrolment in the unit, which is the vast majority, their reflections on the increased workload were often favourable because of the ways in which the pedagogical structures facilitated their learning.

Pedagogical design and the time it takes

> I don't feel like it's an online unit. That's not—if anything, it's the other way, because there's much more engagement. I mean you can go to a lecture, and there's six of you there out of the 60 that should be there, and then you have your 45-minute tutorial. I think this—although there's a lot more online stuff, doesn't feel as remote as sitting and listening to a lecture for 2 hours. It feels more engaging, and it feels more personal, which is a bit bizarre really. Now I'm thinking about it … it feels more personal. It doesn't feel as remote as sitting in front of someone who's lecturing for two hours, even though they are physically there with you. So, I don't feel like I'm in a digital classroom at all really.
>
> *(Lisa, Mature Age Student)*

Regardless of the medium through which a unit of study is taught, quality pedagogy results in better learning (Driscoll et al., 2012: 325). Many a university educator recognises the importance of enhancing the student experiences through curriculum renewal based on sound pedagogical approaches, but as O'Flaherty and Phillips (2015: 94) point out, there is a clear need for significant support to develop teacher skills to enable more systematic use of technologies and for 'translating conceptual thinking into planned learning sequences'. Shifting emphases away from teaching content to learning processes, from disciplinary cultures invested in teaching how we were taught (Salmon and Wright, 2014) towards a more process-focused pedagogy focused on step-wise, reflective forms of learning aimed at reducing cognitive load (Abeysekera and Dawson, 2015) requires a commitment to pedagogical design that can be daunting in the time required to enact these transformations. Yet, as O'Flaherty and Phillips (2015: 93) point out, the intensity of effort required to develop interactive materials is rarely acknowledged in the flipped classroom literature. They suggest this poses serious obstacles in some higher education institutions in terms of resource allocation and a lack of information technology (IT) support.

While we are not claiming any particular skill with regards to curriculum design, we do want to stress the importance of recognising unit content as only part of the curriculum equation. In order to enhance active learning, it is important for the classroom teacher to 'get out of the way' so that learning activity can actually take place, a process that requires a high degree of trust in the ability of engagement with the key ideas to do much of the content work. A necessary cultural shift needed for this to take place requires ongoing recognition of the limited pedagogical value of the face-to-face lecture (Bain De Los Santos et al., 2016; Crossley, 2016; Hamilton, 2012; Nathan, 2005). Knowledge retention rates from lectures are strikingly low, and possibly worsening (Bligh, 2000; Dale, 1969) and, as Lisa suggests above, lectures can feel quite alienating. As she reports it, her sense of alienation from the learning process is heightened by a realisation that more people are absent from the lecture theatre than are attending it.

Tales of dwindling numbers of students at our beautifully crafted lectures traverse the globe (Pursel and Fang, 2012; Rodgers, 2001). While it is apparent that many students have already given the classroom the flip, the message this delivers is not necessarily well received by staff. In a particularly perceptive paper questioning academic commitments to the large lecture, Hamilton (2012: 12) suggests the need to find fresh, more temporally and culturally attuned ways of inspiring students to take up a 'life of the mind'. Digital technologies can help in this challenge, especially if we accept having reached a point in time where the large group face-to-face lecture is no longer necessary. It is a point Hamilton (2012: 6) emphasises in noting that:

> Technology offers ways to deliver content, meaningfully connect with students, and model rigorous academic discourse without the difficulties and challenges associated with assembling five hundred students and their phones, tablets, and laptops in one room to watch a small figure forty rows away read through his or her PowerPoint slides for an hour.

Lisa's response to being in the digital classroom reported earlier is entirely consistent with Hamilton's observation that technology can help personalise the relationship between students and instructors in ways that using the lecture theatre as the main arena of instruction cannot. Producing video lectures aimed at an online audience shifts the focus towards one-to-one engagement, especially when coupled with a commitment towards communicating to students not just what they need to know, but also what they need to *do* in order to be well prepared for the upcoming engagement with their colleagues in the classroom. Another student in the 2016 Australian Society class commented in a similar vein to Lisa:

> In the lecture, you just sort of – this is terrible to lecturers – but you're being spoken at, as opposed to spoken to. When you're doing it yourself

[online], you're not just listening to someone lecturing at you, someone has given you the basic concepts and then you have to work it out for yourself. And so I definitely think that for me particularly that works. Even though, again, it's more time intensive, it definitely helps me grapple with the ideas a lot better.

(Sasha, Science/Arts Major)

Elena, a female international student in her mid-20s, suggests that the digital format enables her to better control the pace of her learning:

You can take your time with everything. It's not like you have to sit down and learn everything at once like you'd have to in a lecture, you can take your time, and I feel like I can digest the concepts a bit better, tak[ing] lectures bit by bit, and sort of being washed over by a massive amount of information, and just 'alright, how do I absorb, how do I absorb?' You can sort of take it at your own pace.

Elena's comments point to the ways in which the digitising of unit content allows her to manage the cognitive load imposed by her studies. Consistent with this, the step-wise constructivist models of the participatory pedagogies associated with the flipped classroom can help students better manage 'working memory' (Clark et al., 2005) than lecture-focused pedagogical models normally allow (Abeysekera and Dawson, 2015).

In keeping with the commitment to active learning associated with the flipped classroom alongside an emergent interest with 'assessment for learning' approaches in higher education (Black et al., 2004; Brown, 2016; Knight, 1995; Martinez and Lipson, 1989; Pokorny, 2016), the Australian Society unit is structured around a research assignment for which the students are expected to interview a young Australian and write a sociological biography of that person. To prepare for this exercise requires engagement with social theory, with the practicalities and skills of conducting a semi-structured research interview and also with the skills of writing an essay marrying life-history to appropriate social theory. The F2F classes are vital to this process as this is where the theory is processed by the students and where skills of interviewing and writing are practised. A female student in her early 20s summarised the approach as follows:

From the outset that assignment was, you know, 'This is your final product,' so every week we'd be doing a little bit more on it. Obviously, there's still that big rush at the end but you sort of had yourself prepared to do it, and he did go − [the coordinator] did go − through, like, the techniques of how to interview people and we got to practise doing those. And then also the, like, I guess the lecture content or the actual content of the unit was useful in sort of figuring out which concepts to draw on when I went and analysed my transcript.

Students reported the classes as being more intense than usual, and from the outset:

> It's very full-on for the start, whereas all your other units kind of take a little while to build up to having a lot of work whereas this one was intense from the beginning.

> But just in the beginning I was very frustrated that it was – it just seemed like so much work and I didn't really get why I was doing it and by – it was like halfway through the second week I was already on board; I like it a lot more.

> You really have to be switched on all the time. So, I like it. It's a lot more work to do than previous units in any sort of ones that I feel I've done.

Placing all of the unit material online has a concentrating effect that can be daunting for students. Seeing the series of video lectures, readings and a variety of instructional text guiding students towards reflective writing and summarising of learning makes the amount of expected work more visible than usual. In formulating and designing the weekly programme, Forsey has noticed that stepping out the learning processes for students creates a greater sense of obligation to present students with enough work to occupy them for eight hours or so per week, matching with the 150 hours of study that is recommended for any unit of undergraduate study at the university. Even though very few students report meeting the recommended time allocations of the unit, one possible effect of seeing all of the required work in one spot in the Learning Management System is to drive some students away. Whereas in the past the Australian Studies unit always finished with more students than started it, the numbers have tended to drop slightly since it was flipped. The reasons for this are not clear; it is difficult to reach those who are not there.

For the students interviewed by Page, once they overcame the surprise of the workload, most found it useful, exciting even. The online environment enabled a much stronger sense of engagement with the unit material and they came to appreciate the ways in which this led them into learning. Alan, a biology major on exchange from the USA, commented on the Australian Society unit being the second flipped classroom he had experienced:

> The one thing I get from both of these is there's a better sense of individual responsibility, like you have to take time—well you don't have to, you can choose not to do any of the work, and sort of take it for what it is at face value, but it definitely puts some weight on your shoulders to do the reading, watch the lectures, and I feel you get so much more out of class and so much more out of the discussion if you do those things.

Alan's observations about the approach to learning encouraged through the flipped format link to directions from adult-education theory and practice that Haggis (2009) urges teachers in higher education to pursue more vigorously than is currently evidenced in the research literature she reviews. She argues that the long history of debate about teaching methodologies in adult education associated with self-directed and experiential learning underpinned by ideas associated with 'learner responsibility' and 'autonomy', 'are either still relatively new to higher education, or ... often exist in higher education contexts in rather simplistic and reduced forms' (Haggis, 2009: 388). Alan's comments, alongside the number of others captured, point to potential enrichment of the pedagogical theory and practice in higher education by renewed commitments to active, engaged learning sparked by so-called flipping of lecture-focused course design. A student offering formal feedback at the conclusion of Forsey's unit when it was run in 2014 offered further support as she reflected upon a unit that offered 'so much structure, yet so much independence'. The comment resonates deeply with Forsey's main hopes for the revitalised curriculum.

Structure, autonomy and higher education in late modernity

In writing a sociological biography of a young Australian, which students are required to do as the major assessment piece of the Australian Society unit, they are invited to contemplate the degree to which they believe their interlocutor is impacted by the individualising imperatives of late, or second modernity (Beck and Lau, 2005; Giddens, 1991). It is sobering to contemplate the degree to which the moves towards the forms of self-responsibility demanded by the flipped form of teaching described earlier reflect these same impulses, and could in turn be read as a form of neoliberal deinstitutionalisation, shifting responsibility from the collective to the individual (see Ball, 2012).

It is not at all surprising that changes in higher education reflect broader cultural change, which must be treated with the same spirit of critical appreciation generally encouraged in the social sciences. Returning to Feenberg's (2015) rather sanguine appraisal of the relatively benign effects of digital technologies on university teaching and learning, it is well to recall, as O'Flaherty and Phillips (2015) have shown, that the reporting on the moves towards the digital classroom and the sorts of flips this can facilitate has so far been generally positive. That this reporting has largely been from individual case studies based on the authors' experiences of flipping the classroom is cause for caution about reading too much into the effectiveness of such pedagogical forms. There is no doubting the need for more systematic, less personally invested studies in this arena; however, there are good and sound pedagogical reasons for embracing the possibilities digital technologies are providing in delivering more flexible and engaging forms of unit delivery to students whose lives in late modernity are increasingly stretched spatially and temporally.

Returning to Hamilton's (2012) telling proclamation that we need to teach the students we have rather than the students we were, it is worth acknowledging that university students on the whole are less inclined to hang around their university campus, they are also putting in less time to their studies at the same time as they are tending to work longer hours in paid employment than students did in the past (Hamilton, 2012; James et al., 2010).[5] There are a variety of reasons for these patterns, and it is not simply about decreasing state support for tertiary education exacerbating student hardship, there are more complex cultural imperatives and patterns driving the structured agency of youth practice in late modernity as they seek more individuated experiences and opportunities than previous generations sought.

Switching voice for a moment, Forsey's experiences are also telling in this regard. While very alert to critique of our consumerist, individualising neoliberal present, as well as to the tendency to see what one wants to see when involved in a reform of practice that requires so much effort, I can report feeling much greater personal satisfaction in teaching in the flipped mode. I sense students are better prepared for class. They are much more willing and able to engage in discussion of the materials and ideas of the unit and in general are discussing and writing much more fluently about them. I also derive a much greater sense of pleasure from the interactions with the classes, a pleasure that derives in equal part from the enjoyment felt in getting to know students better because of working so much more closely with them, and from the satisfaction I get from the enhanced levels of excitement about the ideas of the unit. If decibels are any sort of measure of success, there is no doubt that the classes are noisier and infused with more spirited engagement than they would otherwise be. Learning, and more significantly, improvements in learning are notoriously difficult to measure. It certainly feels as though the learning is richer and deeper, and as Abeysekera and Dawson (2015) suggest, the self-paced preparatory work associated with flipped models of teaching may well enhance student motivation and their ability to manage the cognitive load associated with the limited memory capacity faced by most humans when dealing with, and learning about, complex problems (see also Clark et al., 2005).

Conclusion

There are good reasons for believing that the opportunities presented by recent, and not so recent, technological development enhance our abilities to effectively flip traditional teaching styles on their head. The poles highlighted earlier by Frisk's claims about university teacher enthusiasm for the digital classroom being repressed by inadequate infrastructure and by Eassom's depiction of 'recalcitrant academics' sitting in their sheltered workshops unwilling to change is unprovable at either end (Wells, 2016). Our experience suggests that colleagues are in more complex spaces than this simple dichotomy allows for. It seems clear among those around us that there is a real mix of motivation and willingness to deepen the embrace of the digital classroom, remembering of course that few, if any, can escape this reality anymore.

That said, the engagement with digital technology will continue to increase and deepen. What we are attempting to do here then is to offer some form of reassurance to those who are willing to take up the challenge, and perhaps even those not so willing to do so. It does take time to shift practice. While flipping the classroom carries the promise of having a unit embedded in an online environment that can be used without the need for ongoing development for several years, Forsey's experience suggests it would be a mistake to pin too much hope of time-relief to this sort of future investment.

Shifting to the first-person voice again for a few moments, returns on Forsey's temporal investment were contingent upon the vagaries of university administration: I experienced three different Learning Management Systems in the first four years of my 'flip'. Additionally, it is foolhardy to believe one will get it right the first time. For many of us these moves into the digital classroom are experimental, or at least at the individual level they are. Consequently, the desire, and sometimes even the need to revitalise is ever present as new ideas emerge or as student feedback points to the bits that are not working as well as they might or as instructor dissatisfaction hits. I have already indicated increased satisfaction in the move, and I can also report a certain relaxation about my teaching practice as my confidence in the reforms grow and as I become less preoccupied about not having to be the one who is responsible for delivering a raft of knowledge to students. Trusting the process of active learning can cause a downturn in levels of stress, if not effort, as the pedagogical methods and dispositions take hold in one's habitus.

While we feel it is premature of The New Media Consortium in publishing their *Technology Outlook for Australian Tertiary Education* to declare the flipped classroom to be almost universal in its uptake (Adams Becker et al., 2016), it is clear that a number of universities in various parts of the globe have started to mandate flipped or blended approaches to learning and teaching. It is unlikely for this trend to be reversed in the short to medium term. With this in mind, let us close on a note of optimism as expressed by one of the students interviewed by Page. Unbeknownst to her, the student is assuring us that the flipped classroom carries the promise of impacting student practice well beyond its immediate impact in the classroom:

> I like it. It's a lot more work to do than previous units that I've done, but it's definitely worthwhile. And at the same time, this isn't really to do with the unit [content] itself, I can see that the approach and the learning techniques that it's making me use, by the fact that I have to do all these things, is certainly going to be useful in the future.

Notes

1 Brown (2016) suggests up to two-thirds of students enrolled in degree-seeking programmes in higher education had received instruction with online tools. He cites Radford (2011) for evidence of this claim. There are two problems with Brown's claim. Firstly, Radford's research was of distance education in the USA. Suggestions of universality are therefore questionable. At the same time, it is difficult to reconcile Radford's short report on distance education with Brown's figure of two-thirds. The highest figure we could locate in the data presented was 59% of students aged 23 years or younger primarily received at least one unit of study delivered using live, interactive audio or videoconferencing, pre-recorded instructional videos, webcasts, CD-ROM or DVD, or computer-based systems delivered over the internet (Radford, 2011: 11).

2 Forsey's initial experiences in flipping the sociology class are reported in Forsey et al. (2013).

3 An even greater proportion agreed with the statement 'the mix of online delivery and face-to-face sessions made this unit a good educational experience': 38.7% 'strongly agreed' and 33.9% 'agreed' (*N*=62).

4 While the word cloud provides us with a neat visual representation of student responses to the unit format, it is not without its limitations. Most significantly, it does not necessarily reflect the *most important* descriptors of the student experience, it merely illustrates the frequency of the word's usage. Nevertheless, the cloud presents markers of student experience of the flipped classroom, helping to emphasise some of the more important analytical points to be made about design and time.

5 James et al. (2010) report that in the first decade of this century the average amount of time Australian full-time students spent on campus steadily declined, with fewer hours in class each week (17.6 hours per week in 1994 compared with 15.9 hours per week a decade later). This trend is accompanied by a significant rise in the proportion of full-time students committed to paid employment (47% in 1994 compared with 55% in 2004).

References

Abeysekera, L, and Dawson, P. (2015) Motivation and cognitive load in the flipped classroom: Definition, rationale and a call for research. *Higher Education Research and Development* 34: 1–14.

Adams Becker, S, Cummins, M, Davis, A, and Yuhnke, B. (2016) *NMC Technology Outlook for Australian Tertiary Education: A Horizon Project Regional Report.* Austin, Texas: The New Media Consortium.

Archer, W, Garrison, DR, and Anderson, T. (1999) Adopting disruptive technologies in traditional universities: Continuing education as an incubator for innovation. *Canadian Journal of University Continuing Education* 25: 13–30.

Bain De Los Santos, S, Kupczynski, L, and Bain, S. (2016) The lecture method is D-E-A-D. *Focus on Colleges, Universities, and Schools* 10: 1–7.

Ball, S. (2012) Performativity, commodification and commitment: An I-spy guide to the neoliberal university. *British Journal of Educational Studies* 60: 17–28.

Beck, U, and Lau, C. (2005) Second modernity as a research agenda: Theoretical and empirical explorations in the 'meta-change' of modern society. *The British Journal of Sociology* 56: 525–557.

Black, P, Harrison, C, Lee, C, Marshall, B, and Wiliam, D. (2004) Working inside the black box: Assessment for learning in the classroom. *Phi Delta Kappan* 86: 9–21.

Bligh, D. (2000) *What's the Use of Lectures?* New York: Jossey-Bass.

Blin, F, and Munro, F. (2008) Why hasn't technology disrupted academics' teaching practices? Understanding resistance to change through the lens of activity theory. *Computers & Education* 50: 475–490.

Brown, MG. (2016) Blended instructional practice: A review of the empirical literature on instructors' adoption and use of online tools in face-to-face teaching. *Internet and Higher Education* 31: 1–10.

Clark, RC, Nguyen, F, and Sweller, J. (2005) *Efficiency in Learning: Evidence-Based Guidelines to Manage Cognitive Load.* San Francisco: Pfeiffer.

Conole, G, de Laat, M, Dillon, T, and Darby, J. (2008) 'Disruptive technologies', 'pedagogical innovation': What's new? Findings from an in-depth study of students' use and perception of technology. *Computers & Education* 50: 511–524.

Crook, C. (2015) Should all university lectures be automatically recorded? *The Conversation*, 8 April. Available at: http://theconversation.com/should-all-university-lectures-be-automatically-recorded-39158 (accessed May 2016).

Crossley, M. (2016) The lecture is dead, long live the lecture. *Sydney Morning Herald*, 19 January. Available at: www.smh.com.au/comment/comment-merlin-crossley-on-lectures-20160119-gm8uuy.html (accessed May 2016).

Dale, E. (1969) *Audiovisual Methods in Teaching*. New York: Dryden Press.

Driscoll, A, Jicha, K, Hunt, A, Tichavsky, L, and Thompson, G. (2012) Can online courses deliver in-class results?: A comparison of student performance and satisfaction in an online versus a face-to-face introductory sociology course. *Teaching Sociology* 40: 312–331.

Faculty Focus. (2015) *Flipped Classroom Trends: A Survey of College Faculty*. Madison, WI: Magna Publications.

Feenberg, A. (2015) The online education controversy and the future of the university. *Foundations of Science*. doi: 10.1007/s10699-015-9444-9.

Forsey, M. (2010) Teachers and the re-production of middle-class culture in Australian schools. *International Studies in Sociology of Education* 20: 67–81.

Forsey, M, and Low, M. (2014) Beyond the production of tourism imaginaries: Student-travellers in Australia and their reception of media representations of their host nation. *Annals of Tourism Research* 44: 156–170.

Forsey, M, Low, M, and Glance, D. (2013) Flipping the sociology classroom: Towards a practice of online pedagogy. *The Journal of Sociology* 49: 471–485.

Giddens, A. (1991) *Modernity and Self-Identity: Self and Society in the Late Modern Age*. Stanford: Stanford University Press.

Haggis, T. (2009) What have we been thinking of? A critical overview of 40 years of student learning research in higher education. *Studies in Higher Education* 34: 377–390.

Hamilton, D. (2012) Rethinking the large lecture: Teaching and learning at scale. Presentation at *Teaching Science through the History & Philosophy of Science*, Boston University. Available at: www.bu.edu/hps-scied/files/2012/12/Hamilton-HPS-Rethinking-the-Lecture-Teaching-and-Learning-at-Scale.pdf (accessed October 2013).

Inglis, F. (2011) Economical with the actualité. *Times Higher Education Supplement*, 6 October. Available at: www.timeshighereducation.com/features/economical-with-the-actualit/417654.article (accessed May 2016).

James, R, Krause, KL, and Jennings, C. (2010) *The First Year Experience in Australian Universities: Findings from 1994 to 2009*. Melbourne: The Centre for Study in Higher Education. Available at: www.griffith.edu.au/__data/assets/pdf_file/0013/52303/FYE_in_Australian_Universities.pdf (accessed October 2016).

Knight, P. (1995) *Assessment for Learning in Higher Education*. London: Kogan Page.

Lambert, C. (2012) Twilight of the lecture. *Harvard Magazine*, March–April. Available at: http://harvardmagazine.com/2012/03/twilight-of-the-lecture (accessed September 2013).

Lorenzetti, JP. (2014) Thinking horizontally and vertically about blended learning. *Faculty Focus*, 20 November. Available at: www.facultyfocus.com/articles/blended-flipped-learning/thinking-horizontally-vertically-blended-learning/ (accessed September 2016).

Martinez, M, and Lipson, J. (1989) Assessment for learning. *Educational Leadership* 47: 73–75.

McNally, B, Chipperfield, J, Dorsett, P, Del Fabbro, L, Frommolt, V, Goetz, S, Lewohl, J, Molineux, M, Pearson, A, Reddan, G, Roiko, A, and Rung, A. (2017) Flipped classroom experiences: Student preferences and flip strategy in a higher education context. *Higher Education* 73: 281–298.

Nathan, R. (2005) *My Freshman Year*. Ithaca: Cornell University Press.

Noble, D. (1998) Digital diploma mills: The automation of higher education. *Science as Culture* 7: 355–368.

O'Flaherty, J, and Phillips, C. (2015) The use of flipped classrooms in higher education: A scoping review. *The Internet and Higher Education* 25: 85–95.

Olsenn, M, and Peters, M. (2005) Neoliberalism, higher education and the knowledge economy: From the free market to knowledge capitalism. *Journal of Education Policy* 20: 313–345.

Pokorny, H. (2016) Assessment for learning. In: Pokorny, H, and Warren, D (eds) *Enhancing Teaching Practice in Higher Education*. Los Angeles: Sage, 69–90.

Pursel, B, and Fang, HN. (2012) *Lecture Capture: Current Research and Future Directions*. Pennsylvania: The Schreyer Institute for Teaching Excellence, The University of Pennsylvania.

Radford, AW. (2011) Learning at a distance: Undergraduate enrollment in distance education courses and degree programs. Stats in brief. NCES 2012–154. National Center for Educational Statistics. Available at: https://nces.ed.gov/pubs2012/2012154.pdf (accessed September 2016).

Rodgers, J. (2001) Recording lecture effects: A panel-data study of the effects of student attendance on university performance. *Australian Journal of Education* 45: 284–295.

Salmon, G, and Wright, P. (2014) Transforming future teaching through 'carpe diem' learning design. *Education Sciences* 4: 52–63.

Selwyn, N. (2014) *Digital Technology and the Contemporary University: Degrees of Digitization*. London and New York: Routledge.

Sharples, M. (2003) Disruptive devices: Mobile technology for conversational learning. *International Journal of Continuing Engineering Education and Lifelong Learning* 12: 504–520.

Strayer, J. (2012) How learning in an inverted classroom influences cooperation, innovation and task orientation. *Learning Environments Research* 15: 171–193.

Wells, J. (2016) Academics do want new uni business models: Open universities official. *Campus Review*, 2 June. Available at: www.campusreview.com.au/2016/06/academics -do-want-new-uni-business-models-open-universities-official/ (accessed June 2016).

9

A LABOUR OF LOVE

A critical examination of the 'labour icebergs' of Massive Open Online Courses

Katharina Freund, Stephanie Kizimchuk, Jonathon Zapasnik, Katherine Esteves and Inger Mewburn

Introduction

In recent years, Massive Open Online Courses (commonly known as MOOCs) have made university-level courses at prestigious universities available to anyone with an internet connection. The academic discourse around MOOCs has become polarised, with advocates claiming all kinds of democratising benefits and critics bemoaning the upcoming 'disruption' of higher education. To date, there is little written about the process of making MOOCs, what labour is involved and who pays (or not) for this labour to be performed. This chapter critically examines the complexity of the labour involved in making MOOCs, in particular labour that becomes invisible (Star and Strauss, 1999). This chapter raises important questions about the true cost – for individuals and institutions – of making university courses 'free' and 'open' online.

Since MOOCs have proliferated at a rapid speed, there has been little attention paid to the types of labour involved in building and operating a MOOC, or what can be better described as the 'behind the scenes' work. This is work done largely by teaching professionals and casual staff. This chapter situates itself within existing trends in the field of higher education studies concerned with labour force dynamics; in particular the discussions of institutional pressures of being an academic (Chowdhry, 2014; Gill, 2009; Isenbarger and Zembylas, 2006; Ogbonna and Harris, 2004) and increasing levels of casual or short-term contract-based employment (Coates et al., 2009; Kimber, 2003). This paper contributes to a critical discourse about MOOCs (Rhoads et al., 2013) and the inequalities experienced by those producing and managing MOOC content.

MOOCs are usually built around a 'star teacher'. Hidden from view is the labour of attendant satellite support staff – academics, graduate students and professional staff. Some of these satellite staff supply essential, but unpaid labour, without which

MOOCs could not be built or run. The interesting analytical question is: why? If this unpaid labour is so essential, why does it so easily fall away from view to the extent that it is sometimes not even seen *as* labour? Susan Leigh Star and Anselm Strauss (1999) point out that what 'counts' as labour tends to be work that is visible and has tangible effects. Digging a hole, for example, involves physical movement and sweating and produces a hole as a tangible effect of the labour. By contrast, other forms of labour, particularly those that do not have visible effects, tend to be ignored and/or misrecognised, thus increasing the risk that they become invisible. Labour that has become invisible is easily devalued (Suchman, 1995). University courses are full of labour that easily becomes invisible as most of the work to write, produce materials, enrol students, book rooms and so on is hidden from the view of students themselves – and even from managers. For example, the manager sees a project is delivered to a timeline (or not); students only 'see' the lecturer and their presentation of the material, not the rest of the 'labour iceberg' that lies beneath. It is this MOOC 'labour iceberg' which we would like to examine here.

Some forms of labour – regardless of the workplace context – are inevitably privileged over others. MOOCs can be thought of as an assemblage of various forms and modes of labour, some of which is difficult to recognise as labour at all and might be better described as forms of 'articulation work' (Strauss, 1988). Articulation work is all the 'other' work that it takes to get something done: 'the work you do in order to do the work you do'.[1] The articulation work we observed in the process of putting this MOOC together and running it was often immaterial, affective and intellectual. This is precisely the kind of work that Suchman (1995) points out is more likely to become invisible, particularly to a 'managerial gaze'. Michael Hardt and Antonio Negri (2000: 292) have suggested that immaterial labour is 'where labour produces immaterial goods such as a service, a cultural product, knowledge or communication'.

As Rosalind Gill and Andy Pratt (2008: 8) note, however, Hardt and Negri's definition symbolises a contradictory process: incorporating not only the exploitation brought about by the acceleration of information, but also the pleasure that derives from expanding social networks. It is this precariousness, or rather ambiguity, that binds together the various forms of labour discussed in this chapter. For example, intellectual labour (Žarkov, 2015) and emotional labour (Chowdhry, 2014; Isenbarger and Zembylas, 2006; Ogbonna and Harris, 2004) are two modes of labour that have been explicitly referred to in the context of higher education. What both of these labours have in common is a discourse of denial and ingratitude that form the 'hidden injuries' of academia, such as reviewing of journal manuscripts (Žarkov, 2015) or excessive workloads (Gill, 2009).

The complexity of these types of labour – and their various degrees of visibility – have been virtually ignored by the literature on MOOCs to date. Our contention is that MOOCs involve many complex forms of labour that are highly likely to become invisible. Consequently, it is important for universities to recognise this labour is part of the 'price of free' (Carr, 2009). In this chapter we describe some of the types of labour we observed ourselves doing while building the 'How to

Survive your PhD' MOOC on edX in 2014. We also draw on our experience of designing, building and running the MOOC at the Australian National University in late 2015. This MOOC was designed to encourage conversations about common issues and problems amongst doctoral students, supervisors and other interested parties, such as partners and families. Various techniques were employed to enable the interaction to 'spill' onto other social spaces, such as Twitter, Instagram and Facebook. This work involved invisible forms of labour which, we contend, are crucial to keeping these huge, ambiguous digital spaces functioning as useful teaching and learning environments.

It is critical to unpack and examine these invisible forms of labour in MOOCs because they are often unrecognised, ignored and – importantly – uncompensated. This devaluation is part of a larger trend of free labour in the digital economies of advanced capitalist societies (Terranova, 2000). Drawing in part on Kuehn and Corrigan's notion of hope labour (2013), we argue that this work tends to be unexamined and undervalued, in part because it is emotional and intellectual work geared primarily towards supporting students. In this chapter we describe some of the invisible work performed by satellite staff in our MOOC through examining the personal reflections by the MOOC moderators who offered voluntary labour to this project. These data speak of the effects of blurred boundaries between teacher and student, and between paid and unpaid worker. We call into question the claims for MOOCs to be spaces of liberation from conventional academic arrangements and hierarchies.

Massive Open Online Courses and academic labour

As an emerging body of literature, MOOC scholarship has largely been concerned with evaluating the usefulness of the MOOC platform as a pedagogical tool. MOOC literature has been overshadowed by issues like participant interaction, commitment and success in the digital economy. One strand of the literature focuses on the potential of the platform to reach mass audiences (Johnson et al., 2015; Terras and Ramsay, 2015; Rodriguez, 2012, 2013), patterns of engagement amongst participants (de Barba et al., 2016; Chang et al., 2015; Kop, 2011; Veletsianos, 2013; Veletsianos et al., 2015) and attention to the emerging role of social media (Alario-Hoyos et al., 2016; Stewart, 2010). Another strand of literature responds to the observation that MOOCs tend to suffer from low completion rates. Scholars have attempted to identify reasons for diminishing participant motivation and how to maximise retention rates (Clow, 2013; de Freitas et al., 2015; Koutropoulos et al., 2012; Pursel et al., 2016). Stein and Allione (2014) explored how different kinds of activities contribute to attrition rates, especially during the early stages of a MOOC. To date, 'provider focused' research (Liyanagunawardena et al., 2013) has given some thought to dealing with the volume of marking (Sadigh et al., 2012), 'teacher' identity in an online context (Ross et al., 2014) and including professional staff (for example, librarians) into MOOC course design (MacIsaac, 2012; Mahraj, 2012). Finally, there is literature on course design (Breslow et al.,

2013; Liyanagunawardena et al., 2015; Rayyan et al., 2016; Salmon et al., 2015). There remains a gap in the literature about MOOC production and the labouring that is essential to bring MOOCs into being.

MOOC providers, such as edX, Coursera and Udacity[2] function similarly to other new media industries and the social web (Facebook, YouTube and so on), whereby the company does not actually produce any content themselves, but relies entirely on user-generated content for their business model (Jenkins, 2006). Gregg observes that participating in Web 2.0 content building, such as writing a status update on Facebook or posting a picture on Instagram, is a labour of love that is a normalised practice in the social media age: 'characteristic of online and hacking cultures [this] fits neatly with the profit-seeking, crowd-sourcing aspirations of both established and budget-conscious start-up media companies' (Gregg, 2010: 183). Jarrett (2014) describes this digital labour as the way that internet users provide content, social organisation, beta-testing and community policing for digital corporations, and generate the user data that are sold to advertisers. As Andrejevic (2011: 97) explains, this digital labour is doubly free – freely acquired by the corporations, and freely given by the users:

> When we explore what people do on Facebook or MySpace and the forms of community such sites enable, we must also keep in mind what gets done with the products of this activity, who controls its use and re-use, who profits from its transformation into commercial commodities and marketing campaigns, as well as who is targeted by these campaigns and to what end. Contrary to conventional wisdom, social networking sites don't publicize community, they *privatize* it. [emphasis in original]

What is important to note in all these discussions of user-generated content is that this 'free' content generation is not normally recognised as a legitimate form of work because it is unpaid. The assumption is that content creation provides some kind of intangible benefit to the individual or the social groups with whom the social network corporations are engaged. As will be explored later, pay structures for MOOCs (at the Australian National University) almost exclusively focus on production costs and not on the time or intellectual labours of the staff creating the content or delivering the course. Following Hall's (2016) discussion on the 'Uber-fication' of higher education, while the decentralised users/students of MOOCs benefit from discounted access to education and universities build the platform by providing the content, it is the owners of the data management intermediaries (the MOOC platform, edX) who take the profits.

Although the exploited labour involved in social media participation is equally distributed between men and women, the affective and performative dimensions of social media work are explicitly gendered. According to Jarrett (2014: 15), '[t]he "feminine skills" of flexibility and constant adaptability demanded within current precarious employment systems' are currently visible in digital media work and industries; indeed: 'It often seems as if immaterial labor was only "invented" when it moved out of the kitchen and onto the Internet'.[3] The work of creating and maintaining online social networks and communities is socially in line with what is perceived as 'women's work', the work in the social sphere that creates social cohesion (Fortunati, cited in Jarrett, 2014). This labour in the immaterial realm is not necessarily exploitative, but can bring significant affective pleasure as well as exhaustion, 'burn-out' and other negative consequences. This is something taken further by Brooke Erin Duffy (2015: 441), who examines how discourses of authenticity and branding produce highly gendered ways of engaging with social media. In particular, by participating in such activities that promote the 'promise of social and economic capital', the labour that gets put into social media often goes unrewarded and only reproduces problematic assumptions around gender and work.

The 'How to Survive Your PhD' MOOC

Led by Director of Research Training Inger Mewburn, the 'How to Survive Your PhD' MOOC ran from August to December, 2015, delivered by the Australian National University's edX platform, ANUx. This MOOC ran after only a handful of other courses had run.[4] Press coverage of ANU's partnership with edX suggested it was in response to publicity generated after the University of Melbourne became a partner of Coursera, a competing MOOC platform (Palmer, 2013). Mewburn was chosen by university management to lead this MOOC project because of her previously successful open educational work on the 'Thesis Whisperer' blog.[5] Mewburn was given an open brief to do a MOOC aimed at improving research supervision and a budget of AUD$25,000. Working extensively with the ANU Online team, Mewburn developed a proposal for a MOOC that would explicitly encourage interaction and engage with the global PhD student and supervisor communities. The MOOC would focus on building networks and emotional resilience. Each module of the ten-week-long course was structured around an emotion common to the PhD journey, such as frustration, loneliness, fear and love. As the course explicitly focused on emotions, the content was designed to foster discussions in the edX course forums, on Twitter and in the weekly live video chats hosted using Periscope.[6]

The MOOC was developed over a period of 18 months, with a significant amount of design, building, marketing, video production, training and project management work completed by an ever-widening group of satellite staff. This included a professional video production crew from the university marketing department, technical and project management support, educational design consultation and, in particular, training of volunteer moderators. Only a small percentage of the labour that was undertaken during the 'How to Survive Your PhD' MOOC was visible to those outside the course team: specifically, the text and the videos of Mewburn introducing the topics. The $25,000 budget disappeared quickly. Most was spent engaging a professional writer (whose content was wholly re-written by Mewburn), film editing and graphic design. As with all the other MOOCs at ANU, content was generated by university workers as 'in-kind labour'. Mewburn estimated that hours spent on the weekend and at night over the 18-month period would have amounted to around \$108,000 if overtime was paid to academics (which, under the ANU Enterprise Bargaining Agreement, it is not).[7]

It was clear towards the end of the development process that the MOOC would require a group of moderators, but there was no budget left. Mewburn initially put out a call for participation to an internal list of academics who had completed some professional development activities at the Centre for Higher Education Learning and Teaching (CHELT). She asked for volunteer moderators who were willing to engage with the MOOC as an opportunity to learn skills in online moderation and social media platforms for their own teaching portfolios. It was imagined that this volunteer work would be appealing to early career researchers, who make up the majority of this list cohort, but only one person, a PhD student (Stephanie Kizimchuk), answered the call. Stephanie enlisted a friend and, largely through word of mouth, a group of six moderators was formed: four PhD students and two professional staff who were members of the ANU Online team.

As the project progressed, it became apparent that the workload that had been imagined in the design process was nowhere near what the moderators were being asked to contribute, so the final part of the budget was expended in giving each PhD student moderator a \$500 honorarium. The two professional staff members were unable to be paid the honorarium and it was assumed that this MOOC work would therefore have to fit within their budgeted work hours (it did not). As a consequence, the majority of work by teaching staff on the project was unpaid. Without this unpaid labour, the MOOC would not have run, yet this cost never appeared on any budget spreadsheet. Most of the costs to ANU were not recovered from running the course; only a minority of students (around 50) opted-in for a 'verified certificate' of completion, which in the case of this course cost around \$50.

When the 'How to Survive Your PhD' MOOC opened, the discussion forums and Twitter discussions quickly became an unmanageable flurry of activity, 24-hours a day, with more than 15,000 students enrolled, and 5,000 to 8,000 participants every week from all parts of the globe. This represented a significant workload for the moderators, but what kind of work was it?

Labour in online courses

In this MOOC project, there was a deeply problematic separation of private (unpaid) and public (paid) work. When courses are delivered fully online to a global audience, they exist on a 24-hour schedule, seven days a week. Participants in the MOOC course came from all parts of the world, and their engagement with the course was not constrained by a Canberra-based work-day schedule. While it was never expected that the moderators would be available 24/7 for the course, the types of technologies and platforms used for MOOCs are those that can easily invade personal and social online spaces. It is extremely difficult to 'firewall' the social media spaces used for professional and personal reasons. Indeed, the course was designed to incorporate social spaces such as Twitter and Instagram, and participants were encouraged to create their own Facebook groups and other sites. Once a week, a scheduled live chat was held in the evenings (from 7pm) which required several moderators to be present on campus to facilitate the class, and engage before and after the live chat using Twitter. As tweets directed to the team came at all hours, and Twitter and other social media accounts are available on smartphones and tablet devices, it was nearly impossible to avoid getting notifications and updates about the course in the evenings, weekends and while on holidays. Social spaces previously used for personal reasons (or not used at all) became inhabited by 'work'-related content.

This blurring between professional, office communication (such as via email) and personal, social communication (on Twitter and other social media sites) is identified as a form of presence bleed by Gregg (2011: 145):

> If the office exists in your phone, how is it possible to claim the right to be away from it for any length of time? Indeed, how do employees assert the right to avoid work-related contact if the bulk of their colleagues are friends? [...] Like never before, communications technologies grant access to the workplace beyond physical constraints, just as workplace intimacies trouble the sense of what is coerced or freely chosen labour.

This issue of presence bleed, facilitated by constant access to Wi Fi and devices, is a common one within higher education as a sector. Academics are required to have a constant awareness of work outside of work hours, and are often required to work from home to complete the tasks that build up during the work-day. In particular, responding to emails is frequently done outside of the office as a method of dealing with workload. This form of 'anticipatory labour' involves completing work tasks *before* going to work as a way of dealing with anxiety about work (Gregg, 2008, 2011).

As teaching in a MOOC context is unconstrained by class times and time zones, the labour of teaching spilled across hours and personal spaces. While answering a handful of tweets or forum posts each night seems like a small expenditure of time for each person, it accumulates rapidly over the length of a course into a significant amount of unpaid labour. But, as Gregg (2010: 189) argues, by 'routinely discounting the amount of time and attention their job takes from other pursuits, academics have often been guilty of normalising the self-exploiting tendencies'. This is a kind of labouring on the self which is largely invisible. Much of the invisible (unpaid) work done by the moderators was this form of emotional labour. Often the immaterial, unmeasurable labour of affect and emotion is not considered work, and is also primarily undertaken by women (Gregg, 2008, 2010, 2011).

This labour is both directed at oneself, as well as towards others. Like air hostesses (Hochschild, 1979), moderators had to work on themselves in order to project an appropriate 'moderator self' online, as Moderator Kat notes in her diary:

> As I prepare for my role as moderator in this MOOC, I've been reading the text of the course, and going through articles on e-moderating and

e-moderating skills. But I'm sure nothing will prepare me for it. It scares me that the topic is on emotions and that it will take more than mastery of the content to moderate the discussions. With this, there is no right or wrong answer. I wonder how I will respond to forum posts. Do the students want a response in the first place? Are they asking a question or just sharing? You know that feeling when you are talking to a friend and just pouring your heart out? You're not seeking any advice. You don't want to hear anything. You just want someone to listen to you. And it's really annoying when they start giving advice. I surely don't want to annoy anyone.

What is more deeply troubling about labouring in MOOCs is the question of who is doing the work? The four moderators were all PhD students and contingent academic workers. It is to this issue that we will now turn our attention.

Casualisation and higher education

Higher education has long been reliant on exploited, underpaid casual and sessional staff to deliver teaching (May et al., 2013; Percy et al., 2008). This 'significant but largely invisible' cohort of teachers and short-term contract staff are defined by job insecurity, low rates of pay and negligible benefits (Kimber, 2003). In the name of 'flexibility', both in terms of budgets and staffing, casual and contract positions in higher education now make up roughly half of all teaching staff, and this is a gendered trend. Crimmins (2016: 46) points out that 'women casual academics are *generally* absent, as authors or protagonists, in discourses around higher education, and sessional staffing more specifically'. According to a participant in Crimmins' narrative study of casualisation, 'I don't think we're deliberately left out, I think we're just forgotten about' (2016: 52).

Casual workers are particularly susceptible to issues of presence bleed and unpaid labour. In our experience at ANU (and we have reason to believe this is widespread), budgets for MOOCs rarely include such measures for adequate payment of moderators or teachers, or for office space or devices for MOOC facilitators or moderators. While it is possible that formal structures of how to pay staff for their work on MOOCs have not caught up to this relatively new form of delivering teaching online, it is still symptomatic of the wider problem of unrecognised academic labour. Typical sessional teaching pay is calculated by the 'contact hour' for face-to-face teaching, based on how much time they spend in a physical classroom and how many students they have. In an asynchronous online course like this MOOC, which runs around the clock and has more than 15,000 enrolled students (and 5,000 to 8,000 participating each week), the issue of how to adequately reimburse sessional teachers for their moderation work becomes increasingly complex: especially if, as Gregg (2011) maintains, casual academics feel pressure to match full-time colleagues' work practices in relation to communication standards.

It was assumed that full-time staff would deliver the course as part of their regular workload, and that PhD students or volunteers from the community would work to moderate courses and supply their own 'tools'. Mewburn reported an extreme, and ultimately unpaid, workload in preparation, but as she was employed on a long-term contract she could presumably manage her workload to off-set these hours (given the institutional pressures, however, this did not happen). However, not only were the 'How to Survive Your PhD' MOOC facilitators unpaid for their work, they were not considered 'workers' in the traditional sense. It was assumed by the course team that each member would have access to their own devices, internet access, working or office space, in order to play the role of moderator.

As this kind of work will never be compensated monetarily, what are the implications for MOOCs on this segment of the higher education workforce? Do contingent workers pay a higher price for the existence of MOOCs? If so, why do they do it? The adage, *cui bono* 'to whose profit' is worth returning to when considering teaching and learning in the context of online MOOCs. In this section, we look at the benefits and costs that involvement in the MOOC had for the moderation team, as expressed in their reflective narratives.

Weighing up the costs and benefits of participation

If they were not being paid, why did the moderators take part in the project? There were both extrinsic and intrinsic benefits for being part of the moderation team. Moderator Steph outlined some of her reasons for participating in the course in her application email to Inger, which she also included later in her journal:

> I am excited about the prospect of being involved in a MOOC and would welcome the opportunity to experientially learn the differences that such a format and scale make upon pedagogic practice. I would embrace this chance to be mentored, make a contribution to the learning of others, and in turn, further develop myself professionally.

Moderator Kat wrote in her diary:

> The course is actually about surviving your PhD .... Great. How am I supposed to moderate a course when I have no idea what it feels to be doing your PhD? After that initial meeting with Inger and Katie, I felt like backing out. I don't think I can give justice to the role. I am confident with my moderation skills but I also need to know about the topic or content to give insightful comments. But my desire to learn is greater than this feeling of insecurity and 'unworthiness'. So, I think I will swallow my pride and focus on the things that I will learn instead of chickening out. I am looking forward to learning about the edX platform, the behind the scenes of putting together a MOOC, meeting new people, using Twitter in a MOOC environment, and moderating a massive 'class'.

Moderator and eLearning designer Katie pointed to the wide range of tasks the moderators were asked to do, which went far beyond that which was advertised:

> There was really no other way, and many of the moderators went above and beyond ten times over during the course. But since we were so short-staffed and so desperate for help, we needed the moderators to do work far outside of what they signed up for (in particular, beta-testing and other technical work).

The extrinsic benefits were established within the initial recruitment email. This framed moderation as a unique and 'unusual opportunity' and explicitly linked this to rewards such as mentoring and professional development (Mewburn, 2015). Social prestige was mobilised through marketing the opportunity as one where volunteers would 'work with', 'learn from' and 'be mentored by' the 'successful' 'Thesis Whisperer' who would 'personally train and support you in acquiring any of the skills you might need' (Mewburn, 2015). As the labour involved was unpaid, moderation was framed as being a 'learning opportunity' recognised by the ANU's Academic Professional Development programme including the offer of 'a certificate in recognition of your contribution'. Exclusivity was also heightened through inclusion of a pre-selection process requiring interested parties to directly email the 'Thesis Whisperer' with their CV and reasons for wanting to participate. Mewburn positioned the bid as a form of internship, which is traditionally a form of free labour. All moderators were told they would receive personal guidance from the 'Thesis Whisperer', who also offered to provide professional references on request.

This initial framing affected the way the experience of moderation was perceived and received by moderators. An internship is free labour positioned as an opportunity to break into an industry, but that definition is stretched in this case. What does (and doesn't) count as membership of academia is fuzzy. All the moderators were functioning members of the so-called 'academic precariat' and thus performing various forms of paid academic labour and treated as academics by the human resources (HR) department. When free labour is firmly positioned as a positive enterprise replete with rewards and esteem, it becomes what Kuehn and Corrigan (2013) label 'hope labour': labour offered with the hope there will be some, probably non-monetary, reward down the track. The project quickly expanded in scope and complexity after the moderators came on board. Mewburn attempted to recognise that the amount and complexity of the labour did not fall into the initial 'internship' bid by arranging an honorarium for the moderators' efforts. However, this came as an unexpected surprise, so it cannot be said to be an inducement to participate.

The initial framing of free labour as a 'learning experience' appeared throughout moderators' reflective narratives including within their expressions of intrinsic benefit. These are strongly linked to 'positive' emotions where the reward of effort is simply the love of the task or joy in learning a new skill. Kat, for example, observed that 'it was really an effort for me to use Twitter . . . BUT, I love reading things from Twitter'. Jonathon also reflected that 'I'm really finding the Twittersphere enjoyable . . . I'm also looking forward to giving Storify a go'. Steph shared this enthusiasm, writing: 'I had never used Storify before but immediately fell in love with it . . . Each Storify took me a very long time but it was incredibly satisfying to create them.'

The intrinsic emotional benefits of moderation led to this work being perceived as a haven from other less rewarding outside responsibilities. Kat noted 'I probably spent an hour-and-a-half reading [MOOC related] articles before I realised that I was at work and should be "working"'. Likewise, Jonathon observed 'it was really difficult to divorce myself from my phone so I could teach that afternoon, but I got my fix afterwards on the bus home'. This discourse of inherent personal benefit led to the collaborative experience of working in a team to be viewed in a positive light, despite multiple challenges. Steph summed up a common feeling within the team, writing that 'It felt really wonderful to be included and part of a good quality team that cares about what they do and for a project that is actually making a difference in people's lives. It made me really happy.'

All moderators also felt personal satisfaction from moderating online, facilitating interaction and observing communities form. Katie felt 'lifted up by the wonderful comments from the participants: they were excited, eager, and interested in the topic and looking forward to it!' Kat also 'enjoyed' reading posts and 'was fascinated and entertained by the different topics that the participants are researching'. Jonathon noted that seeing communities form 'made me feel warm inside, especially the threads that were busting at the seams with replies'.

Moderators also overtly identified with the initial discourse that situated their free labour as being a 'learning experience' to the point of linking this with their own constructions of self. Margaret noted she was filled with 'awe' and the 'excitement of discovering this new world, and my place within it'. Kat shared this sentiment: 'curiosity was the main reason why I volunteered . . . Curiosity is what fuels me every day'. Steph added, 'I love learning. . . That is what drives me as a person and as a moderator'. The implications of this are that those more oriented towards seeing their work as enjoyable and mutually beneficial tended to self-select for this opportunity.

Even though there were benefits to being a moderator, considerable personal costs were involved, despite training attempting to mitigate some of these. All moderators were also balancing other major commitments such as family, employment responsibilities and PhD studies. The costs on the team predominantly impacted upon time, psychological and emotional wellbeing and physical health. All moderators reported feeling emotionally and psychologically overloaded at the beginning and early stages of the MOOC. Katie, for example, observed that 'I am finding my brain racing constantly to ensure all the little things, big things, and in-between things get finished in time' and she had an 'an emotional crash once the initial excitement wore off'.

The sheer scale and intensity of the MOOC heightened these feelings. There were at least 1,200 students per team member, and even to an experienced moderator like Katie the volume felt 'tough' and 'nerve-wracking'. Jonathon shared that 'reading bio-after-bio fast became an anxiety inducing task'. Kat also initially froze due to the scale of the online interactions:

> I was not able to do any moderating . . . it's as if [I] was stuck in an intersection with no clear road rules and I could not decide (or have the balls) to drive forward and cross the roads. I needed more time to study the traffic around me.

As the MOOC progressed, some moderators experienced physical exhaustion, nightmares and insomnia. Steph noted that this 'was a major challenge' and that she often felt 'utterly and completely exhausted'. Katie also reflected after the first week that she felt 'pretty numb right now' due to lack of sleep. Further emotional labour was also required to keep the team itself running smoothly, in addition to dealing with participants. Katie captures this well when recording her feelings about taking on an extra moderation shift:

> I am not feeling very well today and I just don't know how much energy I have to continue to empathise with the participants in the course . . . I am covering a moderation shift for someone else today and I just don't have it in me to enact the emotional labour required.

The emotional nature of the MOOC's topics heightened the intensity of their work. Kat distinctively felt that she was continuously 'walking on eggshells' and that she had 'never felt so sensitive about my e-moderating . . . I don't want to rock the boat especially in such an environment when people are emotional'. Consequently, she was 'always on the lookout for participants who seemed distressed and needed counselling more than academic support'. Steph also consciously conducted triage, noting that the majority of her time was spent 'doing the following searches: cutting, self-harm, suicide, anxiety, depression, death, violence, PTSD, kill, murder, rape'. Katie found it 'overwhelming' and 'heart-rending' to read 'posts begging for advice, for help, asking if they should quit their degrees, asking if others felt as drained and depressed'.

The emotional labour needed to sustain work in this intense environment affected the psychological wellbeing of moderators and caused high levels of stress and anxiety despite briefings on self-care. Stress was often compounded by limitations of the forum infrastructure itself which was 'an absolute nightmare' to navigate and made sustained interactions difficult. Several moderators were psychologically triggered at different points by the content and participant contributions. Kat observed she was surprised that 'what I read has a big effect on my mood and emotions' and that 'every time I was on duty as a moderator, I feel anxious'. This anxiety was a shared team experience and was also attributed to the intense and rapid up-skilling required, fears over performance or concerns regarding participant safety. The impact of exposure dealing with very distressing posts such as those relating to suicide, took its toll and remained with moderators long after their shifts.

A labour of love?

The MOOC was truly a 'labour of love' for all involved in making and running it. Love is essential to the functioning of the contemporary academic workforce, even if it is often only tacitly or obliquely acknowledged. Institutions seem to be committed to MOOCs and the platforms themselves are expanding their role as brokers of a new higher education economy. At the time of writing, Coursera had released its first TV spot,[8] which featured appropriately diverse 'students' speaking about the career benefits of participation. There is, unfortunately, no time to fully do justice to the messages in this ad which explicitly draw on conventions of university advertising elsewhere. By taking up these aesthetic tropes, Coursera visually positions itself as part of the conventional higher education landscape, and its heritage of care for students and their futures, despite not actually being the provider of the content or the teaching.

Caring for student wellbeing has long been a part of the professional responsibility of an academic, though Selwyn (2014) notes that the holistic view of the academic's professional role has been devolved and disaggregated by digital technologies. Nevertheless, teaching is what Sara Ahmed (2004) calls an 'affective economy', where emotions work by 'binding' teachers and students together in often unpredictable ways. As teachers, we are conditioned to relate to students in particular ways and the circulation of emotions propels us in certain directions which might be at odds with what is best for us mentally, physically or emotionally. Crimmins (2016) highlights how the pleasure of teaching and good experiences with students keep casual academics coming back even though they know they are being exploited. Likewise, Hughes (2011) addresses the complexity of pleasure in academic work as it is experienced amongst doctoral candidates. Despite moments of guilt, anxiety and a felt lack of deservingness, it is often balanced by moments of 'intellectual *jouissance*', such as the ability to express oneself and develop independent judgement. Related to experiences of academic writing, casual teaching can also be thought of in terms of *jouissance* or addiction, as Mewburn (2016: 40) observes:

> The addicted sessional teacher is willing to endure the low pay, uncertainty and knock backs because they are hooked on that classroom experience. This teaching addiction explains why there is such a ready supply of people willing to do casual sessional work, when it clearly doesn't pay their bills.

In the context of this MOOC, an expected 'drug' was the weekly Periscope/Twitter broadcasts. Added almost as an afterthought, these weekly live broadcasts brought members of the team physically into Mewburn's office once a week. Catching up and sharing the week's work over chocolate and then broadcasting live and talking to course participants in real time created a 'buzz' in the office. Since these broadcasts happened at 7pm there was a feeling of being back 'after school' without permission, which made these evenings feel 'more like fun than work' as Mewburn noted in her diary as she mused on how the moderators had transitioned in her mind from student/volunteers to friends – but with an uneasy professional distance that still had to be maintained:

> I feel like I have to be the grown up sometimes, when all I want to do is muck about after school with the kids. I'm doing so much 'back stage' work, largely with Katie, to hold this group together and get us to the finish line. Everyone needs something different from me and interpersonal tensions in the team make it worse. I'm the Boss, but not the Boss, which makes it all so much harder. I can't really tell people what to do here. All I can do, I suppose, is model the behaviour I expect.

This mingling of work and pleasure, professional and personal troubles the very idea of what counts as labour and what it means to be 'boss' and 'worker'. Unlike traditional modes of face-to-face teaching, which rely on lectures and other 'contact hours' and assessment and feedback moderated by the teaching team, the MOOC teaching experience is wholly different. With no clear 'hours' to be worked at any given time, no assigned cohorts and no marking to complete, the experience of delivering this course became a 24-hour barrage of discussion across forums and personal social media channels. Despite this, the team often enjoyed the work and found it very rewarding. If you are having fun, is it still work? If you are having fun, were you coerced into labour that you might not otherwise have thought to offer? We recognised, as Gregg (2011) notes, that one can be happy to do the work because you enjoy it, but still recognise it as overworked, underpaid and not supported by an employer.

This tension is typical of modes of work in advanced capitalism under the impact of digital technologies and globalisation, where 'increasing numbers of workers in affluent societies are engaged in insecure, casualized, or irregular labour' (Gill and Pratt, 2008: 2). Despite the temporary nature of precarious work, the odd hours and the collapse of boundaries between work and play, participants in these creative industries find it extremely pleasurable and have a deep attachment to their work: '[...] They are toxic, individualized but thoroughly structural features of workplaces that include [...] the neoliberal university' (Gill and Pratt 2008: 16). New technologies like MOOCs tend to adversely affect those who are already vulnerable, including precarious workers (Selwyn, 2014). Similar to Uber drivers and Airbnb hosts, precarious academic workers who labour to deliver MOOCs are creating profits for a software company and are not considered 'employees' (Hall, 2016).

Conclusion

We think this account of our MOOC journey raises important questions for higher education workers and managers. MOOCs are spaces full of invisible, ambiguous, emotional and hope labour. Fully online teaching in free courses is the 'perfect storm' of ambiguous, invisible and exploited labour in the higher education sector; yet they can also be sites of innovation, playfulness and pleasure. The implication of the resulting workplace intimacy and 'presence bleed' means that labour in this context may not feel like 'work' even though the cost to the individual worker is real, if invisible. The course team felt strongly, as indicated in the reflections earlier, that their unpaid labour was in the cause of a greater good. The free labour was considered 'worth it' as it directly helped students who were struggling and had a real-world impact. However, this situation also raises serious questions about whether the practice of on-selling this labour to Web 2.0 companies that then convert it into profit for their shareholders and venture capital investors is actually ethical. If MOOCs are to be the next stage in online education for universities, we must begin to ask the hard questions and consider whether the costs ultimately outweigh the benefits, and for whom.

Notes

1 We are indebted to Dr Ben Kraal for this phrase.
2 edX www.edx.org/; Coursera www.coursera.org/; and Udacity www.udacity.com/.
3 In this case, we are taking immaterial and invisible labour to mean the same thing.
4 Previous courses included an astrophysics series (2014–continuing), Engaging India (2014) and Ignorance (2015).
5 www.thesiswhisperer.com.
6 Periscope is a live-streaming app which allows for interactive live video presentations.
7 This sum is calculated using Mewburn's day hourly rate, assuming time-and-a-half for overtime pay, over a six-month period. The enterprise agreement is available to view online: https://services.anu.edu.au/human-resources/enterprise-agreement.
8 https://youtu.be/_0p6x4kY0cc, accessed 6 October 2016.

References

Ahmed, S. (2004) *The Cultural Politics of Emotion*. New York: Routledge.
Alario-Hoyos, C, Muñoz-Merino, PJ, Pérez-Sanagustín, M, Delgado Kloos, C and Parada, HA. (2016) Who are the top contributors in a MOOC? Relating participants' performance and contributions. *Journal of Computer Assisted Learning* 32: 232–243.
Andrejevic, M. (2011) Social network exploitation. In: Z Papacharissi (ed), *A Networked Self: Identity, Community, and Culture on Social Network Sites*. New York and London: Routledge, 82–101.
Breslow, L, Pritchard, DE, DeBoer, J, Stump, GS, Ho, AD and Seaton, DT. (2013) Studying learning in the worldwide classroom research into edX's First MOOC. *Research & Practice in Assessment* 8: 13–25.
Carr, N. (2009) The price of free. *New York Times Magazine* 13 November 2009. Available at: www.nytimes.com/2009/11/15/magazine/15FOB-Phenomenon-t.html (accessed 7 April 2017).

Chang, RI, Hung, YH and Lin, CF. (2015) Survey of learning experiences and influence of learning style preferences on user intentions regarding MOOCs. *British Journal of Educational Technology* 46: 528–541.

Chowdhry, S. (2014) The caring performance and the 'blooming student': Exploring the emotional labour of further education lecturers in Scotland. *Journal of Vocational Education & Training* 66: 554–571.

Clow, D. (2013) MOOCs and the funnel of participation. Proceedings of the Third Conference on Learning Analytics and Knowledge, International Learning Analytics and Knowledge Conference, Leuven, Belgium, 185–189.

Coates, H, Dobson, IR, Goedegebuure, L and Meek, L. (2009) Australia's casual approach to its academic teaching workforce. *People and Place* 17: 47–54.

Crimmins, G. (2016) The spaces and places that women casual academics (often fail to) inhabit. *Higher Education Research and Development* 35: 45–57.

de Barba, PG, Kennedy, GE and Ainley, MD. (2016) The role of students' motivation and participation in predicting performance in a MOOC. *Journal of Computer Assisted Learning* 32: 218–231.

de Freitas, SI, Morgan, J and Gibson, D. (2015) Will MOOCs transform learning and teaching in higher education? Engagement and course retention in online learning provision. *British Journal of Educational Technology* 46: 455–471.

Duffy, BE. (2015) The romance of work: Gender and aspirational labour in the digital culture industries. *International Journal of Cultural Studies* 19: 441–457.

Gill, R. (2009) Breaking the silence: The hidden injuries of neo-liberal academia. In: R Ryan-Flood and R Gill (eds), *Secrecy and Silence in the Research Process: Feminist Reflections*. New York: Routledge, 228–244.

Gill, R and Pratt, A. (2008) In the social factory? Immaterial labour, precariousness and cultural work. *Theory, Culture & Society* 25: 1–30.

Gregg, M. (2008) The normalisation of flexible female labour in the information economy. *Feminist Media Studies* 8: 285–299.

Gregg, M. (2010) Working with affect in the corporate university. In: M Liljeström and S Paasonen (eds), *Working with Affect in Feminist Readings: Disturbing Differences*. London and New York: Routledge, 182–192.

Gregg, M. (2011) *Work's Intimacy*. Cambridge and Maldon: Polity Press.

Hall, G. (2016) *The Uberfication of the University*. Minneapolis: University of Minnesota Press.

Hardt, M and Negri, A. (2000) *Empire*. Cambridge: Harvard University Press.

Hochschild, AR. (1979) Work, feeling rules, and social structure. *American Journal of Sociology* 85: 551–575.

Hughes, C. (2011) Pleasure, change and values in doctoral pedagogy. *Studies in Higher Education* 36: 621–635.

Isenbarger, L and Zembylas, M. (2006) The emotional labour of caring in teaching. *Teaching and Teacher Education* 22: 120–134.

Jarrett, K. (2014) The relevance of 'women's work': Social reproduction and immaterial labour in digital media. *Television & New Media* 15: 14–29.

Jenkins, H. (2006) *Convergence Culture: Where Old and New Media Collide*. New York: NYU Press.

Johnson, L, Adams Becker, S, Estrada, V and Freeman, A. (2015) *NMC Horizon Report: 2015 Higher Education Edition*. Austin, Texas: The New Media Consortium. Available at: www.nmc.org/publication/nmc-horizon-report-2015-higher-education-edition/ (accessed 10 May 2016).

Kimber, M. (2003) The tenured 'core' and the tenuous 'periphery': The casualisation of academic work in Australian universities. *Journal of Higher Education Policy and Management* 25: 41–50.

Kop, R. (2011) The challenges to connectivist learning on open online networks: Learning experiences during a Massive Open Online Course. *International Review of Research in Open and Distance Learning* 12: 19–38.

Koutropoulos, A, Gallagher, MS, Abajian, SC, deWaard, I, Hogue, RJ, Keskin, NÖ and Rodriguez, O. (2012) Emotive vocabulary of MOOCs: Context & participant retention. *European Journal of Open, Distance and E-Learning.* Available at: www.eurodl.org/index. php?p=archives&year=2012&halfyear=1&article=507 (accessed 14 April 2016).

Kuehn, K and Corrigan, TF. (2013) Hope labor: The role of employment prospects in online social production. *The Political Economy of Communication* 1(1): 9–25.

Liyanagunawardena, TR, Adams, AA and Williams, SA. (2013) MOOCs: A systematic study of the published literature 2008–2012. *The International Review of Research in Open and Distributed Learning* 14. Available at: www.irrodl.org/index.php/irrodl/article/view /1455/2531 (accessed 14 April 2016).

Liyanagunawardena, TR, Lundqvist, KØ and Williams, SA. (2015) Who are with us: MOOC learners on a FutureLearn course. *British Journal of Educational Technology* 46: 557–569.

MacIsaac, PL. (2012) What a librarian can bring to your open online course development team. Available at: http://auspace.athabascau.ca/bitstream/2149/3218/2/MacIsaac_ MOOCs_and_Information_literacy_draft.pdf (accessed 14 April 2016).

Mahraj, K. (2012) Using information expertise to enhance Massive Open Online Courses. *Public Services Quarterly* 8: 359–368.

May, R, Strachan, G and Peetz, D. (2013) Workforce development and renewal in Australian universities and the management of casual academic staff. *Journal of University Teaching & Learning Practice* 10. Available at: http://ro.uow.edu.au/jutlp/vol10/iss3/3/ (accessed 10 May 2016).

Mewburn, I. (2015) Work with the Thesis Whisperer – Professional development opportunity in online tutoring/moderation, 3 March 2016. Email circulated through professional development listing at ANU.

Mewburn, I. (2016) The addiction. *Advocate* 23: 40. Available at: www.nteu.org.au/library/ view/id/6823 (accessed 11 May 2016).

Ogbonna, E and Harris, LC. (2004) Work intensification and emotional labour among UK university lecturers: An exploratory study. *Organization Studies* 25: 1185–1203.

Palmer, C. (2013) ANU joins MOOCs rush with edX partnership. *The Conversation.* Available at: https://theconversation.com/anu-joins-moocs-rush-with-edx-partnership-12379 (accessed 3 October 2016).

Percy, A, Scoufis, M, Parry, S, Goody, A, Hicks, M, Macdonald, I, Martinez, K, Szorenyi -Reischl, N, Ryan, Y, Wills, S and Sheridan, L. (2008) *The RED Report, Recognition – Enhancement – Development: The Contribution of Sessional Teachers to Higher Education.* Sydney, Australia: Australian Learning and Teaching Council. Available at: http://ro.uow .edu.au/asdpapers/135/ (accessed 10 May 2016).

Pursel, BK, Zhang, L, Jablokow, KW, Choi, GW and Velegol, D. (2016) Understanding MOOC students: Motivations and behaviours indicative of MOOC completion. *Journal of Computer Assisted Learning* 32: 202–217.

Rayyan, S, Fredericks, C, Colvin, KF, Liu, A, Teodorescu, R, Barrantes, A, Pawl, A, Seaton, DT and Pritchard, DE. (2016) A MOOC based on blended pedagogy. *Journal of Computer Assisted Learning* 32: 190–201.

Rhoads, RA, Berdan, J and Toven-Lindsey, B. (2013) The open courseware movement in higher education: Unmasking power and raising questions about the movement's democratic potential. *Educational Theory* 63: 87–109.

Rodriguez, O. (2012) MOOCs and the AI-Stanford like courses: Two successful and distinct course formats for Massive Open Online Courses. *European Journal of Open, Distance and*

E-Learning. Available at: www.eurodl.org/index.php?p=archives&year=2012&half-year=2&article=516 (accessed 14 April 2016).

Rodriguez, O. (2013) The concept of openness behind c and x-MOOCs. *Open Praxis* 5: 67–73.

Ross, J, Sinclair, C, Knox, J, Bayne, S and Macleod, H. (2014) Teacher experiences and academic identity: The missing components of MOOC pedagogy. *MERLOT Journal of Online Learning and Teaching* 10: 57–69.

Sadigh, D, Seshia, SA and Gupta, M. (2012) Automating exercise generation: A step towards meeting the MOOC challenge for embedded systems. Proceedings of the Workshop on Embedded Systems Education (WESE). New York. Available at: www.eecs.berkeley.edu/~sseshia/pubdir/wese12-mooc.pdf (accessed 4 May 2016).

Salmon, G, Gregory, J, Lokuge Dona, K and Ross, B. (2015) Experiential online development for educators: The example of the Carpe Diem MOOC. *British Journal of Educational Technology* 46: 542–556.

Selwyn, N. (2014) *Digital Technology and the Contemporary University: Degrees of Digitization*. London and New York: Routledge.

Star, SL and Strauss, A. (1999) Layers of silence, arenas of voice: The ecology of visible and invisible work. *Computer Supported Cooperative Work* 8: 9–30.

Stein, RM and Allione, G. (2014) Mass attrition: An analysis of drop out from a Principles of Macroeconomics MOOC. PIER Working Paper No. 14-031. Available at: http://dx.doi.org/10.2139/ssrn.2505028 (accessed 10 May 2016).

Stewart, B. (2010) Social media literacies and perceptions of value in Open Online Courses. Available at:http://portfolio.cribchronicles.com/wp-content/uploads/2012/11/612701_Social_Media_Literacies_MOOCs.pdf (accessed 14 April 2016).

Strauss, A. (1988) The articulation of project work: An organizational process. *The Sociological Quarterly* 29: 163–178.

Suchman, L. (1995) Making work visible. *Communications of the ACM* 38: 56–64.

Terranova, T. (2000) Free labor: Producing culture for the digital economy. *Social Text* 63: 35–58.

Terras, MM and Ramsay, J. (2015) Massive open online courses (MOOCs): Insights and challenges from a psychological perspective. *British Journal of Educational Technology* 46: 472–487.

Veletsianos, G. (2013) Learner experiences with MOOCs and open online learning. *Hybrid Pedagogy*. Available at: http://hybrid-pedagogy.github.io/LearnerExperiencesInMOOCs/ (accessed 14 April 2016).

Veletsianos, G, Collier, A and Schneider, E. (2015) Digging deeper into learners' experiences in MOOCs: Participation in social networks outside of MOOCs, notetaking and contexts surrounding content consumption. *British Journal of Educational Technology* 46: 570–587.

Žarkov, D. (2015) On intellectual labour and neoliberalism in academia – Or, in praise of reviewers. *European Journal of Women's Studies* 22: 269–273.

10

DIGITAL METHODS AND DATA LABS

The redistribution of educational research to education data science

Ben Williamson

Introduction

The proliferation of digital technologies and data analytics in recent years appears to challenge the legitimacy of the social sciences to interpret and comment on social practices (Burrows and Savage, 2014). Many aspects of social research are currently being redistributed to sites such as commercial research and development labs, social media companies and new kinds of data analytics experts, where analyses are performed and insights generated with software, algorithms and data analytics technologies (Marres, 2012). New 'digital methods' that involve the use of digital devices to 'perform a cultural and social diagnostics' (Rogers, 2013: 3) have the capacity to detect patterns in huge quantities of data and to augment how people and societies see and know themselves, but are often not of social scientific provenance. The redistribution of research also entails a remediation of methods as social research is refashioned through digital data-processing technologies that affect how social phenomena can be known and explained (Ruppert, Law and Savage, 2013).

This chapter explores the challenges facing social researchers in one specific field of methodological redistribution and remediation: that of education research performed in higher education institutions. Claims to authoritative forms of data analysis and knowledge production in educational research are now being made through 'education data science', an emerging field of educational research that deploys new digital methods and algorithmic data analytics technologies alongside psychological theories to measure, know and understand institutions, practices and processes of learning. Education data science represents a nexus of big data analysis and educational research and instantiates a new transdisciplinary professional infrastructure for educational knowledge production and theory generation. Originating in the data scientific study of higher education institutions and practices, the influence of education data science has since spread to studies and interventions that cross primary, secondary and tertiary sectors. It has become a trans-sector form of specialist educational expertise. Similarly, while the transdisciplinary practices of education data science originally emerged in academic higher education contexts – particularly in US education research departments – it has subsequently become distributed across academic, commercial and non-governmental settings and organisations. The current growth of education data science raises significant implications for the future of educational research, particularly in relation to methodological expertise, knowledge production and theory development. More widely, it is illustrative of emerging tensions and debates about the use and analysis of big data in higher education.

Some enthusiasts view big data as a source for 'building a smarter university' (Lane, 2014). Others have noted that big data pose distinctive challenges for disciplines such as the social sciences and humanities (Kitchin, 2014; Lupton, 2015). Referring to the 'knowledge infrastructures' of data-driven discovery, Edwards et al. (2013: 1) note that:

> Enormous transformations have occurred over the last 20 years in our systems for generating, sharing, and disputing human knowledge. Changes associated with Internet technologies—such as social media, "big data," open source software, ubiquitous computing, and Wikipedia—have altered the basic mechanics by which knowledge is produced and circulated. … Knowledge institutions like universities, libraries, and government agencies (and increasingly private entities like Facebook, Google, and Twitter) have begun to adjust, opening up vast stores of anonymised data to analysis and exploitation.

Increasingly, the expert subject capable of working within the emerging knowledge infrastructure of big data analysis must be a digital academic, or a 'digitised knowledge worker', who is skilled in the practices of digital data collection, storage, analysis, visualisation and communication. The education data scientist is a prototypical digital academic, a digitised knowledge worker whose digital methods and algorithmic techniques of big data analysis are challenging existing practices and perspectives in educational research. Working within an emerging professional knowledge infrastructure, educational data scientists are practising a form of digital academia that is sometimes locked in to proprietorial algorithms, intellectual property and platform patents.

Understood as a new professional knowledge infrastructure of educational research that criss-crosses university departments and commercial settings, education data science is increasingly privately owned, sponsored and regulated. As will be detailed in this chapter, education data science represents a redistribution of educational research, knowledge production and theory development to new sites of methodological expertise, technical capacity and financial power. It is a professional infrastructure that is also wedded to a data infrastructure, since big data 'connects myriad distributed people (computer scientists, data handlers, mathematicians, platform designers) and technologies (computers, devices, software, algorithms)'

(Ruppert, 2015). It is through such an interdependent infrastructure of people and technologies that education data science is being accomplished, and through which it is creating social, cultural and economic influence for itself as a powerful field of digital data-driven knowledge production and theory generation.

Methodological fields of expert power

Considered as a 'field', educational data science can be understood analytically through Bourdieu's (1993) notion of 'fields of power', particularly as it has been applied in relation to education policy and methodological innovation. As detailed in the education policy context by Simons, Olssen and Peters (2009: 64), a field is a relatively autonomous domain of action in which agents and groups vie over socially valued resources, and it is through such processes that a field can develop its own 'distinction' or institutional niche from others: 'within the education policy field, like in all other fields, agents struggle and compete over (cultural, economic and social) capital and strategise in order to secure their own position and social power.' Each field is a site for the creation of a particular kind of capital, or an institutionalised resource, including economic capital in the form of money and other financial assets; cultural capital, or socially valued knowledge and credentials; and access to social networks, or social capital. A field consists of structures and relations as well as the dispositions and schemata of perception of those who inhabit it. Education data science therefore needs to be understood in terms of its access to economic capital in the shape of funding and resourcing, its cultural capital in terms of the production of new specialist knowledge such as research findings derived from new expert methodologies and the social capital it gains through its wider networks of affiliations, partnerships and connections. Educational data science is, in other words, a nascent methodological field of power creating its own distinction through assembling a combination of economic, cultural and social capitals. It consists of structures and relations between actors and organisations – which will be traced later – as well as particular dispositions, perceptions and practices.

The notion of fields can also be considered in relation to the formation of methodological domains. Ruppert, Law and Savage (2013) have proposed interrogating the 'social life of methods'. By this they mean exploring specific methods genealogically to identify the theoretical, epistemological and methodological trajectories that animate them, and then to identify how such methods contribute to the production of knowledge or theory generation which influences subsequent thinking and decision-making. From this approach, sociological research has produced studies of particular academic fields, their historical origins and development, the structures and relations within them, their distinctive modes of perception and practice and their methods of knowledge production – such as the various emerging branches of data scientific practice associated with big data (Ruppert et al., 2015). Gehl (2015: 414), for example, has offered a 'partial genealogy of the data scientist, exploring how both big data and the subject who mines it have come to be, how they interact and how they are managed'. As an emerging field, educational data science can be subjected to such a study, with the aim of understanding how its development in the recent past – and its accumulation of economic, social and cultural capital – might influence the modes of perception, practices, methods, knowledge and theories of educational research in the near future.

Studies of digital methods also pay attention to the software, algorithms and data-processing devices that enact them, which 'have a structuring and shaping effect on what data are able to be collected, what data are considered important and what data can be stored for analysis' (Lupton, 2015: 49). Digital methodological devices are fundamentally reconfiguring the ways in which social science can be performed, and the kinds of analyses, interpretations and insights into social worlds that are made possible. For education data science, as with data science more generally, the key to analysis is algorithm design, which can then be deployed to conduct automated analyses of huge and complex quantities of data. Such algorithms can then be considered calculating actors that are involved in the generation of information and the production of knowledge from data.

As a methodological field of expert power and algorithmic calculation, education data science is significant because of its capacity to shape future educational knowledge, to influence the production of new educational products and pedagogies and to displace existing theories and explanations in educational research. It is a field defined by a particular schema of perception, a style of thinking and a mode of expertise in the evaluation of – and intervention in – education. This initial mapping of educational data science attempts to trace the influences, institutions and individuals – as well as the data analytics methods, practices and algorithmic techniques – that have come together in the present moment to make it a legitimate field of expert thought and practice in educational research.

Data scientists and algorithmists

Data science has emerged as a rapid growth discipline of the early twenty-first century, particularly with the emergence of big data. In technical terms, big data refer to datasets that are huge in volume (at the scale of petabytes, exabytes and zettabytes), highly diverse in type and nature, generated continuously at great velocity in or near real time and exhaustive in scope (enabling the capture of entire 'census' populations – or 'n=all' – rather than sampled selections) (Kitchin, 2014; Mayer-Schönberger and Cukier, 2013). To a significant extent, big data are dependent for their generation and analysis on specific kinds of expert data practices. Hilbert (2016: 139) suggests that the 'full name' for big data is 'big data analytics', since, 'independent from the specific peta-, exa- or zettabytes scale, the key feature of the paradigmatic change is that analytic treatment of data is systematically placed at the forefront of intelligent decision-making'. Building on established statistical methods and models, new data analytics and data-mining technologies and techniques have been developed in recent years to detect, classify and extract associations and patterns from large datasets utilising advances in information management and storage, data handling, modelling algorithms, machine intelligence and expert systems (Kitchin, 2014).

Given the technical complexity of conducting big data analyses, the figure of the data scientist has accumulated particular expert status and power. Gehl (2015: 414) has characterised the data scientist as a new kind of 'knowledge worker' who can use algorithms 'to tame the excesses of our constant sharing and mine it for new knowledge and produce valuable new techniques of social management'. As the ideal-type knowledge worker of the big data era, the figure of the data scientist is a hybrid product of statistical analysis, computational power, advances in algorithms within the field of computer science, new forms of information storage and retrieval, new programming languages and entrepreneurialism. New data scientific experts have been termed 'algorithmists' – multidisciplinary specialists in computer science, mathematics and statistics, as well as policy, law, economics and social research – who can undertake big data analyses across commercial, political and scholarly domains (Mayer-Schönberger and Cukier, 2013). Perhaps most notably, the data scientist is understood as an expert who can generate new knowledge and ideas from data that may have potential for commercialisation or management and control. In other words, knowledge can be put into action in the shape of 'new products and services, potential new vectors of value-realisation' (Gehl, 2015: 418).

However, data science is not simply a neutral and unbiased field of expertise. Beer (2016) observes that the technical fact of big data is underpinned by a loaded and powerful concept that has taken on commercial, organisational and economic force and power and come to define contemporary life in many ways. As Kitchin (2014) notes, big data analyses and data science have often been accompanied by grand claims about a 'paradigm shift' in various kinds of research, one that emphasises the inherent truthfulness of data and impartiality of analytics algorithms. The data-intensive statistical exploration and mining of phenomena that are characteristic of data science reflects a 'data-ist' belief that there is no need for *a priori* theory, models or hypotheses and that 'data can speak for themselves' unencumbered by human interpretation and meaning-making. But as Kitchin (2014: 136) elaborates, data are always generated through systems designed to accomplish very specific purposes according to particular scientific theories, methodological preferences and ways of working, while making sense of data is also framed by interpretive lenses:

> Even if the process is automated in some way, the algorithms used to process the data are imbued with particular values and contextualised within a particular scientific approach. [...] [D]ifferent analysts will draw different conclusion from the same analytics. Interpretation then is always in the eye of the beholder regardless of how neutral or value-free they claim to be. [...] As such, data never simply speak for themselves.

These points highlight the fact that data scientists work in specific disciplinary, professional and scientific contexts as part of a thought community with its own distinctive style of thinking, mode of expertise, specialist language and methodological practices and theories, which can all be organised into explanations and arguments. It is through its empirical, data-driven style of thinking that data science is able to project itself as a distinctive field of power, with access to the resources, networks and expertise to produce new knowledge and understandings in diverse domains, including education.

Disruptive education data science

The figure of the algorithmist is now being brought into being in the field of education in the shape of the education data scientist. Education data science itself is an emerging, transdisciplinary field, building on data scientific practices as well as the psychological learning sciences and psychometric techniques. Though its original focus was on applying data analysis to the institutions and practices of higher education institutions, its promoters are increasingly developing techniques to be applied to primary and secondary schooling too. Schools and universities have, of course, historically produced large quantities of data, such as test scores, attendance records, student administrative records and so on. The promise of education data science is to expand the possibilities of data collection and accelerate its analysis, not just in higher education but as a methodological logic of practice that extends homologously across education sectors. Piety, Hickey and Bishop (2014: 3) date the emergence of education data science from 2004–2007 as 'educational data mining' and 'learning analytics' experts and communities began to coalesce around shared questions, problems and assumptions – particularly with the formation of specific professional associations, conferences and academic journals – to form a field that 'has begun to receive combined attention from both federal policymakers and foundation funders and is often seen as the community dealing with "Big Data" in education'. They highlight how new forms of evidence – log files, conversational records, peer assessments, online search and navigation behaviour, among others – are disrupting traditional ways of working in educational research, 'acting in a way similar to *disruptive innovations* that alter cultural, historical practices and activity systems' (Piety, Hickey and Bishop, 2014: 5).

The institutional infrastructure for education data science is emerging across higher education institutions and commercial settings, and there is a substantial and fast-growing body of educational data mining and learning analytics literature (e.g. Clow, 2013; Siemens, 2013). The corporate computing companies IBM and Microsoft have launched major data analytics platforms for schools and universities, making the technologies and practices of education data science into parts of the everyday systems of schooling and higher education alike. Siemens (2016) has also documented the formation of the Society of Learning Analytics Research (SoLAR), its dedicated *Journal of Learning Analytics* and the Learning Analytics and Knowledge (LAK) conference it has held annually as a professional association since 2011. These developments have been supported with significant commercial sponsorship from organisations including the computing company Intel. As a governing organisation for education data science, SoLAR has had explicit goals both in technical research and development (R&D) and pedagogic innovation:

> Advances in knowledge modeling and representation, [...] data mining, analytics, and open data form a foundation for new models of knowledge development and analysis. The technical complexity of this nascent field is paralleled by a transition within the full spectrum of learning (education, work place learning, informal learning) to social, networked learning. These technical, pedagogical, and social domains must be brought into dialogue with each other to ensure that interventions and organisational systems serve the needs of all stakeholders.
>
> *(Siemens, 2016)*

These aims express the highly normative trajectory of educational data science, which pivots not just on the production of knowledge from educational data but on powerful programmatic norms and aspirations to educational innovation and intervention. Beer (2016: 5) suggests that 'the concept of Big Data as a programmatic mode of reasoning also brings with it the values and norms that provide the means for evaluating and judging'. As a field defined by a particular style of thought and schemata of perception in relation to the statistical evaluation of educational processes and practices, education data science draws its distinction from cutting across academic and commercial domains of activity, and implies new norms, values and forms of expertise for educational knowledge production.

Methodological expertise

These disruptive developments bring major implications for technical and methodological expertise in education research. Buckingham Shum et al. (2013: 278) have identified that:

> while the learning analytics and educational data mining research communities are tackling the question of what data can tell us about learners, relatively little attention has been paid, to date, to the specific mindset, skillset and career trajectory of the people who wield these tools.

They term education data scientists a 'scarce breed', and note that they would need to be experts in both learning analytics and educational data mining, as well as in a host of related computational, analytic and algorithmic techniques. Likewise, Piety, Behrens and Pea (2013) have traced the disciplinary origins of education data science to computer science techniques of computational statistics, data mining, machine learning, natural language processing and human-computer interaction. Cope and Kalantzis (2016: 9) argue that one implication of education data science is that researchers will need to reposition themselves as 'data collaborators' who can work alongside software designers since the division is blurred 'in the era of big data' between the data used for pedagogic design and 'the data used by researchers in the educational data sciences'. Added to this, the education data scientist is likely to need to work in collaborative social networks that criss-cross academic and commercial domains, since many of the major technological platforms to conduct big data analyses are emerging from industry contexts rather than scholarly settings.

The methodological expertise of education data science is also producing new practices that can be enacted within educational institutions such as schools and universities. As Siemens (2013) has noted, education data science focuses both on techniques – such as the production of algorithms for analysing masses of educational data – and the design of applications that can be used by practitioners. Learning analytics and adaptive learning platforms are applied technologies of education data science that can be inserted directly into the institutional infrastructures of teaching and learning. Learning analytics platforms are now widely used in higher education to enable institutions to mine data directly from the instructional or pedagogical process. The data generated can be used to identify students that are 'at-risk' or even, via machine learning techniques of predictive analytics, to produce probabilistic predictions of students' future progress and outcomes. Adaptive learning platforms can then be mobilised to 'personalise' the learning experience around each individual. The commercial software system Knewton, for example, performs the task of both a learning analytics and adaptive learning platform. Widely used in higher education institutions, it is increasingly present in schooling systems via its partnership with Pearson, the world's most powerful education business, which sells its e-learning and online learning products worldwide. Through companies such as Knewton and Pearson, as well as other educational technology vendors such as IBM and Microsoft, the distinctive practices and systems of thought associated with education data science are being applied at the core of educational institutions.

Institutionalising educational data science

Education data science is attaining legitimacy and status as an emerging field of educational big data analysis through the advocacy and lobbying of a few key institutions, both operating within higher education and in the commercial educational technology domain. One dominant site of field-building in education data science is the Lytics Lab at Stanford University. Short for 'Learning Analytics Laboratory', the Lytics Lab was established in 2012 to 'advance the science of learning through the use of data and digital technology' (https://lytics.stanford.edu/about-lytics). Its focus is on understanding online learners, including dropout prediction tools and analytics of attainment gaps and studies that evaluate 'digital instruction', as well as the development of new 'learning tools' such as social learning platforms and systems that 'provide feedback at scale'. Its staff includes academics and doctoral students from a cross-disciplinary selection of 'Computer Science, Learning Science, Communication, Psychology, Statistics, Design, and Sociology'.

In 2014, the Stanford University Learning Analytics Workgroup published a report on 'building the field of learning analytics at scale' (Pea, 2014). It was authored by Roy Pea, then director of the Lytics Lab, and co-funded by the Bill and Melinda Gates Foundation and the MacArthur Foundation, two major philanthropic foundations for educational technology in the US. The working group members included Stanford University researchers who would subsequently establish the Lytics Lab; John Behrens of Pearson (then the incoming director of Pearson's Center for Digital Data, Analytics and Adaptive Learning); staff from commercial online learning platform providers (Khan Academy, Coursera); individuals from commercial computing businesses including Intel; philanthropic donors from the Gates Foundation; academics working on learning analytics development in technology-focused research centres from other universities; and governmental officials from the White House Office of Science and Technology Policy and the US Department of Education's Institute of Education Sciences. In Bourdieu's terms, a great deal of economic and social capital — in the shape of funding and cross-sectoral social networks — became available to the Lytics Lab through its centrality to this working group and the various task forces it generated.

In the report of the working group, Pea (2014) proposed a new 'specialised' field combining the sciences of digital data and learning, and the construction of a 'big data infrastructure' for learning consisting of data science and computer science techniques that could be harnessed for the challenge of analysing large volumes of educational data. The report established the need for a new 'professional infrastructure in the field of learning analytics and education data mining, made up of data scientists (straddling statistics and computer science) who are also learning scientists and education researchers' (Pea, 2014: 17). Specifically, it identified 'several competencies for education data science' to contribute to this professional infrastructure:

- Computational and statistical tools and inquiry methods, including traditional statistics skills [...] as well as newer techniques like machine learning, network analysis, natural language processing, and agent-based modelling.
- General educational, cognitive science, and sociocultural principles in the sciences of learning.
- Principles of human–computer interaction, user experience design, and design-based research.
- An appreciation for the ethical and social concerns and questions around big data, for both formal educational settings and non-school learning environments.

(Pea, 2014)

Elsewhere in the report, expertise in psychometrics and educational measurement, cognitive neuroscience, bioinformatics, computational statistics and other computational methods are promoted. These disciplinary competencies delineate the style of thinking underpinning educational data science, particularly its computer science and data science origins twinned with primarily psychological, cognitive and neuroscientific theories of learning.

As already noted, one member of the Learning Analytics Working Group was John Behrens of Pearson. Pearson is the world's largest educational publisher, announcing US$7.9bn revenue in 2014 with operations in over 70 countries and over 40,000 employees. Recently Pearson has significantly extended its operations and ambitions to include R&D in digital learning and big data analysis in education. Its Center for Digital Data, Analytics and Adaptive Learning (CDDAAL), a research and development centre dedicated to the analysis and use of digital data for educational improvement, was established in 2012 (http://researchnetwork. pearson.com/digital-data-analytics-and-adaptive-learning). The founding director of CDDAAL, John Behrens, is an expert in measurement and statistics, while other staff in the centre are described as 'research scientists' with expertise in data mining, computer science, algorithm design, intelligent systems, human–computer interaction and data analytics tools and methods. In a CDDAAL publication, data science is positioned as a 'transformative' methodology:

> Once much of teaching and learning becomes digital, data will be available not just from once-a-year tests, but also from the wide-ranging daily activities of individual students … in real time. … [W]e need further research that brings together learning science and data science to create the new knowledge, processes, and systems this vision requires.
>
> *(DiCerbo and Behrens, 2014)*

The authors argue that combining 'learning science' with data science methods will enable researchers to mine students' data for patterns, based on the understanding that 'faced with a very large number of potential variables, computers are able to perform pattern identification tasks that are beyond the scope of human abilities […] not only to collect information but also detect patterns within it' (DiCerbo and Behrens, 2014: 16). The aim of CDDAAL's R&D programme is to produce 'actionable data' that might be used to intervene at the level of the school, the course or the individual learner, but also to produce new explanatory theories. Behrens (2013: 18) provides an upbeat assessment of how insights extracted from the generation of huge quantities of educational data will challenge current theoretical frameworks, as 'new forms of data and experience will create a theory gap between the dramatic increase in data-based results and the theory base to integrate them'. Through its big data analytics methods, Pearson proposes that it can generate new insights into and understandings of learning itself, using the results of data analysis to build new theories.

As mentioned earlier, a significant aspect of Pearson's work in educational data science is its partnership with the learning analytics and adaptive learning platform provider Knewton. Since 2011, Knewton has provided the back-end analytics platform to much of Pearson's content and distribution, promising to 'usher in a new era of personalised and customisable education products':

> The Knewton Adaptive Learning Platform™ uses proprietary algorithms to deliver a personalised learning path for each student.... 'Knewton adaptive

learning platform, as powerful as it is, would just be lines of code without Pearson,' said Jose Ferreira, founder and CEO of Knewton. 'You'll soon see Pearson products that diagnose each student's proficiency at every concept, and precisely deliver the needed content in the optimal learning style for each. These products will use the combined data power of millions of students to provide uniquely personalised learning'.

(Knewton, 2011)

Knewton's 'proprietary algorithms' have the capacity to calculate students' probable future progress through predictive analytics processes, and then to 'personalise' their learning through pathways deemed appropriate by the algorithm. Underlying these algorithms are complex psychometric calculations designed to predict student progress and outcomes, each of which has been scientifically tested and refined by Knewton's in-house 'data science community' (Naeff and Nichols, 2015). The proprietary nature of Knewton's platform indicates that the predictive knowledge generated by educational data science systems and experts is itself shaped by, and locked into, privately owned infrastructures with their own regimes of intellectual property and platform patents, as well as being structured by complex underlying mathematical models and psychometric theories of psychological measurement and prediction (Perrotta and Williamson, 2016).

Pearson's role in education data science – as a commercial actor with serious economic, social and cultural capital to enforce its centrality to this methodological field – raises significant implications for educational research. It suggests that insights into learning itself are increasingly likely to emanate from private companies with their own proprietorial systems, intellectual property claims and market ambitions. These companies are staking their claim to expertise in the conceptualisation of learning through their ownership of the systems required to calculate big data.

Re-theorising education through data science

The algorithmic and data analytics techniques of educational data science – and the style of thinking that animates them – represent a set of distinctive challenges for educational researchers and their participation in knowledge production and theory development. Notably, the machine-learning algorithms that underpin most analytics packages need to be trained to learn from:

A data sample that has already been classified or labelled by someone. The existence of the classifications is crucial to the work of the techniques. The classification becomes what the data mining techniques seek to learn or model so that future instances can be classified in a similar way.

(Mackenzie, 2015: 433)

Data analytics platforms, including adaptive learning analytics such as Knewton, produce algorithmically learned knowledge that can be deployed to shape future activities, though this is dependent on the classificatory labour of the algorithm designers behind the platform. In relation to education data science, Piety, Hickey and Bishop (2014: 9) acknowledge that its technologies 'encode various theories of learning that manifest themselves in the data the tools provide'. The underlying theories of learning contained in the information architectures of educational data science are therefore consequential to ways of both theorising and acting practically upon individuals.

For Cope and Kalantzis (2016: 11) these issues of data classification raise the necessity of careful theory development in education data science:

> Statistical patterns in machine learning data are to a significant extent creatures of patterns already built into supervised training models. In the case of unsupervised machine learning, the statistical patterns make sense only when they are given explanatory labels. For these reasons indeed, theory is needed more than ever to frame data models, to create ontologies that structure fields for data collection, and for model tracing.

This point about increasing the importance of theory in big data analysis is welcome, though it raises important questions about the sites of expertise where such theory generation might occur and the kinds of theories that are considered desirable. As the Stanford Lytics Lab, SoLAR and Pearson's centre indicate, educational data science is being concentrated in well-resourced research centres, labs and socially networked associations. Their concern for theory development is largely driven by data scientific interests in ontology creation and model-building that are, in turn, framed by psychological, psychometric and sometimes neuroscientific conceptualisations of learning. In addition to this, the field is dedicated to highly normative views of how learning processes and environments can be improved or optimised, with Lytics lab, SoLAR and Pearson all proposing alike to use data scientific digital methods to produce actionable knowledge for active intervention. The theories of education data science are in this sense part of its aspirations to turn data into new knowledge, ideas, services and products that have the potential for value-realisation – whether economically in terms of product commercialisation, socially in terms of network-building and consolidation, or culturally in the shape of credentials and academic kudos.

This returns us to the idea of educational data science as a 'field of power', whereby it can be understood as a distinctive set of relations and structures between a range of actors seeking to establish economic, cultural and social capital. Educational data science has begun to accumulate significant economic capital in the shape of research funding and institutional resources. It has developed strong social capital through its own socially networked professional associations, conferences and journals, plus links to commercial industry, prestigious academic institutions and governmental supporters. It has also assembled cultural capital through its innovative methodological and algorithmic production of new knowledge, and has significant ambitions for future theory generation too. That this field is concentrated among well-resourced labs and centres such as those associated with Stanford and Pearson raises real questions about its capacity to generate new theories that might themselves reshape the ways in which processes of learning are known, understood and accepted more widely in the educational research field and beyond.

Mirroring sociological concerns that social science is increasingly being performed in the in-house research departments of wealthy social media companies (Burrows and Savage, 2014; Marres, 2012), education data science is displacing educational research to well-connected networks of specialist labs and research centres. Few education departments in universities have the big data infrastructure or research capacity to conduct the advanced data scientific studies of Pearson or Stanford. This means that as big data gains credibility as the source for educational knowledge production and theorising, it is likely that legitimacy and funding will flow toward those centres that are able to conduct such analyses, which will then be able to publish and share their findings as new authoritative knowledge.

In a recent article, Ruppert (2015) asks 'who owns big data?' She notes that big data are the product of different actors and technologies involved in its generation and analysis. The actors involved in these practices can in many ways be seen to 'own' big data. These observations point to important issues about the ownership of the insights that come from big data as they are extracted from the everyday traces people leave as they interact with one another and transact with services digitally, since the few for-profit companies that own the data and the tools to mine it – the data infrastructure – possess great power to understand and predict the world (Nielsen, 2014).

In the educational context, in other words, there is a political economy dimension to educational theorising as it migrates toward commercial research centres like those of Pearson or academic institutions with close industry and governmental connections such as Stanford. These sites constitute both a professional and a data infrastructure for educational data science. How learning is conceptualised and theorised looks increasingly to be led by actors with the economic, social and cultural capital to generate insights from big data, some of which, like Pearson, might then stand to gain commercially by designing and patenting e-learning software products on the basis of the theories they have generated. Watters (2016) provocatively suggests that the 'technological future of education' is one where software '*patents become the theory*', which 'does not guarantee that these companies have developed technologies that will help students learn' but 'that there will be proprietary assets to litigate over, to negotiate with, and to sell'. Knowledge production and theory generation based on data analytics have the potential for value-realisation by the institutions that have invested in educational data science as a professional and data infrastructure.

For educationalists, this makes it essential to consider the specific question of 'who owns educational big data?' The ownership of educational big data, the development of educational theory and the application of such theories within proprietorial systems, intellectual property rights and software patents may be leading to a near-future scenario where private companies with market imperatives become increasingly dominant sites of expertise into learning and teaching processes. In this context, how learning is understood looks likely to become a kind of intellectual property for privately resourced research centres.

Conclusion

Lupton (2015: 68) has described digital academics as 'participants in the digitised knowledge economy'. Data scientific digital academics tend to assume that 'data speak for themselves' – that data are objective, calculable, neutral and free of human bias or pre-existing theory (Kitchin, 2014). Education data scientists are proto-typical of the particular form of digital academia that is 'data-ist' in outlook and methodology, informed by data scientific ways of thinking and professional styles of practice. As an emerging field of power in educational research, educational data science represents an attempt to replicate the figure of the data scientist, or the entrepreneurial 'algorithmist', in the educational field. This is a figure armed with new kinds of expertise, new epistemologies and new methodologies – as well as new schemata of perception and normative aspirations – associated with big data. Data scientists, as Kitchin (2014) notes, have particular epistemological outlooks, professional ways of working and methodological approaches that are often techn-icist, functionalist and instrumentalist, and that tend to neglect the social, cultural, political and economic factors that contribute to the phenomena they analyse. Many data scientists have 'little time for theory' or 'the ethics around [...] the social impact of algorithms' (O'Neill, 2016). Their practices are also underpinned by 'a vision for particular types of calculative or numerical knowing about individuals, groups and the social world' (Beer, 2016: 5).

As an emerging field of power in educational research, education data science casts a particular schema of perception over the processes of teaching and learning that sees them in measurable terms rather than as socially, culturally, politically and economically determined practices. With its promises of accelerated insight genera-tion and real-time pedagogic intervention, the digital academic associated with edu-cation data science is becoming a source of methodological expertise, knowledge production and theory development that is challenging the existing discipline of educational research. It is becoming a distinctive field of power, one with significant sources of economic, cultural and social capital. As educational institutions gener-ate increasing quantities of digital data, education data science might therefore be understood as assembling a new form of 'methodological capital'. Methodological capital in this context refers to competence in big data analyses, securing funding and the capacity to produce knowledge that is effective in the competition for control over contemporary understandings of education. This chapter has detailed some of the ways that education data science as a field – consisting of digitised knowledge workers from both academic and commercial settings – has assembled its methodological capital. Its deployment over future years is likely to have significant implications for educational researchers, not least as its insights will be generated within complex mathematical and proprietorial systems that most non-specialists from outside the field itself will find impenetrable.

References

Beer, D. (2016) How should we do the history of Big Data? *Big Data & Society* 3. Available at: http://journals.sagepub.com/doi/10.1177/2053951716646135 (accessed 5 February 2017).

Behrens, J. (2013, April) Harnessing the currents of the digital ocean. Paper presented at the Annual Meeting of the American Educational Research Association, San Francisco, CA.

Bourdieu, P. (1993) *The Field of Cultural Production: Essays on Art and Literature*. Cambridge: Polity.

Buckingham Shum, S, Baker, R S J, Behrens, J, Hawksey, M, Jeffery, N and Pea, R. (2013) Educational data scientists: A scarce breed? In: *LAK'13 Proceedings of the Third International Conference on Learning Analytics and Knowledge*, Leuven, Belgium, April 8–13, 278–281.

Burrows, R and Savage, M. (2014) After the crisis? Big Data and the methodological challenges of empirical sociology. *Big Data & Society* 1. Available at: http://journals.sagepub.com/doi/full/10.1177/2053951714540280 (accessed 5 February 2017).

Clow, D. (2013) An overview of learning analytics. *Teaching in Higher Education* 18: 683–695.

Cope, B and Kalantzis, M. (2016) Big data comes to school: Implications for learning, assessment and research. *AERA Open* 2: 1–19.

DiCerbo, K E and Behrens, J T. (2014) *Impacts of the Digital Ocean*. Austin, TX: Pearson.

Edwards, P N, Jackson, S J, Chalmers, M K, Bowker, G C, Borgman, C L, Ribes, D, Burton, M and Calvert, S. (2013) *Knowledge Infrastructures: Intellectual Frameworks and Research Challenges*. Ann Arbor: Deep Blue.

Gehl, R. (2015) Sharing, knowledge management and big data: A partial genealogy of the data scientist. *European Journal of Cultural Studies* 18: 413–428.

Hilbert, M. (2016) Big data for development: A review of promises and challenges. *Development Policy Review* 34: 135–174.

Kitchin, R. (2014) *The Data Revolution: Big Data, Open Data, Data Infrastructures and Their Consequences*. London: Sage.

Knewton (2011) Knewton and Pearson partner to advance next generation of digital education. Available at: www.knewton.com/press-releases/pearson-partnership/.

Lane, J E. (2014) *Building a Smarter University: Big Data, Analytics and Innovation*. New York: SUNY Press.

Lupton, D. (2015) *Digital Sociology*. London: Routledge.

Mackenzie, A. (2015) The production of prediction: What does machine learning want? *European Journal of Cultural Studies* 18: 429–445.

Marres, N. (2012) The redistribution of methods: On intervention in digital social research, broadly conceived. *Sociological Review* 60: 139–165.

Mayer-Schönberger, V and Cukier, K. (2013) *Big Data: A Revolution That Will Change How We Live, Work and Think*. London: John Murray.

Naeff, R and Nichols, Z. (2015) On the limits of psychometric testing in online education. *Knewton*. Available at: https://tech.knewton.com/wp-content/uploads/2015/01/OnTheLimitsofPsychometricTesting.pdf (accessed 15 July 2016).

Nielsen, M. (2014) Who owns big data? *Change: 19 Key Essays on How the Internet Is Changing Our Lives. Open Mind*. Available at: www.bbvaopenmind.com/en/book/19-key-essays-on-how-internet-is-changing-our-lives/ (accessed 2 July 2016).

O'Neill, C. (2016) The ethical data scientist. *Slate*. Available at: www.slate.com/articles/technology/future_tense/2016/02/how_to_bring_better_ethics_to_data_science.html (accessed 21 December 2016).

Pea, R. (2014) *A Report on Building the Field of Learning Analytics for Personalised Learning at Scale*. Stanford: Stanford University.

Perrotta, C and Williamson, B. (2016) The social life of learning analytics: Cluster analysis and the performance of algorithmic education. *Learning, Media and Technology*. doi: 10.1080/17439884.2016.1182927.

Piety, P J, Behrens, J and Pea, R. (2013) *Educational data sciences and the need for interpretive skills*. American Educational Research Association, San Francisco.

Piety, P J, Hickey, D T and Bishop, M J. (2014) Educational data sciences – Framing emergent practices for analytics of learning, organisations and systems. In: *LAK'14 Proceedings of the Fourth International Conference on Learning Analytics and Knowledge*, Indianapolis, IN, USA, 24–28 March, 193–202.

Rogers, R. (2013) *Digital Methods*. London: MIT Press.

Ruppert, E. (2015) Who owns big data? *Discover Society*. Available at: http://discoversociety. org/2015/07/30/who-owns-big-data/ (accessed 5 August 2015).

Ruppert, E, Law, J and Savage, M. (2013) Reassembling social science methods: The challenge of digital devices. *Theory, Culture & Society* 30: 22–46.

Ruppert, E, Harvey, P, Lury, C, Mackenzie, A, McNally, R, Baker, S A, Kallianos, Y and Lewis, C. (2015) Socialising big data: From concept to practice. CRESC Working Paper no. 138. Available at: www.cresc.ac.uk/medialibrary/workingpapers/wp138.pdf (accessed 12 December 2015).

Siemens, G. (2013) Learning analytics: The emergence of a discipline. *American Behavioral Scientist* 57: 1380–1400.

Siemens, G. (2016) Reflecting on learning analytics and SoLAR. *Elearnspace*. Available at: www.elearnspace.org/blog/2016/04/28/reflecting-on-learning-analytics-and-solar/ (accessed 11 February 2017).

Simons, M, Olssen, M and Peters, M A. (2009) Re-reading education policies. Part 2: Challenges, horizons, approaches, tools, styles. In: M Simons, M Olssen and M A Peters (eds), *Re-Reading Education Policies: A Handbook Studying the Policy Agenda of the 21ˢᵗ Century*. Rotterdam: Sense Publishers, 36–95.

Watters, A. (2016) Ed-tech patents: Prior art and learning theories. *Hack Education*. Available at: http://hackeducation.com/2016/01/12/patents (accessed 22 December 2016).

11

INTERVIEW

Sara Goldrick-Rab interviewing Inger Mewburn

How long have you been using social media as a scholar and what have you been using it for?

I don't know the exact date when I started using it, but I would say that I've probably been blogging since around 2007 or so. I have been on Twitter probably around five years or so and I am starting to use Facebook a little more as a scholar. I had a personal page like a lot of people do, but I now have a public Facebook page. I have a book coming out and I was encouraged to have a public page to use in a scholarly fashion to assist people with understanding the issues in my book. The Facebook page is kind of supplementing the things that are in the book, talking about some of the more current issues and proposals that are out there, and are related to the book.

I've experimented with a couple of other forms of social media. I'm trying to learn a little more about Reddit and Quora and this sort of thing, but I would say I'm most associated with Twitter – for better or for worse. That's probably where I've done the most work, I would say, in terms of figuring out where that fits into being a scholar. That might be impossible. I mean, the whole thing's an illusion and it's sort of nonsense to begin with: 'Right, there's some sort of goal to be achieved and some sort of perfect way of doing it.' If you ask somebody, 'Have you worked out how you do peer review publications or articles?' I also think they'd be wrong to suggest that they've really got it down. It's difficult and it's an on-going process. Every journal that you publish in you have to learn new ground rules and those rules change with each editor and on what you're trying to write about too and the methods.

Social media for me has been an evolving, constantly challenging part of my life as a scholar. It certainly consumes more of my energy than it used to. I wish it didn't but it's hard – it's emotionally taxing, I'm not good at having a negative interaction on Twitter and just walking away from it. I wish I were. You know, it's become a pretty major part of my professional life at this point.

You've had some very difficult experiences on Twitter, which is easy enough to find online when you Google your name. I think it's the second link that comes up. If you compare it to, say, writing journals obviously social media is far more immediate. You have to deal with a lot more reactions to your work than you would with a conventional publishing mode. Do other colleagues, who do not engage on social media, get as much negative attention?

We get some, but there's nothing you can compare Twitter to, not only because there is a timing issue, but there's a reach issue. Most journals are behind a paywall. Twitter is much more democratic; it's much more wide open and far-reaching in terms of who can engage with it. Peer review journals are behind gates for the most part, so very few people can access them. And that really limits the sheer number of people and the type of people who are going to have the opportunity to even read and react to one's work.

You know, it is enormously frustrating to me that of all the things I've done in the last, say, fifteen years, a Google search will turn up an inaccurate story as a first hit. That story is actually completely factually incorrect. That tweet that had almost nothing to do with my professional life, it was a political attack organised because of who I am as a professional.

I don't think that would happen in a journal. You might be attacked for your ideas in a journal, but they would be the ideas expressed in your professional capacity. Instead, the blow-back I have had has been about things that I have said that are in a professional capacity, but in this case I was targeted because I'm a significant name at a university that politicians have a problem with.

Perhaps you could tell us what actually happened to you that makes Google see you that way?

I tweet a lot. I think it's really important to actually say that I'm a prolific tweeter. I'm actually not just a prolific tweeter; I'm prolific at a lot of things. So, I write a lot; I run a lot of research projects. I'm not somebody who does one thing at a time. I never have.

So, I'm a prolific tweeter, which means there are a lot of tweets out there. And all of this controversy was really about one tweet. It was one of thousands over the course of last spring in 2015. It was a comment that I made about then presidential candidate Scott Walker, who is a Neo-Conservative governor of my then state of Wisconsin (I don't live there anymore). He was behaving in a way that actually shares a lot of characteristics with today's presidential...well, about to be nominee, Donald Trump. He was behaving in sort of a boorish manner, he was being very aggressive to lots of folks. One recent thing he had done was take on the status of tenure among university faculty. He supported and helped to arrange a bill that would change forever the terms of our tenure, including those of us who'd already earned tenure, in the entire university system, across the whole state.

I was sitting on my porch a couple of days after that happened, talking to my grandfather on the phone. My grandfather is in his late eighties – he's a psychoanalyst. We're talking about how I felt and how he felt about what was happening in Wisconsin. I described how attacked I felt. I felt academics were being attacked and that this was McCarthyism again where we're hated for our ideas. I felt this politician wanted to run us intellectuals out of the state. He started with teachers and it went onto professors.

Well my grandfather began an analysis [of the situation], a set of analytic comments, that (actually it's funny), a year later are very commonplace. These are comments discussing the characteristics of this presidential candidate and Hitler. It's quite amazing to me that today people readily say, 'Well Donald Trump is acting in a Hitler-like fashion', and people know what that means. It doesn't mean he's driving people into concentration camps. They're describing Neo-Fascist-type activity.

I often remark on conversations I've had with other people on Twitter. I don't name them by name necessarily, but I went on Twitter later that night and I said: 'My grandfather, a psychoanalyst, just walked me through some similarities between Scott Walker and Hitler. They're terrifying.' Now I didn't say that I thought the two men were alike. It was one tweet. It was one tweet. And the God's honest truth is that weeks passed by and no one said a word. This was not my most favourited tweet, this was not a big deal, I didn't hear from anybody saying, 'We have a problem with it'. Nothing happened.

Almost a month later, the day that Scott Walker's presidential campaign was announced, on the official start date, this tweet was released to the public. It wasn't really released – it had already been public – but it was put out there in the media as evidence that we professors in the state of Wisconsin were a problem. We were all inappropriate and this was not a stupid thing that I had said, but this was evidence that we shouldn't have tenure. And then of course, because there's a public record of all my tweets, people started trawling through my other tweets, looking for other problems they could find. Now the person leading this effort was Scott Walker's son, who's a student at the University of Wisconsin Madison [UW]. He found some tweets I had sent to members of the University of Wisconsin community, sharing information with them about other changes to tenure. A few of those messages had gone to students who were thinking of coming to Madison. I wanted them to know about the changes. Now I still don't view this as a problem, to be honest. I don't think they're children. They're eighteen years old, they've been accepted to a university, they're going to pay a lot of money, and they have no idea that there are major policy changes afoot. So, I didn't tell them not to come to UW and I didn't tell them they were stupid to come or whatever. I said, 'I think you might be interested in this information'. So then the politically motivated latched on to these tweets and said I was targeting prospective students and I was getting in the way of the business of UW. It spiralled.

My work is on college affordability. My work certainly does go to these questions about teachers at colleges and what colleges cost. But again, you know, I was speaking in my capacity as a faculty member who was concerned about who was going to be teaching at the university. This other tweet was just taken out of context. And the saddest part of the whole thing is you would think that this is so blatantly political, so used to driving a Republican's campaign, that any thoughtful academic would not take it seriously. Instead, the chancellor of my institution contacted the head of the university committee and said they needed to do something about me.

Their version of 'doing something about me' was to take an illegal action. They had a meeting, without prior meeting notice, of a subset of the committee in which they wrote a statement deploring my actions, calling me inappropriate and unprofessional. They didn't allude to any political context. They didn't mention anything positive or contributions I'd ever made and they certainly didn't talk about the norms of Twitter and how these things were. They put this on a proper university letterhead, without an official vote, and issued it to the media without warning.

That is how you get a story in *Inside Higher Ed* that says that I've been sanctioned by the faculty senate of the University of Wisconsin Madison. All because of one tweet that started during a presidential campaign and a blatant attempt to destabilise public higher education.

That is certainly a cautionary tale. When I teach students about social media I often get asked, 'Am I going to risk losing my job?' Increasingly, it seems, if you are seen to in any way infringe on the corporate business you are potentially in trouble...

I do think these are cautionary tales. So many people try to tell me – especially my colleagues at Wisconsin – not to make a big deal out of this, to not view it as something bigger. I'm not a sign of anything, that this was a one-off, you know, an irresponsible act and it was appropriately punished. They think it's not a sign of a larger problem and I completely disagree. I've heard so many of these things and I think that, you know, it's a 'canary in a coal mine' kind of issue. I mean, I've tried to explain to my colleagues that we're only as strong as the 'weakest link' and if the university came after me ... I mean, what was amazing to me was also that I wasn't just some easily disposed-of faculty worker. I was clearly somebody who would push back. And I was also somebody who meets those corporate metrics for success. I have a large profile of funded research. You would think that if your eye was on the bottom line, you would want people like me. I mean, I am obviously well known as a liberal, but apart from that, I look and walk kind of mainstream. So it was pretty incredible.

That fall I taught a class on scholar activism, which was already scheduled. I had already decided that I would teach for the first time a graduate seminar on scholar activism. Which was a heck of a thing to teach having gone through what I had just gone through. I mean, I felt like I had PTSD [post-traumatic stress disorder]. I could barely function. As a teacher in that classroom all I could do was sit and listen to them talk and try to guide the discussion, because it was so painful. The students had all had these sorts of concerns. Like, 'Can I, should I, must I participate in social media if I'm going to have a career in this day and age and can I bear these risks?' And it's a tough thing to answer. But boy, it hasn't stopped me one bit. It really hasn't. It's not just because I'm stubborn. The incentives are very strong. I seriously don't think I would have the profile, the positive profile that I have for my work. It wouldn't be known in so many places, to the extent that it is, without social media.

I hope that I will certainly add a piece of proof to this this fall when my book comes out. I think my book is going to do so much better and have so many more people read and listen to it and consider it and debate it and critique it than ever would have if I wasn't on Twitter.

So what ended up happening? What was the end of the story?

[Laughing] Well, there wasn't an immediate end. There were many, many months of trying to recover. The effects lasted a long time. I was still getting comments on it from my colleagues in the fall. I was hearing about it from potential funders, who had problems with the attention. What it really did for me was firm up a growing sense that I had had that the University of Wisconsin was not a place I could work anymore.

It was not the first time I'd felt a leader of the university did not value academic freedom the way that she espoused it, or did not understand the political context in which it worked – and was not willing to stand by faculty. And without tenure, and absent any form of union, I felt fairly certain that this would actually go further in the future. I was sure they would move towards getting rid of me entirely.

Since they announced the changes to tenure I had become very open about the fact that I would seek to leave, and by the fall I was on the job market. And then now I'm a professor at Temple University where yes, I have tenure, legitimate tenure. But I think most importantly I am protected by a very strong union.

I must say, I have been assured at every level and actually do believe that my Twitter account is going to have nothing to do with my treatment at Temple University. They've been supportive, thus far, of my use of social media. Although there was an interesting moment in the new staff orientation that I attended. They spoke to us about the Code of Conduct at the university and the importance of behaving in a professional manner. I was the only one in the room with a question. There were about 60 people and I raised my hand and I said, 'Can you please tell me what it is to behave in a professional manner? What does that mean? Like, what exactly is forbidden? What's allowed? And, in particular, what is the policy with regard to social media?' They didn't have an answer. Then I asked, 'Is there a social media policy?' And they said, 'We're sure there is. Why don't we go online and look for it?' And I looked for it and I found one. It's very brief and it's aimed at the students. So, you know, I am in a situation, frankly, where there is something unwritten here. But again, to me it's the combination of tenure plus union protections that make it possible for one to operate at least with some modicum of security compared to where I was before. It's a strong union. We have a very large fraction of our faculty engaged – and not only our tenured faculty, but also our contingent faculty. So the union has a real role on campus and I certainly sought it out as soon as I decided to come here.

Where do you think it's all going? If you think of your grad students, how do you think – ten years', twenty years' time – social media will affect us as academics?

I tell my students, you know, you don't *have* to become a research university professor. You don't have to be well known, right? You can choose something else.

But if you aim to be high-profile and for your work to be used in a broad way, by people beyond the academy, then I'm not sure social media is optional. And I have had students who have decided to learn it and are actively using it. I'm actually pretty proud of one of them, you know, he wasn't with me when this latest thing happened, but he'd seen me go through some struggles. This former student was named top academic in education on Twitter recently. But in my view, he takes a very conservative approach. You know? It's a sort of, 'just the facts, ma'am', kind of approach. He rarely expresses an opinion or critiques anything. And he's just a very balanced – this is just who he is. But I think what's going to be really hard is that the academy just moves and changes so slowly. You know, even this final move to adopt open access journals – one per discipline or something. My goodness!

It's a job to get here. You know? That doesn't make me very optimistic. The other thing is, though, I am confident social media is here to stay, the forms are going to shift again. I don't see how we're using Twitter in ten years. I think people will be bored. I'm actually getting bored. I've had days when I've been like, 'Oh God, do I have to tweet? This is so boring. This is getting dull'. I can predict virtually every conversation I'm going to have now. Very rarely is somebody saying something new – and I used to get new things all the time. So that's actually a problem. I don't think I'm in an echo chamber, because I follow a ton of people. So maybe that will change with the book and it will refresh things for academics. Maybe I'll learn, something new's going to happen because of it. But I keep thinking there's something after Twitter and I just don't know what it is yet, and if I did I'd be rich. Instead, I'm just an academic. But are we going to face a new wild west situation and have to muddle our way through it?

I almost didn't become an academic because I hated how isolated and insulated the community seemed to be. I wanted to get out there with 'regular people'. And I didn't even know about social media at the time; it barely existed. So the fact that this has come along as a tool to doing that, even though it brings risks, it's certainly helped to make it possible to be an academic, while still having real reach and inter-action with other people.

Note: This interview was conducted with Sara Goldrick-Rab by Inger Mewburn via Skype. The interview was audiotaped and transcribed, and both Mewburn and Goldrick-Rab lightly edited the transcript for ease of reading and to correct any transcription errors prior to publication.

12

INTERVIEW

Jessie Daniels interviewing Inger Mewburn

Could you start by telling us about how long you've been using social media as a scholar and how you've been using it? What is to you as a practice?

My experience with the internet, as we used to say, really predates social media. I started out as a very traditionally trained sociologist. I got my first academic tenure-track job in 1995, at more or less the start of the popular internet. I was intrigued with how the internet was going to be changing our understanding of patterns of social human behaviour, which is what we say we study as sociologists. I started taking my sociology students into the computer lab at that very early stage, the late '90s. It wasn't social media then but it was browsers that don't exist anymore – Altavista, Netscape.

I had them do web pages instead of term papers. There was a lot of resistance to that for a variety of reasons – some personal, some professional. I left that academic post after four or five years and went to work in the dot com company. I felt as if I had a front row seat to the digital revolution at the time. It was a very heady, very exciting time. The firm where I worked was an entertainment company. We did chats with Fortune 500 companies and, like you hear on television: 'Come and chat with Tony Soprano after the show', we would run those chats, using proprietary software. It was what we did before Twitter.

Because I had worked at a company that emphasised chat and discussion boards to build community, I had this sense of where social media comes from. Twitter sort of made sense to me based on my experience with chat. I started putting social media into my teaching, research and publishing; less so in teaching. Despite those early experiments with teaching, I often revert to really analogue methods with my teaching. For instance, I do a lot of close reading of text. I often use index cards – old technology – in the classroom, more so than digital technology. But for me, the real benefit of social media has been changing the way I think and process information. I'm not doing research on Twitter, such as the very ambitious and laudable things like scraping data, creating charts and these magnificent graphs that some scholars are doing. For me it's a conversational place, social media – mostly Twitter.

Social media becomes a place for first drafts of publishing. I've taken tweets and sort of transformed those into longer writing on my blog. I review the scholarly literature, other people's research and do meta-reviews. I've produced a series of blog posts that started as a tweet and turned them into a peer review article. Sometimes it goes the other way. For instance, I may have a peer review article that I then will write a blog post about, or share via Twitter. But it's most often the case that it works in an inductive way, where I start with a tweet and then that grows into, 'Let me put some more words behind that. Let me do a blog post which is not to the level of a peer review article', and then two or three of those blog posts it becomes a peer-reviewed article published in a scholarly journal

As an example, I've done a series on the trouble with feminism. Over a year and a half, I've done a series of about twenty blog posts on the topic of race and gender, around [a] particular version of white femininity and white feminism. I now have around 40,000 words, which is half a book. I'm going to turn that into a formal book proposal and then into a book. It's not what I think of as formal research, but just having conversations and listening in on conversations; observing people's behaviour – some of it bad behaviour – on Twitter and then having a critical think about it on the blog.

Interesting. There is a chapter in this book about a survey of PhD student bloggers and one of the things that they said about blogging and tweeting was that they were worried that it was 'misshapen academic text' that they were putting out there. Yet the way you're speaking about it, then it's more like a seed or a launching pad and it's from these things that your academic texts grow or move backwards and forwards. The PhD student bloggers seem to be picking up on a received attitude from the academy, that a blog post isn't 'real academic work', and they should worry about misshapen texts being out there because they're unformed, or in formation, but you have a very different approach. Do you want to comment on that? Have you seen that attitude around you from other academics?

Sure. There is a famous academic who you probably will know, who is fond of saying: 'I have never known anyone who's gotten tenure for a blog post.' And I think in some ways that's true. I think it's undeniable that that's not what people are getting tenure for, but there are ways that institutions are beginning to take into account public scholarship in ways that value that contribution. And so we have to think carefully about what it is we're doing with social media as a form of intellectual engagement. I think that if you are a scholar, and you are a critical thinker, then that's going to be how you approach these platforms and tools.

We have these new modes of thinking, of creating knowledge, of producing knowledge, of also translating and sharing knowledge, and yet we are steeped in what I refer to as 'legacy institutions', some of which were formed centuries ago. The institutions in which we work are not 'born digital' institutions. They're institutions that have very long histories and they're very slow to change. The kinds of metrics that people are using on hiring committees, on tenure and promotion committees, on grant review committees, are not the same kinds of metrics that we look at on Twitter, or a blog or that sort of thing. That means there's a kind of disconnect between these two sorts of measures, what I would call 'epistemologies': ways of knowing and ways of measuring value. Sometimes they collide – legacy institutions and digital ways of knowing – and that's when people run into trouble.

I'll tell you an example of when they collide. Most of the stories that I hear around this are often cautionary tales that haven't actually happened but somebody asking, 'This could happen, right?' This story is actually one of those, so I say that with this caveat. A senior sociologist at a top-tier university I met at the American Sociological Meeting, told me about a junior scholar who was on the market. This senior scholar's institution had been very keen to hire this junior scholar initially, in part because of their high profile on social media. But when their hiring committee looked at the junior scholar's CV, they realised that most of their activity was on social media rather than in books or peer-reviewed publications. The senior scholar said the hire didn't go ahead because, while they liked the attention this junior scholar had garnered via social media, they were concerned about the lack of scholarly publications to back it up. The junior colleague in question got a very fine job at an institution that values the attention they bring through social media.

But that's the kind of collision that I'm talking about between the digital and the legacy institutions: ways of thinking about what's valuable, what the appropriate balance is between scholarly publications and a presence as a public scholar and what makes someone a strong candidate to hire and promote to tenure.

You're obviously very adept at strategically positioning yourself over both social media and conventional academic publishing. Do you share that knowledge with your students?

It's probably the particular place I'm in, but I don't get to do that as much as I would like to. For example, I started my scholarly blog, *Racism Review*, in 2007 and this fall (2016) will be the first time that I'll be teaching a graduate seminar on race and thus, the first chance I'll have to use the blog to teach students how to write for a public audience. I think it's such an important skill to learn in graduate school.

In some ways, the graduate students that I encounter are either very wedded to the traditional, 'I'm just going to do peer review publication', mode of doing sociology. I think of the US as being a little behind, and the UK and Australia as being ahead of these things. There's a lot of distrust among the graduate (and undergraduate) students that I encounter of being on social media at all. I'm sure they have nuanced reasons for not doing it, but it just gets lumped into, 'It's just a time-suck. I'm not going to waste my time'. That's the usual thing that I hear. I don't have graduate students coming up to me and saying: 'Please tell me how to be on Twitter and blogging.' I just don't get that.

What I try to do more of is encourage both graduate students and my faculty colleagues to make their scholarly writing more available. There's a lot of confusion – especially here in the US – around copyright and open access and what that means. The most common reaction I get when I bring up open access with someone here in the US is, 'Well I can't afford that. I can't afford to pay for open access'. Because they conflate open access with the nefarious schemes by publishers to charge authors (US)$3,000, when it was going to become open access anyway, after an embargo period.

So, I really spend most of my time and energy trying to talk to younger scholars, and more established scholars, about open access. Whether they ever figure out Twitter, or write a blog post, I kind of don't care. But I want them to make their work available in a repository somewhere, so that people who are on Twitter, or who are doing a blog post, can find the work and talk about it. I want them to know they can have an impact in the world, which is why most of them went to grad school in the first place.

Have you had any experience of negative attention on social media platforms?

Well I have to say, the first part of my answer is yes, I have had negative attention. But compared to a lot of other people including pretty much every black woman I know on Twitter, I just haven't experienced that much. So I'll give you my stories, but I just feel like it's so little compared to what other people go through.

Whenever I blog something and then share it on Twitter that attacks or is critical of white supremacists then there is somebody from the far-right that will come back at me. I learnt at one point that I had been put on the 'social justice warrior block list', which is a little point of pride! But it also means that a lot of those folks had just blocked me before I'd even said anything.

Last year, about this time, after the horrible mass shooting in South Carolina (the church where nine people were killed), I was invited to write a short piece for *The New York Times* based on my work. I argued that there's certainly precedent for banning white supremacist speech online. We could do it if we simply had the political will to do it. Anytime I say anything that's critical of the First Amendment or controlling hate speech, I get huge pushback. And, this was in *The New York Times* so I was braced for it. A lot of that pushback was really personal. I'd been out, identified as queer, on several of my online profiles. I don't have it on my Twitter profile now just because I change it every once in a while, but I got a lot of anti-lesbian, anti-gay stuff. Lots of personal attacks about my size, but I was like, 'Wow, really? That's all you've got? I'm fat?' So yeah, those were hurtful but not in a way that I ever felt physically threatened. I never thought anybody was going to come to my apartment and harm me.

And it obviously didn't affect your position, your job?

Right. I have been incredibly fortunate, and privileged, in that I'm in an institution where the President thinks my Twitter presence is just great. I don't think she really follows it or reads it, but years ago, when I was untenured, I got added to some list by a blogger at *Forbes*: '20 Inspiring Women to Follow on Twitter'. I didn't know the woman at *Forbes* but God bless her for adding me to that list. The communications person in our college caught that and noticed it had my affiliation on there. The college put it on the web splash page so every time someone logged into their computer on campus my picture was up there with the silly list that I was on. It was on all the screens in the campus. Anyway, the President just loved it and a colleague said: 'Congratulations – and what's Twitter?' Then, the same person, without understanding what Twitter was, said, 'Well, I guess this means tenure is a lock'.

Social media gave me a kind of prominence that was legible within my institution. I recognise this is not the response that most people get from their institutions about their social media presence. So, I think it's important, especially for junior scholars, to find out what kind of value their institution places on social media. Go find out what the chair and the dean and everyone who decides on your promotion at your institution, thinks about social media.

So young, early career academics are, I suppose, probably looking for how to position themselves as critical, aware consumers in this space – as the consumers of platform capitalisms but also as scholars, activists. So where do you see it all going in terms of a professional academic career?

I think that we're kind of at a point now where there's going to be a lot of pushback to social media in a number of ways. For the past few years, academics have engaged in social media at a moment when it was mostly off the radar of most administrators, a point that Mark Carrigan has made. Most academic administrators didn't know what to do with Twitter or the social media presence of their faculty, so they kind of tended to ignore it. But there have been a couple of cases where things have gone badly. Academics have said unfortunate things, some have lost their jobs, different things have happened. I think that academic administrators are now more aware of what faculty who are affiliated with their institution are saying on social media, particularly when it reflects badly on the college or university. I think that's going to prompt a whole slew of probably very bad policies from administrators, so faculty need to be aware of that and pushback against those policies.

The reality is that the most junior of our academic colleagues have grown up with the internet. They have never known a time without the internet, so it makes sense that social media is just going to be a part of how they conduct themselves as scholars. I think that there has to be some way that we grapple, in a more sophisticated sort of way, both as academic administrators and scholars with these tools and platforms. Right now, it's very much there are no rules, there are no guidelines, there are just a few examples and some cautionary tales. There aren't really guidelines or a set of best practices. I think people in the next few years are going to start making those up, and it's important that these aren't simply 'top down' regulations by administrators whose main concern is conformity to a brand, but rather informed by the needs and desires of publicly engaged faculty.

The other thing that we have to really think critically about is that we're all situated in different institutions and come to these platforms with different embodied selves and social positions. This shapes how these platforms perform for us. So I've had a pretty easy time of it, right? I've had some pushback from unpleasant trolls, but basically Twitter helped me get promoted in my job. That's very much part of being a white woman in the academy. That's not what's happening for many of my African-American colleagues and especially African-American women. They're given a really hard time on the platform. We have to think about this. Should institutions, which benefit in many ways from publicly engaged scholars' labour on social media, be protecting their faculty who get attacked online? I think that's an important conversation to be having as we go forward.

Note: This interview was conducted with Jessie Daniels by Inger Mewburn via Skype. The interview was audiotaped and transcribed, and both Mewburn and Daniels lightly edited the transcript for ease of reading and to correct any transcription errors prior to publication.

INDEX

Figures are given in italics.